THE
GOLF RESORT
GUIDE
(WESTERN EDITION)

THE
GOLF RESORT
GUIDE
(WESTERN EDITION)

Jim and Barbara Nicol

Hunter Publishing, Inc.
300 Raritan Center Parkway
Edison NJ 08818
(201) 225 1900

ISBN 1–55650–276–1

Cover photograph: Banff Springs Golf Course, Banff, Alberta, Canada

Maps by Joyce Huber, Photographics.

A companion volume, THE GOLF RESORT GUIDE
(EASTERN EDITION), is also available from the publishers.

CONTENTS

UNITED STATES
ARIZONA 1
ARKANSAS 31
CALIFORNIA
    NORTHERN CALIFORNIA 38
    SOUTHERN CALIFORNIA 57
    SAN DIEGO AREA 64
    PALM SPRINGS-DESERT AREA 80
COLORADO 100
HAWAII
    OAHU 114
    HAWAII 116
    KAUAI 127
    MAUI 135
    MOLOKAI 149
IDAHO 151
ILLINOIS 158
INDIANA 163
LOUISIANA 166
MICHIGAN 168
MINNESOTA 182
MISSOURI 187
MONTANA 192
NEVADA 198
NEW MEXICO 205
OKLAHOMA 210
OREGON 216
TEXAS 223
UTAH 239
WASHINGTON 242
WISCONSIN 247
WYOMING 259

CANADA
ALBERTA 263
BRITISH COLUMBIA 272
MANITOBA 288

MEXICO

ACAPULCO-GUERRERO AREA	294
YUCATAN PENINSULA	300
IXTAPA-ZIHUATANEJO AREA	303
MANZANILLO AREA	306
MAZATLAN, SINALOA AREA	309

INTRODUCTION

With this new edition we have added many new resorts, including those in Canada and Mexico.

Please keep in mind: the rates we quote for the Canadian resorts are in Canadian funds. To compute cost in American dollars deduct 15 percent. Rates shown for locations in Mexico are in U.S. dollars.

We have frequently been asked which resorts were our favorites. I would be less than candid if I did not acknowledge that we have stayed at a few resorts and played some courses which we felt were a notch or two above the others.

In alphabetical order, here are THE TOP 25 RESORTS as we view them. Our selection was based on the quality of the lodgings, the amenities and general ambience, and the caliber of the golf facilities.

BANFF SPRINGS HOTEL — Banff, Alberta

THE BOULDERS — Carefree, Arizona

THE BROADMOOR — Colorado Springs, CO

*THE CLOISTER — Sea Island, GA

*COLONIAL WILLIAMSBURG INN — Willliamsburg, VA

*THE GREENBRIER — White Sulphur Springs, WV

*KINGS MILL ON THE JAMES — Williamsburg, VA

*THE HOMESTEAD — Hot Springs, VA,

*LE CHATEAU MONTEBELLO — Montebello, Quebec, Canada

LAS HADAS — Manzanillo, Colima, Mexico

MAUNA KEA BEACH HOTEL — Kohala Coast, HI

MARRIOTT'S CAMELBACK INN — Scottsdale, AZ

*MARRIOTT at SAWGRASS — Ponte Vedra Beach, FL

OJAI VALLEY INN & COUNTRY CLUB — Ojai, CA

*PINEHURST HOTEL & COUNTRY CLUB — Pinehurst, NC

QUAIL LODGE — Carmel, CA

*SADDLEBROOK GOLF & TENNIS RESORT, Wesley Chapel, FL

*THE SAGAMORE — Bolton Landing, NY

SILVERADO COUNTRY CLUB RESORT — Napa Valley, CA

SUN VALLEY LODGE — Sun Valley, ID

SCOTTSDALE PRINCESS — Scottsdale, AZ

THE WESTIN LA PALOMA — Tucson, AZ

THE WIGWAM RESORT & COUNTRY CLUB — Litchfield Park, AZ

*WINTERGREEN — Wintergreen, VA

*THE WOODSTOCK INN & RESORT — Woodstock, VT

The book you are reading is the Western Edition. The top 25 resorts with an asterisk (*) beside the name are described in the Eastern Edition, also available from Hunter Publishing.

It is our sincere wish that you find this book helpful and that you will experience the pleasure we enjoyed, whichever resorts you choose to visit.

HOW TO GET THE MOST FROM THIS BOOK

In order to best utilize this book, I suggest you become familiar with the following abbreviations and explanations.

(EP): European Plan. No meals are included in the rates shown.

(MAP): Modified American Plan. Two meals per person are included in rates. Usually these are breakfast and dinner.

(FAP): American Plan. All three meals per person are included in rates shown.

GREEN FEES: Rates shown are per person. When two rates are indicated (for example: $20/$30), the first rate is for weekdays, the second for weekends or holidays.

CART FEES: Rates are per cart for two players for 18 holes. Green and cart fees shown are rates reserved for guests of the facility. Rates are usually somewhat higher for "walk-ons."

LODGING RATES: All rates are based on double occupancy and are for two people unless otherwise noted.

All rates are for resorts' peak golf season. In most cases, they are lower at other times of the year. Some resorts do not have "seasonal" rates and remain the same throughout the year. All resorts reserve the right to change rates without prior notice. Due to this fact, there may be a variation between the rates we indicate and those in effect at the time you make a reservation. The resort costs shown are designed as a guide only.

None of the rates include taxes or gratuities unless so stated. Many resorts automatically attach a certain percentage to your bill which covers gratuities. When making reservations, ask about such extras and what they cover. In some cases, you will find they cover check-in and baggage handling. This is, however, an exception.

CREDIT CARDS: While the great majority of hotels and resorts accept credit cards for payment, this is NOT always the case. Check the policy in advance.

TEE TIMES: When making reservations, be sure to request tee times, at least for the first day you wish to play.

GOLF PACKAGES: By and large, these represent a fair savings. But you must realize that in many cases, due to travel time, on the days you arrive and depart no golf will be possible.

TRAVEL AGENCIES: We strongly urge that you use a travel agency once you have made up your mind to book a reservation. In the great majority of cases there is no fee involved to you and you will find it can make your experience go more smoothly.

PETS: Very few resorts will allow pets. In some instances you may find a kennel in a town near the resort. I suggest you ask the resort when making your reservations if such a facility is available.

UNITED STATES

ARIZONA

THE ARIZONA BILTMORE
24th Street and Missouri
Phoenix, AZ 85002
(602) 955–6600
(800) 528–3696

The word "tradition" sums up the Biltmore very well. A lavishly landscaped resort completed in the extravagant late 1920s, it has not lost its stately atmosphere nor its quiet gentility.

With 500 rooms, including several wings and courts, 18 tennis courts (17 lighted) as well as professionals ready to assist you, enough dining areas to sustain a small city, three pools, a health center, sauna, and therapy pools, it is very complete. The Biltmore Health Center, by the way, offers a highly personalized two-day medical evaluation and is located on the grounds of the resort.

The Biltmore, with its new 39,000-square-foot conference center, is one of only five hotels worldwide to win the coveted McRand Conference Center Award for excellence in quality and service as a convention and meeting site. They are also proud of the fact that for the past 30 years they have been the recipients of the Mobil Five Star Award.

While not owned by the hotel, there are two 18-hole golf courses, located adjacent to the property. The Links Course with a par of 71, playing at 6,300/5,726/4,912 yards, offers a typical resort layout. The Adobe Course reaches out a bit more with yardage of 6,767/6,455/6,094 and parring at 72/73. Although we have played both, and enjoyed each of them, we found the Adobe Course to be the better of the two.

RATES (EP) Traditional room: $210. Classic: $260. Resort: $290. Premier Room: $330. Golf package: (including lodging, golf, cart), $335 per couple per day. MAP and FAP rates are available upon request. Rates quoted are for January-April. Green fees: $60, including cart.

ARRIVAL Air: Phoenix. Car: I-17 off Glendale exit, east to 24th, then south to Missouri.

THE ARIZONA GOLF RESORT
425 South Power Road
Mesa, AZ 85206
(602) 832–3202
(800) 528–8282

Accommodations consist of 150 rooms, some with kitchenettes, some with full kitchens as well as a few one- and two-bedroom suites. Each suite has a living room, dining area and a fully equipped kitchen. There are also fairway suites and casitas.

Dining facilities include Anabelle's Restaurant, plus a lounge as well as the "19th Green" offering a coffee shop menu and cocktail service. There are also a number of outstanding restaurants within a short distance.

The resort also offers the use of four tennis courts, an Olympic-size pool and access to a health club located nearby (within ½ mile—additional fee required).

Golf may be enjoyed on an 18-hole course with enough water hazards and bunkers to keep you honest. Playing 6,574/6,195/5,782/5,124 yards, it pars at 71/72.

RATES (EP) Rooms: $125. 1-bedroom fairway suites: $145. 2 bedrooms: (2 to 4 people) $240. Green fees: $40 including cart. Golf package: 3 nights/2 days (includes 3 nights lodging, daily breakfast, two rounds of golf, cart and tax), $269 per person. The rates shown are for January 1-April 30.

ARRIVAL Air: Phoenix Airport (45 minutes). Car: Maricopa Freeway to Superstition Freeway. Exit on Power Road and continue north to resort.

THE BOULDERS
P.O. Box 2090
Carefree, AZ 85377
(602) 488–9009
(800) 553–1717

Opened in December of 1984, The Boulders is located in the desert foothills northeast of Phoenix. At 2,500 feet it enjoys clear air, and

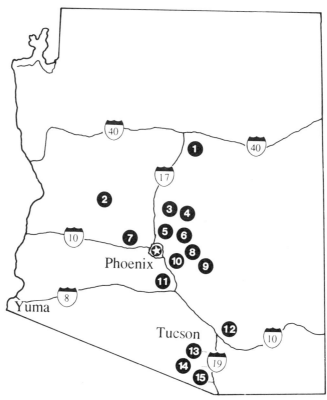

Arizona

1. Fairfield Flagstaff Resort
2. Rancho de Los Caballeros
3. The Boulders
4. Rio Verde Resort & Ranch
5. The Arizona Biltmore
6. Clarion Inn at McCormick
   Ranch
   Hyatt Regency Scottsdale
   Marriott's Camelback
   Inn Resort
   Marriott's Mountain Shadows
   Orange Tree Golf Resort
   The Phoenician Resort
   Pima Golf Resort
   The Registry Resort
   Scottsdale Princess

7. The Wigwam Resort &
   Country Club
8. The Arizona Golf Resort
9. The Gold Canyon Resort
10. Sheraton San Marcus
11. Francisco Grande Resort
12. Loews Ventana Canyon Resort
    Sheraton El Conquistador
13. Fairfield Green Valley
14. Tubac Valley Country Club & Inn
15. Rio Rico Resort & Country Club

a landscape that must be seen to be believed. It is an area of saguaro cactus, Indian paintbrush, hollyhocks and giant boulders shaped by water, wind and time.

Within this majestic setting, the former owners, Rockresorts Inc., put together a complex which, following the normal pattern of their developments, has become one of the premier resorts. In addition to The Boulders, Rockresorts also created the magnificent Mauna Kea Beach Hotel, Caneel Bay, Little Dix Bay and operate the magnificent Woodstock Inn. In other words they know how to put the proper wheels on a resort development.

Built to complement the terrain, the resort used desert tones, textured natural surfaces with flagstone floors, hand-crafted Indian baskets, pottery and original art of the region. The net result is outstanding.

There are 120 individually sited casitas using natural wood, Mexican glazed tile, and adobe plaster surfaces. Each casita has a private patio and a full size wood burning fireplace. They represent some of the most unusual and, I might add, most beautiful accommodations we have visited.

The main building is the site of the Discovery Lounge with its picture window views of the landscape and two of three dining rooms. The very special Latilla is open for breakfast and dinner as well as a fabulous Sunday Brunch, while the Palo Verde dining room is available for all three meals. This part of the resort is also the location of the executive meeting facilities and has a 1,960-square-foot conference room.

The free-form swimming pool, backed by a beautiful waterfall, is a place to relax and enjoy a light meal or a libation. Not a bad way to go after a swim, a game of tennis or a round of golf. Horseback riding is located nearby with picturesque trails to hike, ride or stroll.

Golf, under the direction of PGA professional Bob Irving, may be enjoyed on the resort's 27-hole complex. With three nines available and using a crossover system, you wind up with three 18-hole layouts, each parring at 72. The Boulders/Lake 18 stretches out 7,266/6,459/5,796/4,983 yards; The Saguaro/Boulders combination of nines plays 7,012/6,391/5,703/4,951 yards; while the Lakes/Saguaro combination weighs in at a lusty 6,982/6,344/5,787/4,860 yards.

We have not played the new merging of three nines but we did play the older 18-hole layout. It was a course that could set your teeth on edge. While it was most certainly beautiful, it also could be deadly. There were many hidden problems that you discover only after you have made your play. Looking at the yardage of the new set up I have to assume they didn't make it any friendlier.

There is a complete clubhouse and very well stocked pro shop. The Boulders Club House provides men's and women's locker rooms and a coffee shop. It's actually a bit more than just a coffee shop and we understand it has recently undergone a complete renovation.

RATES (MAP) Casitas: $445 per couple. Green fees, including cart: $75. There are golf packages available during the off season only. Rates are for the January-April period.

ARRIVAL Air: Phoenix. Car: Take I-17 north to Carefree Highway then travel east to Scottsdale Road, then turn north for less than a mile.

INN AT McCORMICK RANCH
7401 North Scottsdale Road
Scottsdale, AZ 85253
602) 948–5050
(800) 528–3130

This resort was originally internationally known for breeding and training Arabian horses. It has an unusual setting for the desert in that it is sited on the shores of a lake.

The Inn has 125 rooms and suites, plus some two- to three-bedroom condominiums. They also have excellent meeting facilities and can handle groups of up to 200 theater-style.

A sample of the activities available includes: a heated swimming pool, a whirlpool and tennis on four lighted courts with a professional staff available to assist. Along with horseback riding (located nearby), biking, sailing, fishing, and golf, there should be enough to keep you busy. The McCormick Ranch is the recipient of the AAA Four Diamond Award.

Golf may be played on The Palm Course measuring 7,021/6,202/5,309 yards with a par of 72 or The Pine Course, stretching out 7,020/6,333/5,494 yards, also parring at 72.

The clubhouse facilities include a very large pro shop, a dining room, as well as a lounge and locker rooms.

RATES (EP) Hotel: $175/$195. Suites range from $275 to $450. Condominiums: $145/$350. Green fees: $65 including cart. Golf packages: 2 nights/2 days (includes lodging, 2 rounds of golf and cart), $586 per couple. Rates are for January to mid-May.

ARRIVAL Air: Phoenix (25 minutes). Car: Scottsdale Road and McCormick Parkway (5 minutes north of downtown Scottsdale).

FAIRFIELD FLAGSTAFF RESORT
1900 North Country Club Drive
Flagstaff, AZ 86001
(602) 526–3232
AZ (800) 352–5777
NAT (800) 526–1004

Flagstaff is one of the only areas within Arizona which experiences four distinct seasons. This is high country with skiing at nearby Fairfield Snow Bowl in the winter, rushing rivers and wild flowers in the spring, warm days and crisp nights in the summer. Fairfield Estates, located right in the middle of this ideal area, is surrounded by more than a million acres of national forest.

Accommodations consist of fully equipped townhouse condominiums.

If you prefer not to "condo it," there is excellent dining available in the Clubhouse, or you might prefer to venture into nearby Flagstaff.

Tennis may be enjoyed on 12 courts (eight lighted) with professionals available to assist. An Olympic-size pool and horseback riding are a few of the other activities available.

Golf is offered on 36 holes under the supervision of the Director of Golf, Jack Wright and staff. One course is closed for member play only. The Elden Hills course is, however, available for guest play. Parring at 72/73, it plays 6,104/5,380 yards. It is well trapped and brings water into play on six holes.

RATES (EP) Townhouse: 1 bedroom and full-size kitchen (sleeps 4), $110. Sleeps up to 6, $145. Green fees: $25/$30, carts $22.

ARRIVAL Air: Flagstaff. Car: Exit I-40 east of Flagstaff, to Country Club Drive.

FAIRFIELD GREEN VALLEY
P. O. Box 587
Green Valley, AZ 85622
(602) 625–4441
(800) 528–4930

On approximately 5,000 acres with 15,000 permanent residents, this resort is actually a retirement community which welcomes visitors seeking a relaxing vacation and who may be interested in buying property.

There are 168 townhouse/casitas available for rental all with living room, one bedroom and kitchen.

As a guest you have access to all of the recreational facilities normally reserved for residents, including six tennis courts and nine swimming pools.

Golf is offered on four 18-hole championship courses. The Desert Hills layout is one of the more challenging courses in Arizona. Though not particularly long, playing at 6,476/6,183 yards, it pars at 72. It is well bunkered and brings water into play on six holes. There are also a number of other courses within the local area.

RATES (EP) Townhouse: $95. Green fees: $22, carts $20. Casitas: 3 nights/4 days, $199; 7 nights/8 days, $455. Rates are for mid-December to April 1st.

ARRIVAL Air: Tucson. Car: south of Tucson (25 miles) on I-19.

FRANCISCO GRANDE RESORT
P.O. Box 326
Casa Grande, AZ 85222
(602) 836–6444AZ
AZ (800) 237–4238
NAT (800) 782–2887

The Francisco Grande, at one time an outstanding destination resort, lost touch with the passing years and suffered. Closed for almost two years, it now has been renovated and brought back to full life. It is amazing what an infusion of several million dollars can accomplish.

The resort is a multi-level hotel with 112 guest rooms and suites. They are also able to handle meeting and conference groups of up to 350.

We understand the food service is as good or better than when we visited here. Dining is now offered in the Palo Verde Room or in a more informal setting on the outdoor veranda.

A few of the activities available include: a huge swimming pool, modern lighted Laykold tennis courts and, of course, golf.

The golf course has undergone extensive renovation with added trees and traps.

Its length remains awesome as it reaches out 7,320/6,975/6,454/5,554 yards and pars at 72.

RATES (EP) Patio rooms: $49. Tower: $85. Suites $99/$159. Green fees: $35/$45 including cart. Golf package: 2 nights/3 days (includes Tower room, green fees and cart, range balls, daily breakfast, taxes and gratuities), $199 per person.

ARRIVAL Car: mid-way between Phoenix and Tucson turn west to Casa Grande. The resort is 4 miles west of Casa Grande on Highway 84.

THE GOLD CANYON RESORT
6100 South Kings Ranch Road
Apache Junction, AZ 85219
(602) 982–9090
(800) 624–6445

The natural beauty of this part of Arizona is legendary. Located about twenty five miles (an hours drive) due east of Phoenix at an elevation of 1,715 feet, the 3,300-acre Gold Canyon Resort has much to offer.

Speaking of legends, Apache Junction is reputed to be the location of the fabled Lost Dutchman Mine. As the story goes, it is somewhere in the Superstition Mountains. Although many have sought and, in fact, are still seeking it, no one has been able to locate the Dutchman's gold.

Each of the resort's southwestern-style rooms and suites is positioned to offer a view of the mountains. The rooms are very spacious, and each has a wet bar, fireplace and patio, with some featuring a private spa.

Their meeting facilities can handle groups of up to 130. The Clubhouse dining room features a varied and delightful menu. There is also and excellent 35-seat lounge.

Tennis, swimming and golf are but a few of the activities available for your enjoyment. Old western-style trail rides, with an experienced wrangler to assist, and guided tours, overnight campouts and cookouts can be arranged.

The golf course, now an 18-hole layout, measures 6,398/6,004/5,686/4,876, with a par of 71/72. It is reputed to be one of the better courses in the area.

Adjacent to the resort is a development of very interesting Casa Townhouses facing the golf course. We do not know if they are available for rental as yet but you can bet they will be eventually. For more information, you may call (602) 983–1000 or (602) 982–8631.

RATES (EP) Rooms: $115. Spa rooms: $130. Golf packages are available. Green fees: $53 including cart. Rates are January 1 to April 30.

ARRIVAL Air: Phoenix. Car: Highway 60 east to Apache Junction; continue 7 miles southeast on 60 to Kings Ranch Road. Turn left to the resort.

HYATT REGENCY SCOTTSDALE
7500 East Doubletree Ranch Road
Scottsdale, AZ 85258
(602) 991–3388
(800) 233–1234

The Scottsdale Regency represents a slight change for Hyatt. The architectural design seems to reflect a definite Moroccan style. Although very pleasing in appearance, it is unique.

While only four stories in height, the hotel appears more massive than it actually is. Perhaps this is due to the manner in which everything seems to unfold. With five different courtyards opening onto the lawn and tennis area, they stretch along the lakefront, overlooking the pools and the golf course. The view from the three-story atrium lobby is absolutely outstanding. All in all, the setting creates a very quiet and relaxed atmosphere.

A magnificent art collection is showcased in and outside the hotel. The art includes sculpture, wall friezes, paintings and carvings. Some of the artifacts date back to 700 B.C. There are 439 guest rooms within the main structure.

There is also a special VIP wing (The Regency Club) located on the third level. Each room has its own air-conditioning control, cable TV, private balcony and a fully stocked, mini service bar. There are also six different categories of suites to choose from. In addition, there are seven Casitas located lakeside.

The Golden Swan, serving lunch and dinner overlooking the lagoon, functions as an indoor as well as an outdoor restaurant. The Squash Blossom, a 300-seat restaurant, provides a beautiful view of the cascading fountain area. Finally, there is the casual Sandolo with its view of the "water playground." While each of the aforementioned restaurants has cocktail service the resort also has Andiamo, a high energy entertainment lounge, as well as the poolside bar and snackbar. Should you go hungry or thirsty at this place, it is your own fault.

Including the 14,000-square-foot ballroom, Hyatt Scottsdale has 23 meeting rooms and can accommodate 1,500 theater-style and 1,200 in a banquet configuration.

The recreational facilities are excellent and include: tennis on eight Laykold surfaced courts (four lighted) with a professional staff and supported by a tennis shop, a health and fitness center, saunas, massage rooms, therapeutic massage, croquet and a four-mile jogging and cycling trail laid out over the 640-acre Gainey Ranch property. Horseback riding is available nearby.

Then there is water in the form of the "water playground", consisting of a half acre of pools with water falls, and a three- story water slide along with a sand beach.

Golf is served up on three distinctly different nine-hole layouts. Designed by Benz and Poellot, each nine pars at 36.

The Arroyo nine features a meandering desert look, which makes sense as "arroyo" means a "desert wash."

The Lakes layout also lives up to its name. It a "showcase nine" in that, while a variety of water hazards come into play in the form of lakes, streams and ponds, it enjoys a garden-like setting.

The Dunes is reminiscent of Scottish courses with its rolling moorlike terrain.

Using a crossover system the Arroyo/Lakes plays 6,818/6,252/5,330 yards. The Dunes/Lakes combination reaches out 6,607/5,975/4,993 yards and the Arroyo/Dunes measures 6,637/6,089/5,169 yards.

Available to assist is a professional staff under the supervision of the Director of Golf, Paul Purtzer.

RATES (EP) Rooms: $275/$325. 1-bedroom suites: $350/$700. Green fees: $75 including cart. Golf package: 2 nights/2 days (includes lodging, 2 rounds of golf, with cart, continental breakfast), $857 per couple. Rates are for January 1 to May 15.

ARRIVAL Air: Phoenix Sky Harbor Airport (45 minutes). Car: from the airport take 44th street north to Camelback Road. Turn right on Camelback and proceed east to Scottsdale Road—turn left and drive north to Double Tree Ranch Road. Turn right (east).

LOEWS VENTANA CANYON RESORT
7000 North Resort Drive
Tucson, AZ 85715
(602) 299–2020
(800) 234–5117

The Ventana Canyon Resort is located in one of the prettiest parts of Arizona, the Sonoran Desert. Situated in the immediate foothills of the Catalina Mountains, the resort structure blends very well with the surrounding area. It is a world of rock spires, guarded by stately saguaro cacti.

While very large (400 rooms), the structure is not a high-rise. The entire setting is park-like, with all the amenities expected of a first-rate resort, but with an added dimension of peace and quiet. All this, plus the fact that you are only about 20 minutes from the downtown area of Tucson.

Each of the rooms or suites has a private balcony and is equipped with a refrigerator and mini-bar. The great majority offer views of either the city of Tucson skyline or the Coronado National Forest.

Loews meeting facilities are quite large, with a capacity of up to 1,300 people. With two major ball rooms and 26 separate function rooms, the hotel provides 37,000 square feet of space for group activities.

You will not want for food or entertainment as there are several restaurants, including The Ventana offering French cuisine, The Canyon Cafe with a general menu, and The Flying V Bar and Night Club for dining and entertainment.

A sample of the activities available include: nature trails, two swimming pools with adjacent hot tubs, jogging, a beautiful tennis complex (10 lighted courts) with a professional staff to assist, Jacuzzis, saunas, a health club and, of course, golf.

The golf course, a Tom Fazio design, plays 6,969/6,380/5,753/4,780 yards, with a par of 72. This layout has now become a private affair, available for member usage only. Guests of the hotel, however, enjoy golfing privileges at The Canyon Course, also a Fazio design.

Parring at 72, The Canyon Course measures 6,818/6,282/5,756/4,919 yards. While the front nine of the Canyon might well be considered conservative, the back side will offer you all the challenge you can handle. Water becomes a factor on only two holes.

RATES (EP) Rooms: $205/$255. 1-bedroom suites: $400/$550. Green fees: $75, including cart. Golf package: 3 nights/4 days (includes lodging, 4 days green fees, cart, bag storage), $1150 per couple. Rates are for January 15 to May 31.

ARRIVAL Air: Tucson.

MARRIOTT'S CAMELBACK INN RESORT
5402 E. Lincoln Drive
Scottsdale, AZ 85253
(602) 948–1700
(800) 242–2635

The Camelback Inn goes back many years. In fact, it dates back to about 1936 and has been a favorite of many well known people since that time. The Inn has not lost its grace nor its subdued splendor. It actually seems to have gained stature over the intervening period. Having established a tradition for excellence, Marriott's Camelback Inn is one of only 21 hotels or resorts in the United States to have continually earned the Mobil Five Star Award. That's quite an accomplishment when you consider the fact that there are over of 20,000 hotels in this country. It truly is a "World Class" resort.

Accommodations consist of 423 rooms, including many adobe casas decorated in a Southwestern motif. The rooms and suites are beautifully decorated and include all of the amenities one would expect of a resort of this caliber.

The Inn has outstanding meeting facilities for large and small groups, and they are handled in the Marriott's usual unbeatable manner.

Their dining facilities are among the finest in the Southwest. The Chaparral Dining Room, while a bit formal, is superb (jackets are required, ties are optional). The Navajo Room, less formal but also outstanding, is available for all three meals. There is also the North Pool for casual dining, and available for breakfast, lunch, and Sunday brunch. Should you have an early tee time, consider breakfast at the Country Club. Again, both the service and the food are excellent.

Just a sample of the activities at your disposal includes: three swimming pools (if you include the Spa pool), 10 tennis courts (6 lighted) with a professional on deck to assist, horseback riding (located nearby) and whirlpool baths. Certainly less strenuous but, nonetheless, very interesting, are the resort shops on the grounds: a ladies' boutique, a men's "Gentry Shop", an Indian Art and Craft Shop and an outstanding Sport Shop featuring tennis, golf, and swim wear as well as casual shoes, etc. There are additional shops offering a wide variety of items.

Golf, located at the Camelback Golf Club, may be enjoyed on two outstanding courses. The Indian Bend layout, a Jack Snyder design, lies in the shadow of Mummy Mountain. Parring at 72, this course reaches out a monstrous 7,014/6,486/5,917 yards. While there is very little water coming into play the undulating fairways, trees and fast greens will more than keep your attention.

The Padre Course was designed by Red Lawrence. It is a bit more in my league with the mileage at 6,559/6,019/5,626 yards. The par is set at 71 for the men and 73 from the ladies tees. Although there is very little water coming into play it is well trapped. The fact that the fairways are lined with beautiful eucalyptus trees also adds to the challenge.

Both courses, as well as the outstanding golf shop, are under the supervision of the Director of Golf, Clay Atcheson.

RATES (EP) Lodging: $210/$235. The variation is location. MAP or FAP plans and golf packages are available. Rates are for January–April. Green fees: $65 including cart.

ARRIVAL Air: Phoenix. Car: north on Scottsdale Road, left on Lincoln Drive.

MARRIOTT'S MOUNTAIN SHADOWS
5641 E. Lincoln Drive
Scottsdale, AZ 85253
(602) 948–7111
(800) 228–9290

Literally in the shadow of Camelback Mountain this resort enjoys a beautiful setting. The general surroundings and the overall atmosphere reflect the grace and enchantment of the southwest.

Accommodations consist of 354 rooms, including six suites.

The Mountain Shadows, now an affiliate of Marriott Hotels, has outstanding meeting facilities. With its large ballroom and 12 separate break-out rooms they are capable of handling groups of up to 1,200.

You may elect to dine at Shells Restaurant, specializing in seafood, or the Cactus Flower, a family oriented dining room. Of course the lovely restaurant at the Country Club is also open to guests of Mountain Shadows. In the evening, a favorite gathering place is Maxfields Lounge, where you may enjoy dancing to live music.

A few of the activities at your disposal include: eight lighted tennis courts, a steam room, sauna, masseur/masseuse, two swimming pools, and a fitness center. Horseback riding is available nearby.

Golf may be played on their 18-hole par-56 course which comes complete with a stream (in fact it has been referred to as a waterfall), highly unusual for this desert area. Tee times can also be arranged on the two fabulous Camelback golf courses. For details on the Padre and Indian Bend layouts see the section on "Marriott's Camelback Inn".

RATES (EP) Rooms: $170/$290. Suites: $275/$410. Golf packages are available. Green fees: Mountain Shadows, $38 including cart. Camelback, $65 including cart. Rates are for December 25-April 30.

ARRIVAL Air: Sky Harbor International Airport (approximately 20 minutes). Car: from Scottsdale Road turn west onto Lincoln Drive.

ORANGE TREE GOLF RESORT
10601 North 56th Street
Scottsdale, AZ 85254
(602) 948-6100
(800) 228-0386

One of the newer additions to the Scottsdale resort scene (opened in January of 1989), this golf and conference center was developed on a beautiful 128-acre site.

Being very careful to blend the resort within the surrounding desert setting, the architects of Orange Tree have been quite successful in capturing the flavor of the southwest without resorting to the traditional and sometimes overwhelming cactus plants, Spanish tile and heavy stucco motif so common within this area. All in all, they have achieved a delightful change of pace.

Accommodations consist of 160 oversized and soundproof rooms along with two executive suites. You may select either a king size bed or a room with two double beds. Following a Southwestern architectural style, the rooms have been arranged in a series of two-story villas, with the majority enjoying a view of the golf course.

A sample of the amenities includes: a 27-inch cable-equipped TV set—plus a 9″ TV located in the bathroom so you won't miss your soap opera while using the whirlpool spa built for two. Other equipment includes a VCR (they will arrange movie rentals) and an AM/FM stereo. These people are not savages—there is also a fully stocked wet bar and ice makers. Each of the rooms has either a private patio or a deck.

With eight meeting rooms (14,000 square feet of meeting space), the Orange Tree can accommodate groups of from 10 to 500.

Dining facilities are offered in Joe's American Grill & Bar. Located within the hotel, and overlooking the 18th fairway, the restaurant offers breakfast, lunch and dinner along with entertainment in the evening. There is, in addition, the Fairway Pavilion situated at the course, presenting a more casual setting. Light snacks and beverage service are also available in the pool area.

Now that you may well have eaten yourself into trouble, let's look at a few of the activities at your disposal. The Racquet & Fitness Club, a 25,000-square-foot facility, features 16 lighted, all-weather tennis and eight racquetball courts, an aerobics center, Nautilus work-out equipment, a heated swimming pool, therapy spas and a sauna.

While the resort is new, the golf course has been in play for over 30 years and, obviously, is very mature. Designed by Johnny Bulla, it features a complete practice area.

The Orange Tree Golf Course stretches out 6,837/6,398/5,618 yards and pars at 72. While relatively flat, it is very well trapped and has enough trees coming into play to create a definite series of challenges.

The new and extremely well-equipped pro shop is under the supervision of the Director of Golf, Mark Rose.

RATES (EP) Rooms $210. Green fees: $60 including cart. Golf package: 2 nights/2 days (includes breakfast, lodging, 2 rounds of golf with cart, club storage, lockers), $684 per couple.

ARRIVAL Air: Phoenix Sky Harbor Airport (13 miles) or Scottsdale Municipal (4 miles). Car: from the Scottsdale Airport drive south to Shea Blvd. Turn west and drive to north 56th. Turn right (north), drive about a block and you have arrived.

THE PHOENICIAN RESORT
6000 East Camelback Road
Scottsdale, AZ 85251
(602) 941–8200
(800) 423–4127

The Phoenician, sited on 130 acres, is located on the southeast side of Camelback Mountain.

While the exterior design is rather unusual, unfortunately it is not at all consistent with the general decor of this area. It is considered by many as being ostentatious, even a bit on the tacky side.

Accommodations consist of 606 rooms and suites, including 132 casitas.

The Phoenician can handle meeting groups and has separate space to accommodate them.

The various restaurants include the Main Dining Room, the Outdoor Terrace as well as The Signature Restaurant. Lighter fare is also available at poolside and at the Cantina.

A few of the activities to be enjoyed include a health spa and 10 tennis courts.

The Phoenician Golf Course designed by Homer Flint plays 6,487/6,033/5,058 yards and pars at 71/72.

RATES (EP) Rooms: $250/$340. Suites: $600 and up. Casitas: $325/$365. Casita suites: $650. Green fees: $75, including cart. Rates are for peak season January through mid-May.

ARRIVAL Air: Phoenix Sky Harbor Airport.

PIMA GOLF RESORT
7330 North Pima Road
Scottsdale, AZ 85258
(602) 948–3800
(800) 344–0262

The Pima Golf Resort offers accommodations in 100 rooms, including 53 two-bedroom suites. Each room is equipped with a guest service bar and, of course, is air-conditioned.

Dining is available in The Patio Room with entertainment provided in The Sand Trap Lounge. The resort can handle meeting groups of up to 200 people.

Other amenities at your disposal: a heated swimming pool and golf. Horseback riding and hay rides can also be arranged nearby.

Golf is played on the resort's own 18-hole championship layout under the supervision of the Director of Golf, Jim Mooney. Playing 6,952/6,449/5,722 it pars at 72/73. There is water coming into play on nine of the 18 holes.

RATES (EP) Rooms: $115. 1-bedroom suite: $145/$165. Green fees: $48 including cart. Golf package: 2 nights/2 days (includes lodging, two rounds of golf with cart, daily breakfast, tax and gratuity), $212/$242 per person. Rates are for January through mid-April.

ARRIVAL Air: Phoenix. Car: North Pima Road runs north and south and is due east of Scottsdale Road.

RANCHO DE LOS CABALLEROS
Wickenburg, AZ 85358
(602) 684–5484

The name translates to "Rancho of the Horsemen." The name is appropriate, as the resort is sited on 20,000 acres of rolling foothills, and is a working ranch. The Rancho is open only during the winter months of October through May each year.

Accommodations consist of rooms in the Inn, plus some 14 one- to four-bedroom bungalows carefully decorated to bring memories of the Old West into each room. There are a total of 73 spacious rooms and suites.

Meals are served in the main dining room, offering a menu which is both varied and imaginative. And, I must hasten to add, the food is outstanding.

The Rancho is capable of handling meeting/conference groups and can handle a maximum of 150 people for group affairs.

They offer riding (60-horse stable), desert cookouts and perhaps a look at a cattle roundup. A few other activities available include complimentary tennis on four courts, skeet/trap shooting, scheduled square dances, swimming and, of course, golf.

Children are welcome here with indoor and outdoor playgrounds and trained counselors to supervise their activities. I know it will break your heart to be left alone to enjoy the resort's other amenities.

It can be cool in the evenings so warm clothing is recommended.

Golf is now offered on the new Los Caballeros 18-hole golf course. With a yardage of 6,965/6,577/5,896 it pars at 72/73. The course circles the entire resort and comes complete with lakes, traps and trees.

Rancho de Los Caballeros provides a clubhouse including a pro shop, locker rooms and a restaurant.

Guest play may also be arranged on the Wickenburg Country Club, located approximately three miles away.

RATES (FAP) Lodgings: $125 per person. Green fees: $35, cart $26. Golf package: 3 nights/4 days (includes lodging in Sun Terrace Room, FAP, golf or riding each day—carts not included), $398 per person. Rates quoted are for February-May.

ARRIVAL Air: Phoenix. Private aircraft: Wickenburg (4,200-foot paved) or the Rancho, 2,600 feet. Car: an hour's drive northwest of Phoenix on Highway 60/89, 2 miles west of Wickenburg on Highway 60.

THE REGISTRY RESORT
7171 North Scottsdale Road
Scottsdale, AZ 85253
(602) 991–3800
(800) 247–9810

The Registry, located in this vacation paradise, is a luxurious 76-acre resort and convention complex.

Accommodations consist of 319 rooms, including suites. The meeting facilities are quite large and very complete with all the modern audio/visual aids at your disposal.

Their restaurants include La Champagne, serving French cuisine, and Cafe Brioche for more casual dining. There is 24-hour room service provided as well. Live entertainment is a nightly feature.

Tennis certainly does not take a back seat to golf at this establishment, with 21 courts, a professional staff and a separate tennis shop. Other amenities include horseback riding nearby, four swimming pools and a health spa.

Golf may be enjoyed on two 18-hole layouts. The Pines, with a par of 72, plays at 7,020/6,333/5,494 yards. This layout brings water into play on six or seven holes and has more than its share of trees.

The Palms course reaches out a substantial 7,021/6,202/5,309, also parring at 72. With water in contention on nine holes and some of the toughest par-3's you want to tangle with, it will offer you all the challenge you could wish for.

RATES (EP) Rooms: $219/$245. 1-bedroom suites: $325. Green fees including cart: $65. Golf packages are available. Rates are for January-mid May.

ARRIVAL Air: Phoenix. Car: about 25 minutes from the Sky Harbor International Airport in Phoenix.

RIO RICO RESORT & COUNTRY CLUB
1550 Camino Ala Posada
Rio Rico, AZ 85621
(602) 281–1901
(800) 288–4746

Rio Rico is nestled in the mountains at an altitude of 4,000 feet. While this altitude produces beautiful clear days it also tends to get a bit sharp in the evening. The magnificent scenery provided by the Santa Cruz Mountains is one of the more spectacular sights in Arizona.

The hotel offers fine dining featuring Mexican cuisine, seafood and steaks. Located only 12 miles from Nogales and the border of Mexico, you are on top of a bargainer's paradise for shopping, along with a wide selection of places to eat and be entertained. The Rio

Rico Hotel has complete meeting facilities for groups up to 500 including eight break-out rooms.

In addition to tennis on four lighted courts, and an Olympic-size pool, the hotel offers riding and trap shooting.

Golf is available on a Robert Trent Jones, Jr. course. It stretches out an awesome 7,119/6,426/5,577 yards and pars at 72/71. It is an interesting layout with undulating terrain on the back side, a rather flat front nine and a liberal supply of water coming into play.

The golf course is two miles from the hotel. Good news: shuttle service is available.

RATES (EP) Rooms: $85. Suites: $115. Apartments: $155. Green fees: $45 including cart. Golf package: 2 nights/3 days (includes lodging, MAP, unlimited golf including cart, bag storage) weekdays $125, weekends $135 per person. Rates are for January-May.

ARRIVAL Car: 57 miles south of Tucson and 12 miles north of Nogales on I-19, Calabasas exit.

RIO VERDE RESORT & RANCH
18815 Four Peaks Boulevard
Rio Verde, AZ 85255
(602) 991–3350
(800) 233–7103

Rio Verde is an adult community consisting of approximately 600 homes and golf villas sited on 700 acres. Located 30 miles northeast of Phoenix, it enjoys a quiet desert setting. The resort is situated among the awesome beauty of the Tonto National Forest. The backdrop of the beautiful McDowell, Superstition and Mazatzal mountains form a spectacular backdrop for this entire area.

Accommodations consist of private homes located either on one of the two 18-hole courses, or very nearby. They range in size from one bedroom and den to three bedrooms and are equipped with two baths, a kitchen (fully equipped for housekeeping), a barbecue unit and a washer/dryer.

The clubhouse features a cocktail lounge and restaurant. In the evening dinner and dancing may be enjoyed in the new Oasis Restaurant.

There are six tennis courts (two lighted) and two swimming pools. Facilities for horseback riding are provided at their 140-acre ranch. As a matter of fact a few of the homes provide their own private swimming pool.

Golf is offered on Quail Run, parring at 72. It plays 6,500/6,228/5,558 yards and is a well bunkered course with water hazards coming into play on eight holes.

The second 18, the White Wing layout, measures 6,456/6,053/5,465 yards, with a par of 71. Both courses operate from a rather small pro shop located in the corner of the clubhouse.

RATES (EP) Casa Bonita weekly: $750. Hacienda: $850 weekly. Golf package: $250 per person—includes 5 rounds of golf with cart. Rates are for January-May.

ARRIVAL Air: Phoenix. Car: northeast of Scottsdale (25 miles). North on Scottsdale Road, right at Pinnacle Peak Road, continue over Reata Pass.

SCOTTSDALE PRINCESS
7575 East Princess Drive.
Scottsdale, AZ 85255
(602) 585–4848
(800) 223–1818

The Scottsdale Princess, at least from an architectural standpoint, is most impressive. Sited on a slightly raised area, using the beautiful McDowell Mountains as a backdrop, it seems to project up out of the desert somewhat like a huge Mexican estate. The general motif of "Old Mexico" complemented by earth tone colors, old stone, cottonwoods, "old brick" courtyards, even a bell tower, combine to produce a very quiet, pastoral setting.

The Princess, in our opinion, must be ranked among the very best in the United States. Although the fabulous structure and layout play a part in the evaluation, it is based more on the overall ambience, the warmth of the hotel staff, and the level of service in the restaurants.

But then they should be good at what they do. While this is the first of the Princess Resorts in the contiguous U.S., they have operated for several years with such world class properties as the Acapulco Princess and the Pierre Marques in Mexico, the

Southampton Princess in Bermuda and the renowned Bahamas Princess Resort & Casino on Grand Bahama Island.

Accommodations consist of 400 rooms and suites in the main building along with 125 casitas near the tennis complex. Each room has three phones, a mini bar and either a private terrace or balcony.

The casitas have a living room with a working fireplace (additional logs are just outside your door), a very large bedroom, a walk-in closet and a bathroom in which you could hold the NBA play-offs. These outstanding accommodations must be seen and experienced to be fully appreciated.

The Grand Ballroom, one of the largest meeting facilities in the state and measuring some 22,500 square feet, can handle groups of 1,550 (school-room style), 2,500 (theater-style) and 1850 (banquet-style). The ballroom can be subdivided into nine separate meeting rooms, each with state-of-the-art audio/visual equipment. There are, in addition, two large "Board Rooms" and eight break-out rooms. Should additional space be required there are also six fully equipped casita meeting rooms available. One other extra—there is a separate check-in and check-out section for meeting groups, keeping them out of the vacationers way, or perhaps it's the other way around. For more detailed meeting information you may call the resort.

There are a total of four dining rooms along with six cocktail lounges. In my opinion, that is a perfect balance.

The newest restaurant, The Marquesa, is in a class by itself, featuring a most unusual cuisine (for this country). It is an intermingling of dishes taken from Catalonia, which includes northeastern Spain, the French region of Roussillon and from an Italian city located on the Island of Sardinia. The combination includes olive-oil, garlic, tomatoes, eggplant, seafood, beef, game, beans and even pasta—it is a delightful culinary experience. There is also La Hacienda for seafood and Mexican fare, Las Ventanas, adjacent to the pool area and the Championship Bar & Grill. The latter is, of course, located at the golf club. Entertainment and dancing is offered nightly in the Caballo Bayo Lounge.

Along with the two golf courses you may enjoy 10 tennis courts, including a stadium court, a health and fitness center with racquetball and squash courts, aerobics, weight rooms, saunas, steambaths, loofas, herbal wraps as well as three swimming pools. Adjacent to the resort is a 400-acre equestrian center with a four-mile cross country course and two polo fields.

The two golf courses, adjacent to the hotel, are public facilities owned and operated by the city of Scottsdale. These two layouts are under the supervision of the Head Golf Professional, Jack Carter, and an excellent and friendly staff.

The Stadium Course, home of the 1988 Phoenix Open, must be considered one of the better layouts in the country. Stretching out 6,992/6,508/6,049/5,567 yards, it pars at 71. A Tom Weiskopf and Jay Morrish design, it is a links type affair, with rolling terrain, multi-level greens, over 70 traps (a few six or seven feet deep) and water coming into play on seven holes. This layout will keep your undivided attention (at least it better had). While fun to play, it is anything but a pushover.

The Desert Course, is a bit more of a relaxing affair. Again, this is a Tom Weiskopf, Jay Morrish design layout. Measuring 6,525/5,877/5,314 yards, it also pars at 71. The courses are supported by an outstanding golf shop offering all the amenities.

RATES (EP) Rooms-Hotel: $200/$260. Cholla Suites: $375. Casita: $475. Green fees: Stadium Course, $80 including cart; Desert Course, $35 including cart.

ARRIVAL Air: Sky Harbor (approximately 1 hour). Private aircraft: (including private jets) Scottsdale Municipal Airport (10 minutes away). Car: the resort is about ¼ mile north of the intersection of Bell Road and Scottsdale Blvd.

SHERATON SAN MARCUS
1 San Marcus Place
Chandler, AZ 85224
(602) 963–6655
(800) 325–3535

The original San Marcus Resort dates back many years—in fact the original structure was completed in 1912. Like many lovely old resorts time passed it by and it was virtually closed in 1979. Only the lodge with its 44 rooms (built in 1961) and the golf course continued to function.

Starting in 1986 a dramatic $19 million rehabilitation and expansion of San Marcus, including the addition of three new wings, was begun. There are now a total of 295 rooms and suites—45 overlooking the golf course, and 250 in the new structures. There are also 11 executive suites. San Marcus has set aside some 30,000 square feet of function space for meeting and convention groups. Included in this area is a 5,500-square-foot ballroom and 13 additional breakout meeting rooms. Of course, in the usual Sheraton manner, they can provide all the state-of-the-art audio/visual equipment which may be required for business groups.

The three restaurants, on the grounds include the 1912 Room, the Cafe, and Mulligan's Clubhouse Grill. During the evening you may choose to relax in the historic piano bar or perhaps dance a bit in the lounge.

In addition to golf, a few of the activities available include lighted tennis courts, swimming, a whirlpool, horseback riding, jogging, bicycling and an on-site fitness center.

The golf course, which recently underwent a complete renovation, measures 6,450/6,117/5,371 yards and pars at 72. While not heavily trapped, there is more than enough sand and, as usual, it seems to be in the wrong place. Water coming into play in the form of three ponds and a canal, involving eight holes, is also a factor. All in all it is a fun layout to play.

RATES (EP) Rooms: $155/$170. Executive Suites: $210. Suites $425. Green fees: $30/$35 including cart.

ARRIVAL Air: Sky Harbor International. Car: off I-10 onto Chandler Blvd. Travel east to intersection of Chandler Blvd. and Arizona Avenue.

SHERATON TUCSON EL CONQUISTADOR
10000 North Oracle Road
Tucson, AZ 85704
(602) 742-7000
(800) 325-3535

The El Conquistador architecturally blends very well into the locale. The 440 rooms, suites and casitas are done in a Western Spanish architectural motif, which is both impressive and beautiful. Their meeting facilities are also impressive: with rooms for groups of from 10 to 1,200.

Dining is available in the White Dove, which specializes in continental cuisine; the Last Territory, presenting Western fare; and the Sundance Cafe for breakfast, lunch or dinner. They have not forgotten thirsty golfers either, as there are three cocktail lounges.

There are 16 lighted tennis courts with a pro shop and tennis professionals available to assist. In addition, there are four racquetball courts, a health club with a full spa program, a swimming pool and riding stables. With their 40 horse stables, the resort is able to set up trail rides, breakfast or dinner affairs along with hayrides.

Golf may be enjoyed on 27 holes: the El Conquistador nine, a par 35 affair, contiguous to the hotel and the Canada Hills Country Club course, located nearby. The Club layout plays 6,698/ 6,215/5,316 yards and pars at 72. Bite off what you think you can handle. While relatively open, it is a fun course and a demanding one.

The PGA professional is Carl Dalpiaz.

RATES (EP) Rooms: $160/$310. Casitas: $280 and up. Green fees: $60 including cart. Golf packages are available. Rates are for January-May.

ARRIVAL Air: Tucson. Car: I-10 north, off at Miracle, then east to Oracle Road, then north.

TUBAC VALLEY COUNTRY CLUB & INN
P.O.Box 1358
Tubac, AZ 85640
(602) 398–2211

The Inn is sited on the original Otero Spanish land grant in the lush Santa Cruz Valley. Just 25 miles from the Mexican border, it is surrounded by the Santa Rita range to the east and the Tumacacories to the west.

Accommodations consist of Casitas (little houses), featuring a wood burning fireplace, a bedroom, and living room. Some have a full kitchen. The Villas have two bedrooms, two baths, living room, and kitchen. The full Villas, by the way, are handled by a local real-estate firm—(602) 398–2701.

Dining is a wonderful experience at the Inn. The Stables and Terrace Dining Rooms are well known throughout the area, for their outstanding food and service. The Territorial Room is primarily used for meeting groups.

A few of the other activities to be enjoyed include a tennis court, a very large swimming pool and horseback riding. Tours of the general area, as well as into "Old Mexico", can also be arranged.

The Santa Cruz River forms the main challenge of this golf course. The trees and many traps also tend to keep your attention. Reaching out a very strong 7,147/6,592/5,442 yards, it pars at 72/71.

RATES (EP) Posadas: $75/$93. Casitas: with kitchen $98/$120, without kitchen $89/$98. Weekly/monthly rates are available. Green fees: $30, including carts. Rates are mid-December to mid-April.

ARRIVAL Air: Tucson or Nogales. Car: south from Tucson on Highway 19, off at exit 34.

THE TUCSON NATIONAL RESORT & SPA
2727 West Club Drive
Tucson, AZ 85741
(602) 297–2271
(800) 528–4856

Located on 650 acres of high chaparral desert, the Tucson National is architecturally very distinctive. Its outward appearance is one of quiet formality.

Accommodations consist of 51 casita rooms, 116 villas and a townhouse—all with private patios or balconies, wet bars and refrigerators. 27 of the Executive Casitas have a living room, bedroom and a kitchen. Some of the accommodations are poolside while others are golf course oriented.

A few years back the Tucson National underwent a major renovation—with the addition of a second swimming pool, 79 poolside rooms more villa suites, and a new 18,000 square foot convention center allowing them to handle larger group affairs.

Dining is provided in the casual setting of the Fiesta.

This resort really gets into the spa plan—with deluxe massage, facials, herbal wraps, and special therapy. There are, in fact, special rates for a "Spa Getaway". There are few spas in the world that can offer the variety of services available at the National.

Golf may be enjoyed on 27 holes—the Gold, Orange and the Green nines. When inter-joined to form 18 holes, you have Orange/Gold at 7,108/6,549/5,764 yards with a par of 72/73. The Green/Orange combination weighs in at a yardage of 6,692/6,215/5,428, parring at 72. The Gold/Green nines play, 6,860/6,388/5,502 and par at 72/73. Water hazards, bunkers and very slightly undulating terrain make them all interesting as well as challenging affairs.

RATES (EP) Lodging: $135/$185. Green fees: $62 including carts. Rates are for January-May 15.

ARRIVAL Air: Tucson (30 to 45 minutes). Car: route I-10 to Cortaro exit, travel 3.5 miles and you are there.

THE WESTIN LA PALOMA
3800 East Sunrise
Tucson, AZ 85718
(602) 742–6000
(800) 876–3683

The Westin La Paloma, which opened in December of 1985, is part of a 792-acre development in Tucson's exclusive Catalina Foothills area.

The hotel, consisting of 487 guest rooms (including 40 suites) arranged in a village-style setting, has used Southwestern-theme furnishings which complement the architecture and suggest a relaxing "oasis in the desert." The entire complex might best be summed up in one word! *SUPERB.*

No one will want for food at this resort. You may choose from: The Desert Garden, the resort's main dining room with seating indoors or out; La Villa, specializing in seafood; "Sprouts," for those who go the health food way; Sabinos for poolside hamburgers; and the Cactus Club, La Paloma's high energy lounge for dancing. Located in the 35,000-square-foot golf clubhouse, you will find another restaurant and, of course, a lounge. If that is not enough there is also excellent room service offered.

The meeting facilities are large enough to match the resort. Consisting of 42,000 square feet, separate break-out rooms and two very large ballrooms, they are more than capable of handling groups of 200 to 2,000.

A sample of the recreational facilities include: 10 lighted tennis courts with clubhouse, two racquetball courts, two swimming pools, one with a swim-up bar, spas, a fully equipped health club, jogging and cycling trails and, of course, a golf course.

The Westin La Paloma Country Club's 27-hole golf course is a Jack Nicklaus Signature layout. While this is, to be sure, a resort course, it is also a championship caliber layout. As Jack Nicklaus predicted during construction, it is "one heck-and-a-half" of a golf course. I can go along with that description. The 27 holes, when played in combination, are as follows. The Hill/Ridge nines reach out 7,017/6,464/5,984/4,878. The combination of the Ridge/Canyon nines plays an awesome 7,088/6,635/6,011/5,125 yards. The final combination of the Canyon and Hill nines weighs in at 6,997/6,453/5,955/5,057 yards. Each course pars at 72.

The various tee placements—on some holes there are as many as five different teeing areas—allow you to take on whatever you feel you can handle and, in some cases, offer a variation of from 80 to 100 yards per hole. For tee times you may call (800) 222–1249.

The La Paloma course offers something quite different. They can provide you with a "Forecaddie" who stays with you throughout your round. He can save you your weight in golf balls and no small amount of frustration by keeping you out of many of the hazards which, many times, are not readily visible.

RATES (EP) Rooms: $265/$310. Suites: $560 and up. Green fees: $85 including cart. Golf package: 2 nights/2 days (includes lodging, 2 rounds of golf, cart, and a caddy), $820 per couple.

ARRIVAL Air: Tucson. Car: 10 miles north of Tucson's business district and 17 miles from Tucson.

THE WIGWAM RESORT & COUNTRY CLUB
Litchfield Park, AZ 85340
(602) 935–3811
(800) 327–0396

I do not know why the better resorts are so hard to write about. The Wigwam falls in this category. They seem to do everything right, making it difficult to describe their facilities without sounding like an advertisement. It starts off with the warmth of greeting upon check-in and continues while you are being escorted to your room. As a matter of fact it never seems to come to an end.

It is true that the Wigwam dates back to the 1918/1919 period (coming into being as a resort in 1929). But, then, many resorts have operated for a lot longer. It may have something to do with the fact that a number of employees represent second and third generation help. I overheard one employee explaining to another guest that if he "goofed up" he was more likely to hear from his grandfather or mother (both employees) than from his supervisor. Any way you care to measure it, the Wigwam must be considered one of the very best resorts in the country.

Not content to stay as is, The Wigwam recently underwent a complete ground-to-ceiling renovation which involved all of the facilities, including the new tennis casitas. The total cost was somewhat in excess of $30 million.

In the past the Wigwam closed during the summer months. They now have decided to stay open for the entire year, offering the same excellent amenities, but at a much reduced rate.

Lodgings consist of 241 guest accommodations. You may choose from rooms or suites located either in the pool, tennis, golf or garden locations. Including the golf courses, the entire property is 475 acres of manicured lawns and flower beds.

The centrally located Main Lodge houses the new and lovely Terrace Dining Room, lounge and private rooms available for all manner of social functions. Another new addition is the Arizona Kitchen restaurant. While ties are required in the Terrace Room, the Kitchen restaurant is less formal. There is also the Grill on the Greens, located in the clubhouse.

The resort's meeting facilities are excellent, with a capacity of up to 600.

Adjacent to the Lodge is a patio and new very large swimming pool—a delightful location for luncheon, a slight libation or perhaps just to relax. While there are gift shops located within the Lodge, the Village, two blocks away, has a number of very interesting retail shops.

Tennis may be enjoyed on eight courts (six lighted), featuring a professional staff to assist, four practice alleys with ball pitching machines and a separate tennis shop. Another new addition is the stadium court allowing spectator attended tournaments.

A few of the other activities include: horseback riding and hayrides (from their own stables), a complete health club providing a massage facility and offering the use of exercise rooms, sauna, and whirlpool. You may also enjoy skeet and trap shooting. Bicycles, ping pong tables, and shuffleboard are all available on a complimentary basis.

If you can not get your fill of golf at the Wigwam, you have a problem. There are three outstanding golf courses. The Gold Course stretches out 7,047/6,504/5,567 yards and pars at 72. The West Course, also with a par of 72, reaches out 6,865/6,307/5,808 yards. The Blue Course plays 5,960/5,178 yards and pars at 70.

The Gold and Blue courses are Robert Trent Jones, Sr. designs, while the West course was designed by the late Robert Lawrence. Rated among the top 100 golf courses in the United States, the Gold layout is something else—gleaming white sand traps, brilliant lakes (beautiful if you can avoid them), and huge greens add to the challenge.

The West Course brings into play a wandering stream and five lakes to keep your attention. The Blue layout offers well bunkered fairways and very large greens, characteristic of Trent Jones, to spice up the action.

The Wigwam recently spent a considerable amount of money on the courses, putting in all new cart paths, cleaning out and redoing all the streams and water hazards and installing pumps to keep the water flowing. It's amazing what can be accomplished with the use of several millions of dollars.

RATES (EP) Rooms: $200/$235. 1-bedroom suite: $340 per couple. Green fees: Gold Course $60 including cart; the West and Blue courses $55 including cart. Golf package: 1 night/1 day (includes lodging, green fees and cart), $280/$311 per couple. Rates shown are for the peak season January-mid April.

ARRIVAL Air: Phoenix Sky Harbor Airport (25 miles). Pick up can be arranged. Private aircraft: Phoenix/Litchfield Municipal Airport (3 miles away, an 8,600-foot paved runway). Car: 15 miles west of Phoenix on Glendale Boulevard, then south on Litchfield Road. Traveling on I-10 take Litchfield Road exit. Travel north to Indian School Road and turn east to resort.

ARKANSAS

THE ARLINGTON RESORT HOTEL & SPA
Hot Springs National Park, AR 71901
(501) 623–7771
(800) 643–1502 Arlington Hotel
(800) 643–1504 Majestic Hotel

The Arlington Hotel is in reality a resort complex consisting of two hotels—The Arlington and the Majestic. Located among the pines of the magnificent Ouachita Mountain Range, it truly has a beautiful setting.

Although dating back to the 1870's the present structure came into being in December of 1924. Over the years many changes have come about. The Board Room was added to accommodate television. For many years "Natural Ventilation" (open the window for Heavens sakes) was the way it was done. Now of course the hotels are air-conditioned. The building of a six-story tower (completed in 1966), installation of three new elevators in 1969, and the new Conference Center, have all helped to bring the Arlington's two-hotel complex into the 20th century.

There are 488 guest rooms, including suites. The Majestic has 310 rooms. The dining facilities, located at the Arlington, consist of the Fountain Room, Venetian Room and the Captain's Tavern (the coffee shop). You may enjoy evening entertainment or, perhaps, a slight libation in either the Lobby Bar or the Silk Saddle Lounge. The Majestic offers dining in the H. Grady Dining Room and, for a more casual experience, the Dutch Treat Room.

Both the Majestic and the Arlington have excellent meeting facilities. The Arlington, with its 10,000-square-foot ballroom, can handle groups up to 900. The Majestic has approximately 4,900 feet of space set aside for group affairs and can handle up to 300.

The hotels have long been known for their thermal mineral baths and massages. A stay here without trying a massage or the whirlpool baths (which, by the way, are maintained at body temperature), would be a real waste.

Tennis is played on eight courts (four lighted) complete with tennis shop and resident professionals to offer assistance. Swimming pools, sun decks, jogging paths, exercise rooms, game rooms and racquetball are just a few of the activities available. Remember, you are within a very large National Park area with several large lakes, including the Ouachita and Lake Hamilton, just begging to be fished.

Golf may be enjoyed on two courses at the Hot Springs Country Club: the Arlington, reaching out 6,646/6,393/6,206 yards, parring at 72/74 and the Majestic Course parring at 72, and playing 6,667/6,286/5,541 yards. There is also a 9-hole, par-34 layout, measuring 2,929/2,717 yards.

RATES (EP) Arlington Rooms: $62/$82. Mineral Water Rooms: $85/$115. Suites: $250/$350. (EP) Majestic Rooms: $43/$62. Green fees: $22, carts $22. Golf package: 2 nights/3 days (includes lodging, golf, cart), $220 per couple. Rates are mid-April through November.

ARRIVAL Air: Little Rock (53 miles). Private aircraft: Hot Springs Airport. Car: from Little Rock take I-30, connecting with State Highway 70 west. Turn north on Highway 7 and continue past Bath House Row to the resort.

DAWN HILL GOLF & RACQUET CLUB
P.O. Box 1289
Siloam Springs, AR 72761
(501) 524–5217

Nestled among 715 acres of tall woods, rolling hills and lush meadows, this resort was planned and designed with the lifestyle of the 1990's in mind. Accommodations consist of two- to three-bedroom townhouse clusters, featuring natural stone fireplaces, loft bedrooms and fully equipped kitchens. There are also some private homes available for rental.

If you decide to dine out, there is the recently remodeled restaurant with a cocktail lounge for dancing.

A few of the amenities at your disposal include tennis on four lighted courts, along with a sauna, whirlpool and racquetball courts. Golf may be played on the Dawn Hill Golf Course. Reaching out 6,768/6,434/5,307 yards it pars at 72. It is an open layout with very little water coming into play. There is a full-line pro

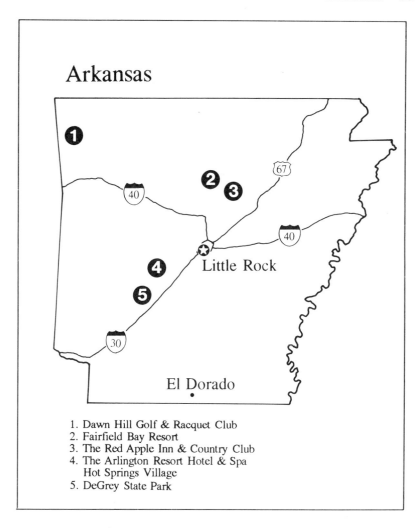

Arkansas

1. Dawn Hill Golf & Racquet Club
2. Fairfield Bay Resort
3. The Red Apple Inn & Country Club
4. The Arlington Resort Hotel & Spa
   Hot Springs Village
5. DeGrey State Park

shop, lounge, restaurant and swimming pool provided to support the golf course.

RATES (EP) Townhouses: $95/$125. Green fees: $18, carts $16. Golf packages are available.

ARRIVAL Air: Siloam Springs (6 miles). Car: Route 68 near the Oklahoma border.

DeGRAY STATE PARK
Box 375
Arkadelphia, AR 71923
(501) 865–4591
(800) 633–3128

DeGray Lodge, and convention center, is on Lake DeGray, within an hour's drive of Little Rock. It is also situated approximately 30 minutes from Hot Springs. The Lodge, a rustic 96-room wilderness structure fashioned from redwood and stone, rises magnificently from an island on beautiful DeGray Lake. While the lodge may be "rustic" the amenities are quite modern. The resort features an excellent restaurant, along with a 10,000-square-foot convention center for meeting and convention groups of up to 500 people.

The park has full camping facilities, along with tennis courts, a swimming pool and a 110-boat marina (boats and motors are available to rent). The lake, which is some 13,500 acres, offers excellent fishing.

Golf may be enjoyed on the DeGray State Park Golf Course. Weighing in at a pretty fair 6,930/6,417/5,731 yards, it carries a par of 72. Water comes into play on eight holes.

RATES (EP) Rooms: $55/$65. Green fees: $12, carts $15.

ARRIVAL Air: Hot Springs (21 miles). Private aircraft: Arkadelphia (11 miles). Car: I-30 exit to Highway 7, northwest 6 miles.

FAIRFIELD BAY RESORT
P.O. Box 3008
Fairfield Bay, AR 72088
(501) 884–3333
Limited Area (800) 482–9826
NAT (800) 643–9790

Fairfield Bay Resorts is in the foothills of the Ozarks. It was built north of Little Rock, and is set on the northwestern shore of Greers Ferry Lake.

Accommodations consist of a total of 350 bedrooms, suites, villas and condominiums. The villas and condos are fully equipped for housekeeping.

The heart of the resort is the conference center. This 14,000-square-foot meeting facility can handle groups of up to 400. It also happens to be the location of the indoor pool, health club, racquet club, lounges and restaurants. Less formal dining is available in the newly opened Village Cafe.

This is a very large layout. In fact it is a year-round community, complete with a medical center, a fire station, several churches as well as riding stables with horses available for all levels of experience. There is also a youth recreation center, a marina (180 boat slips), a beach area, two swimming pools and two 18-hole golf courses.

Tennis may be enjoyed on 10 courts (four lighted), with a professional staff on deck to assist. This tennis complex, by the way, has been rated as one of the top 50 facilities in the U.S.

The Mountain Ranch golf course plays 6,780/6,280/5,760/5,325 yards and pars at 72. Showing tree-lined fairways, with water coming into play on only two holes, it is a nice change from the "Pacific Ocean" type golf courses.

The Indian Hills Country Club layout weighs in at 6,437/5,727/4,901 yards and pars at 71. On this course water is a bit more of a challenge with seven holes involved. We understand that the Indian Hills golf course is now restricted to member play only.

RATES (EP) Rooms: $75. Suites: 1-bedroom $155. 2-bedroom villas: $230. Green fees: $30, carts $20. Golf packages are available.

ARRIVAL Air: Little Rock. Car: 80 miles north of Little Rock. Entrance on Highway 16 west of Highway 65.

HOT SPRINGS VILLAGE
Box 5 DeSoto Center
Hot Springs Village, AR 71909
(501) 922–0303
(800) 643–1000

Hot Springs Village, 16 miles north of Hot Springs, is a very large recreational community. Accommodations consist of townhouses or homes, fully equipped for housekeeping, which may be rented by the day, the week or month. Some have fireplaces and some are equipped with washer and dryer.

Within the village itself there are many activities: tennis on 11 courts, two recreational centers with swimming pools and game rooms and a clubhouse. There is also a marina, with boat docking facilities, on Lake DeSoto. The Coronado Community Center also provides various social activities including square dancing.

I have only touched on the possible amenities at your disposal. For example, within nine to 44 miles there are four lakes with over 2,200 miles of shoreline, providing all manner of water sports action.

There are several excellent restaurants on the property: the Village Bakery and Sandwich Shop, Mary Lee's Restaurant, the DeSoto Clubhouse and Lounge, the 19th Hole and the Wood-N-Iron Restaurant. There are many more in the general area. Also within the village are a grocery store, service station, gift shops, beauty shops, and a laundromat.

Golf is offered up on four 18-hole courses: the DeSoto, The Cortez, The Coronado and the newer Balboa. Three are championship courses, while the Coronado is an executive affair. Each has a pro shop and full facilities. Within a few miles are a total of eight other golf courses available to play.

RATES (EP) Townhouses: $65/$130. Monthly: peak season $675 and up. Green fees: $25, carts $20. Excellent monthly golf rates are also available.

ARRIVAL Air: Hot Springs. Car: Highway 7, approximately 21 miles northeast of Hot Springs.

THE RED APPLE INN & COUNTRY CLUB
Eden Isle
Heber Springs, AR 72543
(501) 362–3111
AR (800) 482–8900
NAT (800) 255–8900

I really don't remember what we expected upon our arrival but it was one of the most pleasant surprises we have experienced. The Red Apple Inn is one of the best resorts in the country. The resort property is nestled in the rolling hills of Arkansas and virtually surrounded by 35,000-acre Greers Ferry Lake. Muted and handsome, sprinkled with works of art, fireplaces, patios, fountains and tapestries, it is a delightful place.

The rooms and suites, which provide a view of the lake, are appointed with hand-carved furniture from Italy and Spain. There are also one- to three-bedroom condominium suites featuring a fireplace, living room and dining room, a fully equipped kitchen and a private deck or patio. The Red Apple is ideal for meeting groups and has an entire wing set aside for this purpose. This is a nice arrangement as it separates the business people from those who are on vacation.

A Spanish gate, retrieved from an ancient castle, welcomes you to the "After Five Room" for cocktails. After dining here and experiencing this touch of French cuisine with a southern accent, you will understand why they have earned the Mobil Four Star Award.

Tennis on five courts (three lighted), water skiing, sailing (with professional sailing instructions available), lake swimming, or the use of two swimming pools and fishing are but a few of the various sporting activities available.

Golf is played on the Red Apple Inn & Country Club's own course. Stretching out to 6,431/6,006/5,137 yards, it pars at 71. Architect Gary Parks blended the rolling terrain and tree-lined fairways to create an interesting layout.

The pro shop, under the direction of professional Mark Brugner, is very well stocked and provides full facilities.

RATES (EP) Inn rooms: $75/$95. Villa suites: 1 bedroom $105. 2 bedrooms: $125/$145. Green fees: $20, carts $18. Rates are for April-October.

ARRIVAL Air: Little Rock. Private aircraft: Herber Springs Airport (3 miles). Car: Highway 65 to intersection of Highway 25— turn right on 25.

NORTHERN CALIFORNIA

THE MONTEREY PENINSULA AREA

One can get deeply involved in the historical background of Monterey and the role it played in the early days of Spanish influence. And it did play a significant part.

Today, Monterey, Pacific Grove and Carmel represent a virtual treasure box of intriguing shops, along with restaurants which can virtually destroy your will to remain slim. There are an almost infinite number of art galleries, photographic studios, antique shops and on and on. You could spend several months, perhaps even years, visiting each of these places and I doubt, even then, that you could see all of them. What makes this area so impressive is that you are not looking at articles of art made elsewhere and sold here but rather at items made or painted by the many local and very talented artists.

But then not everyone likes to shop. So how about a visit to Monterey's museums of history, literature (including the John Steinbeck Library) and art. If that will not do it, then I would suggest a visit to the very new and exciting Monterey Aquarium or to any of several wineries.

If music is your thing why not visit The Carmel Bach Festival, the Monterey Symphony, the Chamber Music Society, the Monterey Jazz Festival or the Monterey Film Festival. To come into this area and not see or visit the famous Carmel Mission would be a shame.

If none of the above activities appeal to you—then consider sailing in the magnificent Monterey Bay, or a hot air balloon ride over the area's vineyards, Or you might consider a helicopter tour over Big Sur and the entire Peninsula.

There is also, of course, the famous Steinbeck's Cannery Row, Fisherman's Wharf, whale watching, and all manner of fishing, as well as the beaches of fabled Carmel-by-the-Sea.

I have saved the best for the last—a drive along the enchanting 17-mile drive, the beach area of Carmel, the white sand, the deer so sure of themselves they almost come to you—the quail, ducks, and the rabbits, and the overwhelming Pacific Ocean as it comes ashore.

Northern California

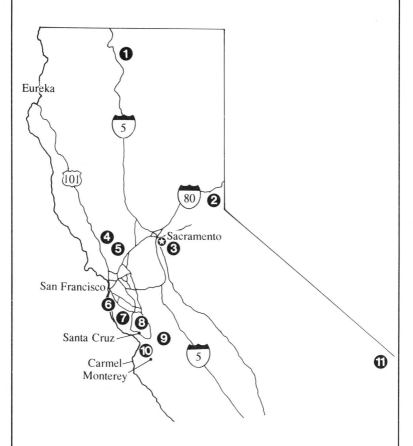

1. Lake Shastina Golf Resort
2. Northstar at Tahoe
3. Rancho Murieta
4. Sheraton Round Barn Inn
5. Silverado Country Club Resort
6. Half Moon Bay Lodge
7. Boulder Creek Lodge
8. Pasatiempo Inn
9. Ridgemark
10. Carmel Valley Ranch
    The Hyatt Regency Monterey
    The Inn & Links at Spanish Bay
    The Lodge at Pebble Beach
    Quail Lodge
11. Furnace Creek Inn & Ranch Resort

When all else fails take a walk along these magnificent shores and you will have enjoyed the best that can be experienced anywhere.

Within this area, and in their way, adding to the magic of this region are five fabulous resorts—the Carmel Valley Ranch, the Hyatt Regency Monterey, the Inn & Links at Spanish Bay, the Lodge at Pebble Beach, and the magnificent Quail Lodge.

CARMEL VALLEY RANCH RESORT
One Old Ranch Road
Carmel, CA 93923
(408) 625–9500
(800) 422–7635

In June of 1987 another lovely Carmel area resort came into being. On 1,700 acres in the scenic Carmel Valley, its presence has added another dimension. The entire complex is nestled high above the clubhouse and the front nine of the course.

The builders and architects should win an award for the manner in which the Lodge and the various buildings were sited. By very careful planning they were able to build around and take advantage of some of the most beautiful and venerable old oak trees we have seen. They created a soft and quiet setting which would not have been possible without the trees.

Featuring 100 luxurious suites, as well as a very beautiful main lodge, the resort has many amenities to offer its guests.

The suites, built in clusters of four to five, range in size from 810 to a little over 1,200 square feet. They feature fully stocked wet bars (including refrigerators with ice makers). Each also provides a living room, a wood burning fireplace, cathedral ceilings throughout, and private decks with views of the mountains, fairways and the valley. Many of the units also have a fireplace in the bedrooms. Eight of the one-bedroom suites include a private outdoor spa. This is one of the few resorts on the Monterey Peninsula with a 24-hour guarded security entrance.

An entire section of the lodge has been set aside to handle conference and/or social gatherings including a Grand Ballroom measuring 3,278 square feet.

The Lodge Dining Room, serving breakfast, lunch and dinner, as well as the Lounge are of contemporary ranch style architecture. Well worth seeing are the many artifacts and antiques on display around the lodge area.

The Golf Clubhouse, with its view of the front nine, is available for breakfast, lunch and afternoon cocktails. Breakfast, lunch and cocktail service are also provided at the 100-seat tennis complex. The tennis complex (12 courts) is supported by a tennis shop as well as a professional staff. A few of the other activities which may be enjoyed include a free-form swimming pool, four additional spas and, of course, the golf course. A Pete Dye design, the Carmel Valley Ranch course plays 6,515/6,055/5,582/5,088 yards with a par of 70. Being a Pete Dye layout, the course has small greens, some surrounded by sand traps with railroad ties forming a border. There are also three man-made lakes and the Carmel River which runs alongside four additional fairways.

While the front nine is a fun, yet a challenging affair, the back side can destroy you. The 10th hole, although tough, is fair. Holes 11 through 14 might best be described as unfair. In fact "Mickey Mouse" was the description given by a group of golf professionals after they played it. When you have passed these monsters and provided you still want to play this game you will find the back nine intelligent. All in all (with the exception of the four holes mentioned above) it is a very well set up golf course, and takes advantage of the elevation changes as well as the rolling terrain of the area.

Located within the clubhouse is the pro shop, restaurant, a bar, and locker rooms.

RATES (EP) 1-Bedroom suites: $225/$250. Spa suites: $375. Master suites: $600/$650. Green fees: $75 including cart.

ARRIVAL Air: Monterey. Car: take U.S Highway 1 just past (south of) the turn off to Carmel and take a left (east) onto Carmel Valley Road. Continue approximately 7 miles. You must exit to the right onto Robinson Canyon Road. This turn-off is very difficult to find. The road is just beyond the shopping center which will be on your right.

HYATT REGENCY MONTEREY
One Old Golf Course Road
Monterey, CA 93940
(408) 372–7171
(800) 233–1234

Including suites, the Hyatt Regency Monterey offers 579 guest accommodations, some quite lavish. The setting of the hotel, surrounded by cypress, pine and gnarled oaks is one of the loveliest we have seen.

Although you are in "Steinbeck Country" where superb food is commonplace, the Peninsula Restaurant at the hotel more than holds its own.

There are three swimming pools and six tennis courts to enjoy. The hotel is capable of handling meeting or convention groups of from 20 to 900.

As a guest of the Hyatt, you enjoy preferred tee times and golf rates at the Del Monte Golf Course or arrangements can be made at several other golf courses including Pebble Beach or Spyglass. The "Old Del Monte" golf course has been around since 1897 and has hosted such famous players as Vardon, Hagen, Hogan and Bobby Jones. The course plays 6,278/6,007/5,431 yards with a par of 72/74. It is a heavily tree-lined course, generally considered one of the more beautiful and lush layouts in the area.

RATES (EP) Rooms: $165/$200. Suites: $275/$550. Green fees: $25, carts $22. The Hyatt does offer special room rates from time to time. Be sure to check.

ARRIVAL Air: Monterey. Car: from the north take Pacific Grove exit from Highway 1. Travel on Del Monte Road to Sloat Avenue, turn left continue and ahead to entrance of the Hyatt Regency Monterey.

THE INN & LINKS AT SPANISH BAY
17 Mile Drive
Pebble Beach, CA 93953
(408) 647–7500
(800) 654–9300

The Inn at Spanish Bay opened in January of 1988. The views of the rolling Pacific Ocean, the manicured golf course and parts of the 17-mile drive are magnificent.

Accommodations at this beautiful inn consist of 270 rooms including 16 suites. Eventually there will be 80 privately owned condominium apartments located a bit north of the clubhouse. Each of the rooms has a gas burning fireplace as well as a mini-bar. Each also has a deck or balcony providing views of the grounds, the forest or the ocean.

With their meeting and conference facilities (14,000 square feet) they are capable of handling groups of up to 550 (school room style).

Dining ranges from the rather formal (The Bay Club) to casual (The Dunes). As one might well expect the food as well as the service is excellent.

The Inn provides several possible activities including: a relaxing spa, eight tennis courts (two lighted), supported by a tennis shop and a professional staff, a lap swimming pool, saunas, steam rooms and a heated pool.

Combining their talents, designers Robert Trent Jones, Jr., Tom Watson and Frank Tatum used the narrow, rolling fairways, large sand dunes and, with the help of restored coastal marshes, created a distinctly Scottish type golf course. The natural beauty of the area also added a dimension which could not be duplicated, providing sweeping views of the Pacific Ocean and the rolling terrain of white sand.

The Links is positioned directly along the ocean with a portion of the famous 17 Mile Drive coming directly through the course. It is not unusual to have cars stop to watch your tee shot. All you can do at this point is to pray you either hit a decent shot or that the car is full of non-golfers and they don't know the difference. One point—if you enjoy strong winds, and I mean constant in nature, you will fall in love with this layout. The course plays 6,820/6,078/5,287 yards, parring at 72. The very impressive new clubhouse accommodates the pro shop, locker rooms, a restaurant, bar and health club.

RATES (EP) Standard view: $220. Forest view: $265. Ocean view: $325. Suites: $500 and up. Green fees: $95 (includes cart). Guests of Spanish Bay Inn also have access to golf at Pebble Beach ($118/$133) and Spyglass Hill ($93). Del Monte green fees are $25, plus cart at $22 (cart is optional at Del Monte). The green fees for The Links, Pebble and Spyglass include carts, which are mandatory.

ARRIVAL Air: Monterey. Car: enter the 17-Mile-Drive at the Pacific Grove entrance.

THE LODGE AT PEBBLE BEACH
17 Mile Drive
Pebble Beach, CA 93953
(408) 624–3811
(800) 654–9300

So much has been written about "The Lodge" I find it difficult to add anything significant. It is everything you may have heard. True, it is somewhat formal, but that too can be a refreshing change of pace. In operation since 1919, it has lost none of its charm, warmth or elegance.

You may choose to dine in either The Cypress Room, with its magnificent views of Carmel Bay, or perhaps patio dining at The Club XIX. Or maybe you would prefer something light from The Gallery overlooking the first tee. Following dinner I would recommend a visit to The Tap Room, where entertainment is provided nightly. You are, of course, in the Monterey Peninsula area with a plethora of fabulous restaurants and places to be entertained.

As a guest of The Lodge you are also on the famous 17 Mile Drive, so by all means see it. These magnificent homes may well inspire you to return home, increase the insurance and start playing with matches. One thing I would add: the trip by cart around the course, even if only one of you plays, is well worth the time and effort. You can see the exposed back side of the houses without the interference of gates and trees. These homes, many built in the heyday of the flamboyant twenties (before income taxes), are truly something to behold.

There are other activities, in addition to golf, to choose from: swimming, tennis on 14 courts, two paddle tennis courts, horseback riding, hiking, bicycling, exercise rooms, saunas, massage, steam rooms, aerobics classes, as well as sailing.

The fabled Pebble Beach Golf Links plays 6,799/6,357/5,197 yards parring at 72. Depending on how the wind changes, this course can turn from tough to a monstrous affair.

Until a few years ago, Pebble Beach was the home of the Bing Crosby Tournament. It is now the location of the AT&T Pro-Am. Though it is sponsored by AT&T, and has been for several years, it will always remain the "Crosby". If you have watched any of these presentations on television, further description of this course is redundant. It is one of the premier golf layouts in the world.

Not only is Pebble Beach golf available to you as a guest, but Spyglass Hill, Del Monte and now the Links at Spanish Bay are at your disposal as well.

RATES (EP) Garden view: $265. Ocean view: $325/$400. Suites: $850/$950. Green fees: (for registered guest) Pebble, $125/$135 including cart; Spyglass, $95 including cart; The Links At Spanish Bay, $95 including cart; and Del Monte, $25, cart $22.

ARRIVAL Air: Monterey. Car: U.S. 101 to Carmel. San Francisco (130 miles). Los Angeles (330 miles).

QUAIL LODGE
8205 Valley Greens Drive
Carmel, CA 93923
(408) 624–1581
CA (800) 682–9303
NAT (800) 538–9516

Quail Lodge is one of only 21 resorts or hotels out of a total of approximately 20,000 such establishments in the United States to have attained the coveted Mobil 5 Star Award. As a matter of fact there are only seven on the entire west coast. This award has come to them again and again over the years. Once you have been a guest here you will understand why the award has been made. They have recently undergone a few changes—for one they have built a very impressive new entrance to the club. There were some changes at the golf club as well.

Quail provides a unique choice of accommodations. Their cottage units consist of five rooms, which can be "personalized" to your specific needs: one or two plus sitting room, or all five. Each suite has a fireplace, fully stocked bar and refrigerator, a stereo unit with tape deck and of course a TV. The Executive Villas also have a partial indoor/outdoor hot tub. The setting of these charming lakeside cottages is outstanding. The view spans 245 acres of the beautiful Carmel Valley Golf & Country Club, offering a view of 10 sparkling lakes, and the lush green valley itself. This is, without doubt, a premiere California retreat.

One definite extra is the resort's location. Situated in the relative shelter of the Carmel Valley, the Lodge remains warm and sunny on many days when Carmel and Monterey are foggy and cold.

Located both at the Clubhouse and the Lodge, the conference facilities are ideal for groups up to 150. Banquet-style the maximum capacity is 250.

The Covy Restaurant which offers both superb selection and quality will please even the most demanding gourmet. The Covey plays no small part in the fact that Quail has received the Mobil Five Star Award year after year. While the dress code is informal, gentlemen are requested to wear jackets when dining in the Covy.

In addition to golf you may choose to walk these beautiful grounds, swim in either of the two pools, enjoy a game of tennis, with professionals on deck to assist, or a round of golf. Or perhaps you would prefer to forget the rest of the world, at least for a little while, and spend some time in the outdoor hot tub.

The Carmel Valley Golf & Country Club measures 6,141/5,453 yards with a par of 71. It is not only interesting but a challenging layout as well. One of most delightful distractions is brought about by the deer and birds that watch, and it seems, in some cases, appear to critique your swing. But then, perhaps I'm getting too sensitive about my game.

The resident teaching professional, Ben Doyle (an outstanding teacher) and the Head Professional, Christopher Lynch, provide all the assistance you could require.

All things considered, Quail Lodge is an outstanding resort.

RATES (EP) Patio rooms: $205. Cottage suites: (sitting room, bedroom, wetbar, fireplace) $265. Executive villas: 1–2 bedroom suites (private hot tub, wetbar/fireplace) $495/$760. Green fees: $70 including carts. Golf package: 2 nights/3 days, (includes lodging, golf and cart), $265 per person. Package plan rate is available Sunday through Thursday.

ARRIVAL South from Monterey, left on Carmel Valley Road, 3½ miles to Valley Greens Drive. Turn right to the Lodge.

BOULDER CREEK LODGE
16901 Big Basin Highway
Boulder Creek, CA 95006
(408) 338–2111

Boulder Creek Lodge and Conference Center is located among the towering redwoods in the Santa Cruz Mountains of north-central California. Accommodations consist of condominiums featuring fully equipped kitchens, wood-burning fireplaces, spacious decks and cable television, with the golf course running throughout the complex. Their meeting facilities can handle groups of up to 230 people.

There are five swimming pools (at various locations within the resort complex), six tennis courts, The Redwood Dining Room, a cozy cocktail lounge and a golf layout.

While very short, playing 4,279/3,970 yards with a par of 65, the Boulder Creek Golf Course offers various challenges. The setting, with towering old trees, is one of magnificent beauty. It is also an interesting layout and one that will keep your attention. If you are not alert, you can easily get mixed up with a wandering creek or a lot of timber, and very fast.

RATES Condos: 1-bedroom $90. There are villas (kitchen, fireplace, 1–3 bedrooms), rates upon request. Green fees: $15/$24, carts $18. Golf package: 2 nights/3 days (includes lodging and golf), $99 per person.

ARRIVAL Air: San Jose. Car Highway 9—just 20 minutes from Santa Cruz.

FURNACE CREEK INN & RANCH RESORT
Death Valley, CA 92328
The INN (619) 786–2361
The RANCH (619) 786–2345

Furnace Creek Resort is quite different for a variety of reasons. Although its location in Death Valley is 200 feet below sea level, the lowest point in the contiguous 48 states, you can see the highest point from here as well—Mt. Whitney.

The resort is truly an oasis in the desert. Its beauty is highlighted by Death Valley, one of the bleakest and most inhospitable places on earth. How anything could survive the parched, burning heat of summer, and yet be so beautiful in the fall and winter, is difficult to comprehend.

We are really talking about two places: the Ranch, more of the Old West in flavor; and the Inn, more on the "posh" side with lighted tennis courts, an "Oasis" supper club and so on. (Coats are required but ties are optional in the evening). The dress code at the Ranch is casual.

There is much to do and see here, including the Borax Museum, the visitor's center and the opportunity to study the fascinating geology of this area. Due to the arid conditions, the landscape has remained virtually unchanged for thousands of years. There are, of course, the more mundane activities available such as swimming, riding and hiking.

Golf is offered on an 18-hole layout playing 5,750/4,977 yards, with a par of 70/71. The many palm trees and the lush greenery provide a startling contrast to the desert. While the course is not long, it does pose its own special challenges.

RATES (MAP) The Inn: $218/$275 per couple. Suites: $300. The Ranch: (EP) $64/$94. Green fees: $25, carts $18. The season is January-May.

ARRIVAL Private aircraft: Furnace Creek (3,040-foot surfaced runway) Car: there are so many ways into Death Valley it is not possible to list them all.

HALF MOON BAY LODGE
2400 South Cabrillo Highway
Half Moon Bay, CA 94019
(415) 726–9000
(800) 528–1234

The Half Moon Bay Lodge is nestled on the fourth fairway of the Arnold Palmer/Francis Duane-designed Half Moon Bay Golf Links. There are 83 rooms, some with fireplaces and kitchenettes, all with either private balconies or patios. Room service is provided by a Swedish restaurant, the Last Whistle, adjacent to the Lodge. The Lodge also has three fully equipped conference rooms to accommodate business meetings.

There is an enclosed whirlpool spa and a swimming pool. In addition to the recreation offered by numerous nearby parks and beaches, there is riding, tennis and fishing.

Located about seven miles north you will find one of the better seafood restaurants to be found anywhere—The Shore Bird. Drive north through Half Moon Bay and turn left at the first signal light (several miles). Though it's a bit removed from San Francisco, make reservations. The San Francisco crowd knows good food when they find it, and this place has been discovered!

Golf on the Links is something else. Designed by Francis Duane and Arnold Palmer and using fully the picturesque setting of the area, it brings water, barrancas (ravines) and bluffs into play. The course has been rated third in Northern California. Parring at 72, it plays 7,116/6,447/5,710 yards. It is one of the more beautiful, and challenging, golf layouts we have come across.

RATES (EP) Rooms: $88/$108. Suite: $114. Green fees: $65, carts $25.

ARRIVAL On Highway 1, 2 miles south of Half Moon Bay. From San Francisco Airport (30 minutes), take Highway 92 to Highway 1 then south.

LAKE SHASTINA GOLF RESORT
5925 Country Club Drive
Weed, CA 96094
(916) 938–3201
(800) 358–4653

The Shastina Golf Resort is about 75 miles north of Redding, California, and about the same distance south of Medford, Oregon. Snow capped Mt. Shasta provides the spectacular background for this resort and its 27 holes of golf.

Accommodations are provided in condominiums located throughout the golf course area with some adjacent to the lake. Each accommodation includes a bedroom, living area and a fully equipped kitchen.

Other facilities include a clubhouse, site of the restaurant and lounge, two tennis courts, a swimming pool and spa. Accessible from the area are river rafting and water skiing. Fishing trips may also be arranged.

The Lake Shastina Golf Course, a relatively flat and open affair, reaches out 6,950/6,317/5,542 yards and pars at 72.

RATES (EP) $89/$139. Green fees: $24, carts $24, Golf package: 2 nights/3 days (includes lodging, unlimited golf and cart), $298/$318 per couple.

ARRIVAL Air: Medford, Oregon or Redding, California. For private aircraft, a 3,800-foot runway (altitude 2,938 feet) is 5 miles from the golf course. Shuttle service to the resort is provided with prior request required. Car: I-5 from either direction approximately 1½ hours.

NORTHSTAR AT TAHOE
P.O. Box 2499
Truckee, CA 95734
(916) 587–0200
(800) 533–6787

Northstar offers super skiing facilities during the winter. Featuring 2200 vertical feet of downhill, 42 kilometers of cross country trails, a 100-instructor ski school, they specialize in ski clinics.

In the spring you may play tennis on 10 courts, enjoy horseback riding through this beautiful mountain area or a swim in the Olympic-size pool.

But summer is the time to take on the very challenging, 18-hole, par-72 golf course. Playing 6,337 yards (white tees) it is rated by NCGA at 72.4. An able professional staff is on deck to help you enjoy this great layout.

Northstar is just seven miles from the California/Nevada border, offering gaming and big name entertainment as well as the awe-inspiring beauty of Lake Tahoe.

RATES (EP) Lodgette: $72. Village suites: (living room, loft, fireplace, kitchen and bedroom), $109. Green fees: including cart $60. Golf packages are available. Rates are June-September. Rates are higher during the winter months. $99 per Night (2 Night minimum) 1 Round of golf

ARRIVAL Air: Reno (40 minutes). Private aircraft: Truckee-Tahoe, 6,400-foot strip. Car: Highway 267 between Truckee and the north shore of Lake Tahoe (approximately 6 miles).

PASATIEMPO INN
555 Highway 17
Santa Cruz, CA 95060
(408) 423–5000

The Pasatiempo Inn is a beautiful "Spanish mood" building. With its 58 rooms, fine restaurant, and cozy cocktail lounge, it is pretty complete.

The Inn can accommodate convention and seminar groups of up to 250. Pasatiempo has recently undergone complete remodeling.

The Pasatiempo Golf & Country Club Course, bordering on the Inn, is one of the older and finer layouts in the state. Little wonder, as it was designed by Dr. Alistair MacKenzie, the same man responsible for St. Andrews in Scotland, the Masters course in Augusta and Cypress Point at Monterey. It has been judged by *Golf Digest* as one of the top 100 layouts in the United States. The course plays 6,607/6,281/5,626 yards, parring at 71.

In addition to the deep barrancas, sand traps and oak trees bordering the fairways, you can enjoy the breathtaking views of shimmering Monterey Bay or the Santa Cruz Mountains each time you approach the ball. All things considered you will find this a beautiful course and a true test of your game. At certain times it might also test your vocabulary.

RATES (EP) Rooms: $75/$85. Weekends: $90/$100. Green fees: $55/$65, Carts $25. Golf packages can be arranged when booking reservations.

ARRIVAL Car: from the north take Highway 17 (I-880) south to Pasatiempo Drive exit. The resort will be on your right.

RANCHO MURIETA
14813 Jackson Road
Rancho Murieta, CA 95683
(916) 985-7200
CA (800) 852-4653

The Rancho Country Club is almost due east of Sacramento. It is one of the few northern California resorts to provide a 24-hour security entrance. A very nice extra.

Accommodations consist of 74 rooms, including 37 executive suites, along the golf course. Each suite has two bedrooms, two baths, living room, kitchenette (not equipped) and private patio. There are also some private homes, townhouses and villas available.

The Country Club, the cocktail lounge and dining room, are in a massive structure of some 40,000 square feet. This resort is well equipped to handle meeting groups.

Right outside the entrance to Rancho Murieta may be found some excellent restaurants as well as a shopping complex. These facilities include a bank, dental and medical offices, a grocery store and many other shops to serve you.

There are six lighted tennis courts. In addition, you may enjoy swimming, saunas, hydra spas, volleyball, badminton, a jogging track, fishing and non-motorized boating. Located nearby is an equestrian center. There is definitely enough going on to keep one from becoming bored!

If it is golf you want, this is the place. It has two 18-hole layouts. The North Course, recently redesigned by Arnold Palmer, stretches out 6,875/6,371/5,642/5,339 yards with a par of 72 /73. The South Course measures 6,886/6,307/5,527 yards and pars at 72. Both layouts are interesting in the manner in which they bring trees, water, bunkers and undulating fairways into the action. The rather large, multi-level greens also tend to keep you awake.

RATES (EP) Room B: $75. Room A: $120. Suite of A and B: $185. Green fees: $55, carts $20. Golf package: 2 nights/3 days (includes golf, cart, tennis, club storage) $215/$270 per person.

ARRIVAL Air: Sacramento (35 miles). San Francisco (110 miles). Private aircraft: Rancho (3,800-foot landing strip). Car: east on Highway 50, south on Bradshaw Road then left on Jackson Road. Approximately 1 hour.

RIDGEMARK
3800 Airline Highway
Hollister, CA 95023
(408) 637–8151

Ridgemark Golf and Country Club has accommodations consisting of cottages, some equipped with Jacuzzi tubs.

The dining room presents a diverse menu and, of course, has cocktail service.

The golf course, due to the mild climate, can be played year-round. It plays 6,834/6,204/5,564/5,724 yards with a par of 72. Tennis courts are also available.

RATES (EP) Rooms: $65/$85. Green fees: $20/$35, carts $25.

ARRIVAL Air: San Francisco (90 minutes). San Jose (45 minutes). Car: south of Hollister (2 miles).

SHERATON ROUND BARN INN
3555 Round Barn Boulevard
Santa Rosa, CA 95401
(707) 523–7555
(800) 325–3535

The Round Barn Inn is in Sonoma County, the heart of the wine country of California, some 55 miles north of San Francisco. Sited on the historic Fountain Grove Ranch the property overlooks the beautiful town of Santa Rosa.

The 247 guest rooms, which are larger than the average, feature oversized desks, several phones, and cable TV. The resort is also well equipped to handle meeting and seminar groups. The two ballrooms, which can be divided into eight separate meeting areas, can accommodate groups of up to 250.

The restaurant at the Red Barn has earned a Four Star Dining Award. They also boast an outstanding wine cellar (it had better be good in this part of California).

Located at 2755 Mendocino Avenue (less than a mile away) is one of the greatest Italian restaurants we have been fortunate enough to find. Very modest in price and featuring an excellent wine list (and a bar), it serves up every type of pasta, chicken, veal, seafood and steaks you could desire. "Fioro's" has been operated by "La Familia DeFiori since 1935. For reservations call (707) 527–7460.

A few of the activities available at the Sheraton include: a swimming pool, a whirlpool and a jogging path. Located at the golf course are five tennis courts. Horseback riding is also nearby. There are a great many wineries (nearly a 100) scattered throughout the greater Santa Rosa area. Tours of a few of them can be arranged by the hotel.

The Fountain Grove Country Club course stretches out 6,797/6,380/5,644 yards and pars at 72. Winding up and down through these beautiful hills it offers not only superb views but also all the challenge you could desire. While not easy it is a fun layout to navigate. Of course if the game gets too much, there are always the wineries. The course is very new and needs some time to reach full maturity. I predict that in due time this layout will be considered one of the finest in northern California.

There is a unique and lovely clubhouse. Done in a Japanese architectural style it houses the small pro shop as well as an outstanding restaurant. A word of warning—the restaurant is not open in the early morning so be sure to have breakfast prior to arrival. The phone number for the course is (707) 579–4653. The Head Golf Professional is J. Michael Jonas.

RATES (EP) Rooms: $90/$120. Suites: $180/$250. Green fees: $35/$55 carts $24.

ARRIVAL Air: San Francisco. Private aircraft: Sonoma Country Airport. Car: from San Francisco travel north on Highway 101. Take the Old Redwood Highway/Mendocino Avenue exit. Stay right. At the first light swing left up the hill. Then take the first left again (up the hill). You are there.

SILVERADO COUNTRY CLUB RESORT
1600 Atlas Peak Road
Napa Valley, CA 94558
(707) 257–0200
(800) 532–0500

Silverado is a little over an hour and a half from San Francisco and only two miles from Napa. It also happens to be the site of a number of California's outstanding vineyards. Many of these venerable old wineries were crafted from hand-hewn stone and are worth the time to visit.

The 270 personalized accommodations range from studios to one-, two- or three-bedroom condominiums. The condos feature extremely well equipped kitchen, living room with fireplace and either a patio or a balcony.

Silverado has, without doubt, one of the better facilities for group meetings. For detailed information check with their sales department.

The two restaurants, The Vintners Court with California cuisine and The Royal Oak, specializing in steak and seafood, are excellent. Jackets are required, ties are optional. There are other fabulous restaurants located in nearby Napa, as well as several a few miles north in Yountville and St. Helena.

A sample of the amenities at your disposal on this 1,200-acre estate include two 18-hole golf courses, eight swimming pools, tennis served up on 23 plexipaved courts (three lighted) along with an able tennis professional staff to assist, a large driving range as well as practice putting greens.

While this is a brief physical outline of Silverado there is really much more: you will enjoy a quiet, soft formality in a relaxing atmosphere. I think the best description is "gracious" with all that word implies. People at the check-in desk start things off right with their warmth and friendliness and it seems to continue right through the golf starter.

Golf is served up on two outstanding courses. The North course, stretching out 6,896/6,351/5,857 yards, pars at 72. The South layout, measuring 6,632/6,213/5,672 yards, also pars at 72. We have played both several times and found each of them all we could handle. The clubhouse houses the pro shop, an excellent restaurant and locker rooms. The Head Professional is Jeff Goodwin.

RATES (EP) Rooms: $130. Studios: $175. Condominiums: 1-bedroom $215. 2 bedrooms: $340. Golf package: 2 nights/3 days (includes lodging unlimited golf and cart), $305 per person. Green fees: $70 including cart.

ARRIVAL Air: San Francisco (62 miles) or Oakland (50 miles). Private aircraft: Napa (5 miles). Car: north end of Napa, east on Trancas Boulevard—then left on Atlas Peak Road.

TAHOE DONNER GOLF & COUNTRY CLUB
P.O. Box TDR #45
Truckee, CA 95734
(916) 587-6046

This four-season, family resort area is in the Sierra Mountains near Donner, one of the most beautiful lakes within California. Its location, just 35 miles west of Reno and 15 miles north of Lake Tahoe, makes reaching the gambling tables an easy chore.

Accommodations consist of one- to four-bedroom condominiums, fully equipped, most with fireplaces.

Rental arrangements must be made through the Truckee Realtors Group. In order to make reservations you may call the following real estate firms handling home rentals in the area: Coldwell Banker (916) 587-5501 or NAT (800) 345-0102; Truckee-Tahoe Realty (916) 587-5990; McCormick Realty (916) 587-2897.

The marina on Donner Lake provides all types of boating activities including sailing and fishing. It is, however, a bit cold for swimming in this lake! *The foregoing is probably one of the greatest understatements you will ever read.* Try the heated pool instead. There is an equestrian center and miles of riding trails. There are also six tennis courts.

Golf may be enjoyed on the Tahoe Donner G & C C Course. This beautiful, tree-lined layout stretches out through the wooded rolling terrain with the following yardage: 6,899/6.635/6,052 parring at 72/74. It is not only a very interesting golf course but it comes complete with tree-lined fairways, ample traps and water on eight holes.

Golfing season runs from late May to late September. Ski season takes over after that time.

RATES Green fees: $45/$65 including cart.

ARRIVAL Air: Reno. Car: 2 miles from I-80 at Truckee.

SOUTHERN CALIFORNIA

THE ALISAL
1054 Alisal Road
Solvang, CA 93463
(805) 688–6411

The Alisal presents a peaceful setting enhanced by the presence of hundreds of wild deer, magpies, acorn woodpeckers, raccoons, bobcats and other wildlife on display.

Accommodations consist of studio/sitting room, two-room suites, two-room loft suites, or private bungalows. A word of warning— there are no phones or TV's in the rooms. Some people think this is fine, others feel cut off.

Alisal provides an outstanding dining room (jackets are required in the evening). There is also the Clubhouse snack bar and cocktail lounge located at the golf course.

The resort has a meeting capacity for groups of up to 135 although in the fall and winter larger gatherings can be handled.

A visit to the nearby town of Solvang (three miles away) is a must. With its delightful shops and Danish style architecture it is charming. There are also several wineries open to the public and, of course, the historic Mission Santa Ynez. To travel here and not see this magnificent Mission would be a shame.

Within these grounds stuffed with 10,000 oak and sycamore trees you have at your disposal: horseback riding, golf, tennis, a hot water spa, a swimming pool, badminton, volleyball, croquet and tennis on seven courts. In addition there is the lake and its many water-oriented activities.

The Alisal Golf Course, framed and studded with oaks, is both beautiful and challenging. Parring at 72/73 it measures 6,286/5,919/5,594 yards. While the course is short, the many trees plus water in the form of a creek wandering throughout the entire layout will more than keep your attention. The course now boasts a new and enlarged pro shop with locker rooms and shower facilities.

Southern California

Bakersfield

Santa Barbara

San Bernadino

Los Angeles

1. San Luis Bay Inn
2. Stallion Springs Lodge
3. The Inn at Silver Lakes
4. The Alisal

5. The Ojai Valley Inn
   & Country Club
6. Sheraton at Industry Hills Resort

RATES (MAP) There is a 2-night minimum. Studio/sitting room: $225 per couple. 2-room suite: $265. Green fees: $35, cart $22. There are also various package plans available.

ARRIVAL Air: Santa Barbara. Private aircraft: Santa Ynez. Car: U.S. 101 to Buellton, turn off to Solvang. In Solvang turn right on Alisal Road (3 miles).

THE INN AT SILVER LAKES
P.O. Box 26
Helendale, CA 92342
(619) 243–4800
CA (800) 228–7209

The Inn has 40 guest rooms, each with either private patio or balcony. There is also a dining room and lounge. The two lakes make available all manner of water sports activities, with the high desert location providing an ideal climate. There is, in addition, a large swimming pool, a sauna, Jacuzzis and four lighted tennis courts.

The Silver Lakes Country Club layout consists of 27 holes. When played in combination they measure as follows: the North/East nines reach out 6,689/6,328/5,465 yards; the South/North, 6,822/6,428/5,564 yards; the combination of the East/South plays 6,747/6,374/5,633 yards. No matter how you mix them, they come out to a par of 72. These are interesting layouts with water coming into play on several holes of each nine.

RATES (EP) Rooms: $65/$79. Golf package: 2 nights/2 days weekends (includes lodging, one dinner, golf and cart), $145 per person. Midweek: $98. Green fees: $20/$25, carts $18.

ARRIVAL Off I-15 between Victorville and Barstow, on the National Trails Highway about 95 miles from Los Angeles.

OJAI VALLEY INN & COUNTRY CLUB
Ojai, CA 93023
(805) 646–5511
(800) 422–6524

The charming Ojai Valley, nestled in the foothills of the Sierra Madre Mountains, is only 14 miles from the Pacific Ocean. As a matter of fact, this area is only about 90 minutes northwest of Los Angeles. It is, however, approximately a million miles from Los Angeles in gentility, customs and culture. The name, "Ojai" is of Indian origin meaning "the nest". This resort has been for many years a hide-away for people from Southern California.

Located within this quiet, peaceful and idyllic setting is the Ojai Valley Inn. Sited on a hillside overlooking the valley, it offers a magnificent view of the countryside. The mountains which surround the area add to its beauty and, because they hold down the wind, they help to produce the warm and gentle climate enjoyed here.

Recently renovated and restructured, the resort now has 218 beautifully decorated guest rooms. Each of course has a mini-bar and is air conditioned. The 15 suites feature a parlor and most have a fireplace. The general motif of the Inn is one of warm Spanish/American design which blends into the surrounding area. All accommodations have either a terrace, patio or balconies. Adding to the beauty is the fact that the entire complex is surrounded by the golf course. They have, by the way, just been awarded The Mobil Four Stars.

The Inn is well equipped to handle meeting groups. With their new Conference Center, eight meeting rooms, a Board Room and the large ballroom, they can accommodate groups of 10 to 550.

Dining at the gracious Vista Room or the more informal Oak Grill and Terrace or at The Club can be a delightful experience. People from the area travel many miles to enjoy the outstanding cuisine offered.

There are eight newly resurfaced tennis courts (four lighted) with a professional staff to assist. This new tennis complex includes a clubhouse, pro shop and snack bar. Other activities to be enjoyed include: two swimming pools, a spa, exercise equipment and fitness classes, jogging trails, the use of bicycles on a complimentary bases and lawn croquet. If you have biked or hiked into the village and have *just plain run out of gas,* you can catch the shuttle bus from Ojai's shopping arcade back to the Inn.

One final suggestion: take the time to really "look" at the quaint village of Ojai. Its old mission style architecture, boutiques, shops, galleries and the museum are more than worth the time.

The Country Club Golf Course originally designed by George C. Thomas, Jr. in 1923 and put together by Billy Bell, has long been regarded as one of the better layouts in California. In order, however, to bring it into the present time period yet continue its almost legendary reputation, Jay Morrish, a leading designer, was engaged. The restoration and updating, including a modern irrigation system, is now complete.

Playing 6,476/6,103/5,487 yards, the Ojai course pars at 70/73. With its lush fairways and rolling terrain, it is in a class by itself. While the front nine is fun, it is not really remarkable. But the back nine is something else. It must be considered one of the most unusual layouts we have had the pleasure of navigating. Wandering through the foothills the backside takes advantage of every tree (and there are more than enough of them), every ravine, gully and hill, to turn this nine into a shot maker's course.

The Inn has provided an extremely well equipped pro shop as well as the assistance of an excellent professional staff, under the direction of Head Professional Scott Flynn.

RATES (EP) Lodgings: $180/$200/$220/$240 per couple. Deluxe suites: $350/$530. Green fees: $66, carts $28. Golf package: 2 nights/3 days (includes MAP, lodging, green fees), weekdays $596, weekends $716 per couple.

ARRIVAL Car: off U.S. 101 at the north edge of Ventura, travel to Highway 33.

SAN LUIS BAY INN
P.O. Box 189
Avila Beach, CA 93424
(805) 595–2333
CA (800) 592–5928

The resort is high above the surrounding terrain looking over the Pacific Ocean and back across an inlet to the golf course. Accommodations feature private balconies, spacious baths with sunken tubs and breathtaking views. The fresh flowers in your room and the beds turned down each night reflect some of the warmth and hospitality extended.

While this resort is small (74 rooms), they can handle meetings and are very well equipped to do so.

The amenities available include four tennis courts and a heated pool. There is sport fishing at Port San Luis, just one mile down Avila Road, where deep sea charter trips can be arranged.

The golf course is a par 71 playing 6,544/6,138/5,286 yards. It is a picturesque layout, as it winds through oak lined canyons, finishing up just a pitch shot from the ocean.

RATES (EP) Room: $114. Ocean view: $145. Suites $190/$289. Green fees: $20/$30, carts $22. Golf package: 2 nights/3 days (includes lodging, 3 days golf, cart, range balls, taxes), $375 per couple.

ARRIVAL From the south, Avila Beach exit 3 miles north of Pismo Beach. From the north, San Luis Bay Drive exit, 7 miles south of San Luis Obispo.

SHERATON AT INDUSTRY HILLS RESORT
One Industry Hills Parkway
City of Industry, CA 91744
(213) 965–0861
(800) 325–3535

This Sheraton hotel, located on a hill overlooking the entire complex, comes packaged with indoor fountains, liberal use of marble, stained glass and a staff that can greet you in Spanish, French, German, Japanese and even in English.

Meeting facilities are available in the usual fine Sheraton style with banquet seating for up to 1,500.

The resort provides many activities to be enjoyed, including 17 tennis courts, 15 miles of riding trails, three swimming pools, whirlpools, saunas and even billiards. A few years back they added an equestrian center featuring a covered arena. The entire resort is referred to as a 650-acre "playground". The location is certainly convenient, just 40 minutes to Disneyland, 50 minutes to Knott's Berry Farm or the Los Angeles Coliseum.

The 17 tennis courts (lighted for night play) are under the supervision of a professional staff. Teaching facilities include closed circuit video tape equipment to allow you to see yourself in slow motion replay. "Do I really look like that"?

Golf is served up on two 18-hole courses: the Dwight D. Eisenhower and the Babe Zaharias layouts. The Eisenhower 18, parring at 72/73, stretches out 6,712/6,287/5,967/5,637 yards. The Babe Zaharias Course, a bit shorter, plays 6,481/5,994/5,426 and pars at 71. You will enjoy the view provided by the St. Andrews station and the golf funicular, which operates on the Eisenhower course, lifting you from the ninth green up to the tenth tee. The entire complex is administered by a Director of Golf and a staff of five PGA and two LPGA professionals. The course is supported by an excellent pro shop.

RATES (EP) Rooms: $105/$150. Suites: $225/$270. Green fees: $33/$45, carts $22. Golf packages are available.

ARRIVAL Car: Highway 60 (Pomona Freeway) to the Azusa Avenue exit. North to Industry Hills Parkway.

STALLION SPRINGS LODGE
Star Route 1 Box 800
Tehachapi, CA 93561
(805) 822–5581
CA (800) 367–0470

This intimate lodge consisting of 66 guest rooms crowns a mountaintop in the rugged Tehachapi range. It is one of the most beautiful settings we have seen.

Accommodations feature studio kings, loft suites and double bedrooms all with a panoramic view of tall pines, greens and fairways.

The conference rooms will accommodate up to 75 people. The very attractive dining room enjoys an outstanding view of the surrounding area spreading out below the hotel.

An equestrian center provides instruction and supervised trail rides. Boarding for privately owned horses can be arranged on a space available basis.

There are two lighted tennis courts, a heated swimming pool, locker rooms with saunas and a lounge offering food and beverage service.

Horse Thief Golf Course is a well maintained, 18-hole layout. Parring at 72, it reaches out 6,650/6,317/5,723 yards.

RATES (EP) Rooms: $69/$79. Loft suites: $105/$125. Golf packages are available. Green fees: $20/$33, carts $22.

ARRIVAL Air: Tehachapi. Car: 56 miles from Bakersfield, 118 miles from Los Angeles. Located 16 miles west of Tehachapi on Route 202. It is not easy to get to this resort. Get local directions in Tehachapi and have patience.

SAN DIEGO AREA

CARLTON OAKS LODGE & COUNTRY CLUB
9200 Inwood Drive
Santee, CA 92071
(619) 448–4242

You will find yourself in a quiet country setting at the Oaks Lodge. Bordered on one side by the 6,500-foot Laguna Mountains, and with rolling hills on the other side, the atmosphere here is one of relaxation.

Accommodations consist of rooms in the Lodge. Air-conditioned, they feature a view of the golf course or tennis courts. A few are equipped with either a full kitchen or a kitchenette. The Oaks is set up to handle meeting or banquet groups of up to 300. Along with a casual dining room and lounge there is entertainment and dancing on the weekends.

The resort's location, in eastern San Diego County (20 miles from downtown San Diego), offers up the beach area and all of its water sport activities, Sea World and the Mexican Border, for your enjoyment. In addition to swimming in the heated pool, tennis may also be enjoyed on four lighted courts.

Recently acquired by a Japanese/Hawaiian investment group, the resort has just concluded a major renovation of the golf facilities. A Pete Dye design, it now plays a very substantial 7,109/6,613/6,084/5,772/4,817 yards and pars at 72. The challenging features of this course are found in a creek that meanders throughout the entire complex, aided and abetted by menacing ponds, rolling terrain and, of course, Mr. Dye's penchant for railroad ties.

RATES (EP) Rooms: $75/$85. Suites: (1-bedroom with kitchenette, some with a full size kitchen) $150/$160. Green fees: $60 including cart.

ARRIVAL Air: San Diego. Car: from Highway 15 turn east on Highway 8, then north on Mission Gorge Road.

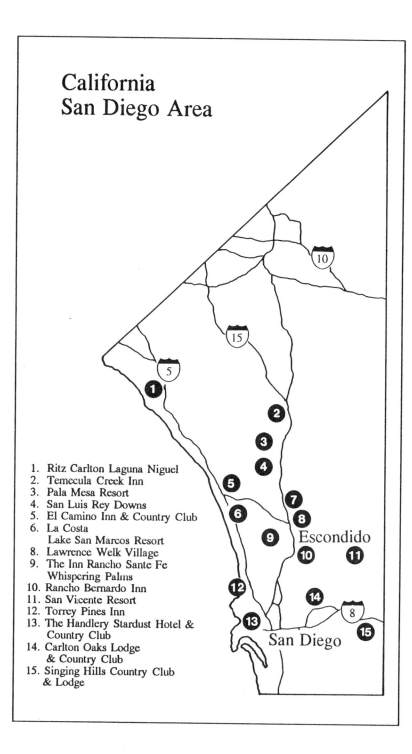

California
San Diego Area

10

15

5

1

2

3

4

5

7

6

8

9

Escondido

10

11

12

14

13

15

8

San Diego

1. Ritz Carlton Laguna Niguel
2. Temecula Creek Inn
3. Pala Mesa Resort
4. San Luis Rey Downs
5. El Camino Inn & Country Club
6. La Costa
   Lake San Marcos Resort
8. Lawrence Welk Village
9. The Inn Rancho Sante Fe
   Whispering Palms
10. Rancho Bernardo Inn
11. San Vicente Resort
12. Torrey Pines Inn
13. The Handlery Stardust Hotel &
    Country Club
14. Carlton Oaks Lodge
    & Country Club
15. Singing Hills Country Club
    & Lodge

EL CAMINO INN & COUNTRY CLUB
3170 Vista Way
Oceanside, CA 92056
(619) 757–2200
(800) 458–6064

The Inn which is adjacent to the El Camino Country Club can offer its guests the privileges and use of all of the services of this private club. Located on a hill overlooking the golf course, the Inn offers 42 rooms. Some feature living rooms, a few with either kitchens or kitchenettes and dining areas. One- and two-bedroom units are available.

The dining room, located at the clubhouse, affords a commanding view of the course and the rolling hills beyond. Private banquets and receptions may be arranged.

In addition to two pools there are seven tennis courts (two lighted) with a professional tennis staff to assist.

Golf is played on the club's 18-hole course. Reaching out 6,774/6,439/5,831 yards, it pars at 72. While water comes into play on only three holes, traps are intriguingly placed around the greens.

RATES (EP) Rooms: $59/$65. Green fees: $20, carts $18. Golf package: 2 nights/2 days (includes lodging, golf, cart, continental breakfast), $230 weekdays, $250 weekends per couple.

ARRIVAL Air: San Diego (35 minutes). Los Angeles (90 minutes). Car: I-5 off on 78 east, El Camino Real north to Frontage Road.

THE INN RANCHO SANTA FE
Box 869
Ranch Santa Fe, CA 92067
(619) 756–1131
(800) 654–2928

Originally developed by the Santa Fe Railroad in the early 1920's, the Inn was sold to the Royce family in 1958 and has been run by them since that time.

Like the inn keepers of days long past, the Royce family feels that each guest is an individual and must be treated as such.

There are rooms as well as cottages which can be set up as one bedroom or multiple arrangements. Each room is air-conditioned and some have fireplaces and wet bars. There are one- and two-bedroom cottages available as well.

The Inn has the capacity to handle small conference groups in separate meeting facilities, with all audio/visual aids available. Opening off the lobby are the Garden Room for breakfast, lunch and dinner and the Vintage Room for lunch, cocktails and dinner. (Jackets are required, ties are optional). During the summer months, the Patio Terrace features dancing under the stars on Friday and Saturday evenings.

There is a large heated pool, and the Inn also has a beach cottage at nearby Del Mar with showers and other facilities. Tennis may be played on three courts.

While Rancho Santa Fe has no golf course of its own, they do have golfing privileges at Rancho Santa Fe Country Club located half a mile away, as well as at Whispering Palms Golf Course, about two miles away.

RATES (EP) Guest rooms: $95/$175. Large bedroom with fireplace and kitchen: $280. Cottages with full kitchen, living room, fireplace, private patio: $280/$450. Green fees—Rancho Santa Fe Course: $90 including cart; Whispering Palms $22/$28, cart $22.

ARRIVAL Air: San Diego. Car: from I-5 turn off at Solana Beach. Now on Lomas Santa Fe Drive (which changes its name to Linea del Cielo) keep straight on and you will run into the Rancho. Trust me. The parking lot is 6 miles from the I-5 turn off.

THE HANDLERY STARDUST HOTEL & C C
950 Hotel Circle
San Diego, CA 92108
(619) 298-0511
(800) 223-0888

The Stardust Hotel is done in an old and lovely Spanish style, but all else is contemporary.

With air-conditioned rooms, lighted handball and racquetball courts, steam rooms, massage, beauty and barber shops, eight tennis courts (four lighted), golf and swimming, what more could you ask for?

Dining facilities consist of The Crane Room, specializing in steak and seafood, and a 24-hour coffee shop.

Golf is offered on 27 holes. Using a crossover system you may play three 18-hole layouts: the Lake/River nines reach out 6,602/6,309/5,734 yards; the Valley/Lake combination plays 6,655/6,357/5,797 yards; and the River/Valley layout weighs in at 6,645/6,356/5,871 yards. All three combinations par at 72. There is also a par three nine available.

RATES (EP) Rooms: $75/$95. Suites: $145/$185. Green fees: $20/$24. Carts: $20. Golf package: 2 nights/3 days (includes lodging, MAP, 2 rounds golf), $295 per couple. Rates are June 16-September 15.

ARRIVAL Air: San Diego. Car: located in the Mission Valley Hotel Circle, near Highways I-5 and I-8.

LA COSTA
Costa Del Mar Road
Carlsbad, CA 92008
(619) 438–9111
(800) 854–5000

La Costa's location, approximately 45 minutes from San Diego, opens up many activities: the wonderful San Diego Zoo, Sea World and of course a trip to Old Mexico.

Accommodations consist of 300 rooms, some in the main hotel, while others are located along the golf course or near the tennis complex. There are also 75 one- or two-bedroom suites.

Each of the five restaurants offers a unique eating adventure. One could go on and on about the variety and quality, but let it suffice to say the food and service is outstanding. Recently we had the privilege of eating at Pisces. Located a short distance away, and specializing in seafood, this restaurant must be ranked among the very best. After dinner you may elect to visit the Tournament of Champions Lounge to enjoy the nightly dancing and entertainment. If this is not your cup of tea, try some duplicate bridge, a movie in your room or one in the hotel theater which, by the way, features first-run films each evening.

The new 50,000-square-foot Conference Center has added a new dimension to La Costa. They are now able to handle groups of up to 650 banquet-style. For details check with their sales and conference department.

La Costa's spa program is widely recognized as one of the very best. Its private club-like complex for women, and a separate one for men, pampers you with facials, massages, whirlpools, loofah scrubs, pedicures, yoga classes, and exercise sessions. If you wish, you can really get into it with Swiss showers, Roman pools, and herbal wraps. The resort also offers a medical fitness evaluation facility conducted by a permanent staff physician.

Tennis may be enjoyed on a 25-court complex, under the direction of well known tennis professional, Pancho Segura and staff. The program is supported by a full-line tennis shop and video instruction equipment. If you are not completely done in at this point, you might consider a swim in any one of the four fresh water pools.

Golf is served up on two beautiful golf courses. The North Course reaches out 6,983/6,596/6,263/5,980, parring at 72/73. The South Course shows a substantial yardage of 6,896/6,534/6,214/5,632 and pars at 72/74. There are, of course, the amenities which are expected at a resort such as this: locker rooms, snack bar, practice area and an extremely well stocked pro shop.

A word of CAUTION. While this is a lovely resort, they handle a great many convention and meeting groups and a twosome can get pushed aside when it comes time to play golf. If you are a twosome be sure your tee times are confirmed in WRITING.

A second word of warning: this is a very busy place and at times the bellmen tend to get very short tempered and seem to forget who is the guest and who is the bellmen.

RATES (EP) Rooms: $205/$275. Suites: $415/$675. There are many different packages: Spa Plan, Golf package, Tennis package, etc. Green fees: $65, cart $25.

ARRIVAL Air: San Diego. Private aircraft: Palomar (3 miles). Car: Los Angeles (2 hours). Take I-5 to La Costa Avenue exit, to El Camino Real, then left to the entrance.

LAKE SAN MARCOS RESORT
1025 La Bonita Drive
San Marcos, CA 92069
(619) 744–0120
(800) 447–6556

Guests of the Inn (Quails Inn) are really entering a private residential community with the lodge fronting on Lake San Marcos.

In addition to rooms in the lodge, there are lakeshore cottages which are equipped with kitchenettes. There are also some private homes available. The meeting facilities, which are quite new, have a capacity for 300 theater- or 160 classroom-style. With their five separate meeting rooms they are able to handle almost any group arrangement.

For dining you have a choice of either the Quails Inn Dinner House, the Country Club or the Coffee Shop. Within a mile of the resort are a wide variety of restaurants at your disposal.

There are four tennis courts, three paddle tennis courts and two swimming pools. Possible water activities include: rental of a kayot party boat, sailboats or canoes.

Golf may be enjoyed on the championship Lake San Marcos Country Club course or on the Lakeview executive affair. The San Marcos layout reaches out 6,474/6,260/5,959 yards and pars at 72/73. The Lakeside, parring at 58, has a yardage of 2,278.

RATES (EP) Rooms: $75/$95. Cottages: 1-bedroom $150; 2 bedrooms $200. Green fees: $55 including cart.

ARRIVAL Air: San Diego. Car: I-5, east on Palmar Airport Road. Right on Santa Fe Road (1,000 feet ahead).

LAWRENCE WELK VILLAGE
8860 Lawrence Welk Drive
Escondido, CA 92026
(619) 749–3000
(800) 932–9355

The Lawrence Welk Village is in the middle of a golfer's paradise 34 miles northeast of San Diego. Within this 1,000-acre village are gift and beauty shops, a fashion parlor as well as medical and dental offices. There is also a market and deli shop.

Accommodations consist of 138 guest rooms available at the Village Inn, plus 256 two-bedroom villas. The villas feature living rooms, dining area and fully equipped kitchens. Each has either a private patio or balcony.

The new Greens Conference Center gives the resort a capability of handling large meeting groups. There are now two excellent dining rooms. The Lawrence Welk Dinner Theater, seating 300, features professional entertainment Tuesday, Thursday, Friday and Saturday evenings with matinees scheduled throughout most of the week. There is, of course, a cocktail lounge.

Between the Inn and the villa location, there are a total of five tennis courts, a swimming pool and spa.

Golf may be enjoyed on The Meadow Lake Country Club course. Reaching out a substantial 6,521/6,312/5,758 yards, it pars at 72/74. Also available is The Fountains 18, an executive affair playing 4,002/3,581/3,099 yards, parring at 62. The resort also has a very short par-3 course of some 1,837 yards. In addition, there are at least 15 championship caliber courses within a few miles of the village.

RATES Inn rooms: standard $95/$110. Villas: minimum 2 nights (up to 4 people) $220. Green fees: $30/$35, carts $20.

ARRIVAL Air: San Diego (33 miles). Car: 8 miles north of Escondido off I-15.

PALA MESA RESORT
2001 South Highway 395
Fallbrook, CA 92028
(619) 728–5881
CA (800) 722–4700
NAT (800) 822–4600

Pala Mesa has long been considered one of Southern California's better resorts. While modest in size, it enjoys a beautiful setting and provides many amenities. Its location doesn't hurt them either. Set in a lovely valley between Los Angeles and San Diego, it has long been known as an outstanding resort.

Accommodations consist of 135 lovely rooms as well as several condominiums fully equipped for housekeeping. Alexander's Restaurant presents a variety of outstanding fare and is supported by an excellent lounge.

For group meetings their eight separate conference rooms can handle 248 classroom- or 400 theater-style.

Tennis is a basic part of Pala Mesa's sports activities and they provide play on four courts with a professional staff to assist. There is also a swimming pool.

This is an excellent golf course. Parring at 72, it plays 6,472/6,151/5,814 yards. While not particularly long it can test your skill as well as your vocabulary. If your problem is a wild hook, I hope you have been a regular at church—as the first three holes might well destroy you. This is an outstanding course and one that we took the time to come back and play a second time—a luxury we rarely have.

The professional staff, under the direction of Chris Starkjohann, are excellent teachers and may be able to help your game. If, however, you can not dispense with your hook, I doubt they will be able to do much for your vocabulary.

RATES (EP) Rooms: $100/$130. Suites: $130/$190. Condominium units: (kitchens) 1 bedroom $125/$150; 2 bedrooms $160/$185. Green fees: $45/$55 including cart. Golf packages are available.

ARRIVAL Air: San Diego. Car: 55 miles north of San Diego on I-15. Off at Highway 76, left, then first right west of I-15, about 2 miles.

RANCHO BERNARDO INN
17550 Bernardo Oaks Drive
San Diego, CA 92128
(619) 487–1611
CA (800) 542–6096
NAT (800) 854–1065

Rancho Bernardo is situated in a beautiful valley just 28 minutes from the San Diego Airport. The Rancho has been a premiere resort for many years. Now after updating and refurbishing it has really matured, evolving into a lovely destination resort. It presents a quiet, soft and very genteel atmosphere—formal where it should be formal and informal when informality is called for.

The Inn's location adds another dimension to your visit and opens up the possibility of a trip to Tijuana perhaps to see a bullfight or visit the Caliente Race Track. It is also close to Sea World, the fabulous San Diego Zoo and, of course, the beautiful beaches found in this area.

The delightful and quaint custom of serving "Afternoon Tea", with a background of piano music, offers a delightful and refreshing pause to the day.

Accommodations, consisting of 287 rooms and suites, provide for every convenience. Lodgings are just steps away from the golf course, tennis courts, restaurants, lounges, the three warm spas and the swimming pool areas. Rancho Bernardo is also well prepared to handle meeting groups. For in-depth information contact their sales department.

Nighttime at the Inn is a delightful experience. You may choose to dine in El Bizcocho, with its three-star gourmet cuisine (jackets required), or in the less formal Veranda Room. Both are supported by an outstanding wine selection. Cocktails are available in two lounges. After dinner you may dance to your heart's content.

Tennis certainly does not take a back seat at this resort. As a matter of fact, the tennis facilities have been rated Five-Star by *World Tennis*. Playing on 12 courts (four lighted), the Inn offers a "Tennis College Program" under the direction of professional Paul Navratil. There are more than 35,000 graduates who will attest to the value of the instruction they have received. Also available: a complete fitness center with massage, steam, sauna and workout rooms.

Golf is enjoyed on one of California's more interesting courses. The West, a par-72 layout, plays 6,388/6,200/5,468 yards. An additional 27 holes are offered on the Oaks executive course, with each nine parring at 30.

Tom Wilson, Director of Golf, and his able staff are available to assist you with tee times and with your game. They also have one of the better stocked and merchandised golf shops.

RATES (EP) Rooms: $175/$200. Suites: $210/$465 up. Golf package: 2 nights/3 days (includes MAP, lodging, golf, cart, club storage, tennis time), $620 per couple. Green fees: $45, including cart. Rates are for January-April 15.

ARRIVAL Air: San Diego. Car: south from Los Angeles, drive I-5 to Oceanside, 78 to Escondido. Highway 15 south to Rancho Bernardo Road exit. From San Diego, travel north on 15.

THE RITZ CARLTON-LAGUNA NIGUEL
33533 Shoreline Drive
Laguna Niguel, CA 92677
(714) 240–2000
CA (800) 442–3224
NAT (800) 241–3333

Sited on a bluff overlooking the Pacific Ocean this Mediterranean style structure is the first major hotel built on the Southern California coast in almost 30 years. The location places you very close to many attractions—fishing, shopping malls, the Mission at San Juan Capistrano as well as many other interesting places.

Accommodations in the four-story hotel structure (393 rooms) range from those with an ocean view, an oceanfront courtyard location or a poolside lanai.

Should you go hungry or thirsty here, it is your own fault—at your disposal are The Dining Room, offering classic and contemporary French cuisine; The Cafe Terrace, an all day restaurant and bar; The Club Bar, featuring live entertainment and dancing; The Library Cocktail Lounge, with its fireplace setting; and "The Bar," with its piano entertainment in the evening. The conference and meeting facilities are quite large, and the hotel is well equipped to handle groups.

The recreational activities available are numerous: two miles of beach front, four tennis courts, two swimming pools, a fitness center with a steam room, sauna, whirlpool, men's and women's massage, and an exercise room are but a sample.

The golf course, an 18-hole affair, was designed by Robert Trent Jones II. With a yardage of 6,243/5,655/4,984, it pars at 70. While obviously a short course it brings into play 88 sand traps, four lakes and three ocean-side holes. While not as easy as the yardage might indicate, it is fun to play.

RATES (EP) Rooms: $185/$360. Suites: from $700 up. Green fees: $55/$75 including cart.

ARRIVAL Air: Los Angeles or San Diego. Car: from San Diego on I-5 take Crown Valley Parkway west to Pacific Coast Highway, then south 1 mile to the hotel.

SAN LUIS REY DOWNS
31474 Golf Club Drive
Bonsall, CA 92003
(619) 758–3762

This golf and tennis resort nestled in the San Luis Rey Valley offers accommodations in 26 rooms, seven with kitchenettes.

There is a dining room, snack bar, pool, lounge and a country club. For the horse lover they offer a thoroughbred training center, one of the largest in the country.

At the present time tennis is played on four lighted, all-weather courts. The resort provides the facilities of an outstanding tennis shop as well as the services of teaching professionals to assist.

The golf course is an interesting one with more than enough trees and water to keep your attention. Parring at 72, it plays 6,610/6,324/5,547 yards.

RATES (EP) Rooms: $68/$89. Green fees: $20/$25, carts $20. Golf package: 2 nights/2 days (includes golf and cart), $205 per couple—weekends $250 per couple.

ARRIVAL Exit I-5 at Oceanside on Mission Avenue. Go east on Highway 76 for 13 miles, then follow signs.

SAN VICENTE RESORT
24157 San Vicente Road
Romona, CA 92065
(619) 789–8290
(800) 765–7323

Stretched over 3,200 acres of California's high desert, the resort has a unique and lovely setting.

Accommodations consist of rooms in the Lodge as well as condominiums (villas). Each villa has from one to three bedrooms, two baths, full kitchen (fully equipped for housekeeping) and a dining area. Specify if you wish to be near the tennis complex or golf course (about two miles between).

San Vicente features a 6,700-square-foot conference center with accommodations for groups of 15 to 400.

There is a dining room in the main lounge just off the first tee.

Tennis, located at the Ranch, is played on 24 courts with eight lighted. The tennis complex is supported by a clubhouse and pro shop. There is also the "Racquets" restaurant/lounge for your pleasure. The 23-acre Western Center offers rental horses and stable facilities.

The golf course, parring at 72, measures 6,585/6,180/5,578 yards. This layout is equipped with more than its share of water. As I recall there were 12 holes in which water hazards came into play.

RATES (EP) Lodge: $65/$85. Condominiums: $100/$180. Green fees: $26/$45 carts $18. Golf package: 2 nights/3 days (includes lodging, golf and cart), midweek $275 per couple; weekends $321 per couple. The phone number given above is for reservations at the Inn, but for condominium rentals call (619) 789–8678 or (619) 789–7070.

ARRIVAL Air: San Diego (38 miles). Car: Highway 67 to Ramona, right on San Vicente Road (7 miles). From Escondido take Highway 78 (19 miles) to Ramona, then straight ahead for 7 miles.

SINGING HILLS COUNTRY CLUB & LODGE
3007 Dehesa Road
El Cajon, CA 92021
(619) 442–3425

The 95-unit lodge, nestled in an ancient olive grove, provides immediate access to the course, swimming pool, the dining area and the tennis courts. Lodgings consist of rooms and suites. The rooms are exceptionally large and very well appointed. Consisting of a bedroom with a large sitting area, along with a walk-in dressing area, and oversized bathroom, they would be considered suites in most resorts.

Facilities are available to accommodate small business groups with banquet seating for up to 300.

Adjacent to the pro shop is a very nice breakfast/lunch dining area and on the other side is their outstanding dining room.

The location of the resort is ideal. You are 20 minutes to the San Diego Zoo, 25 minutes to Sea World and 36 minutes to Tijuana in Old Mexico.

The Willow Glen Golf Course reaches out 6,573/6,156/5,585 yards and pars at 72. The Oak Glenn layout plays 6,132/5,749/5,298 yards with a par of 71. They have utilized raised tees, six lakes, strategically placed bunkers, natural rock outcroppings and the aged oaks and sycamore trees to enhance the beauty and character of this course.

The entire layout is one of the better ones in Southern California. There is also a par-54 executive layout available.

The very friendly professional staff, led by the Director of Golf Operations, Tom Addis, is justifiably proud of these golf facilities and their new 4,000-square-foot pro shop. The golf shop, is extremely well stocked and the merchandise is sensibly priced.

RATES (EP) Rooms: $72/$79. Jr. Suites: $97/$110. Executive Suites: $115/$130. Green fees: $20/$25, cart $18. There are no golf packages during the peak golf season.

ARRIVAL Air: San Diego (30 minutes). Car: off Highway 8 to El Cajon Boulevard to Washington Avenue; jog onto Dehesa Road, then travel 2 miles.

TEMECULA CREEK INN
Box 129
Temecula, CA 92390
(619) 728–9100
(800) 962–7335

The Temecula Creek Inn is situated in the foothills of the beautiful Santa Rosa Mountains. The resort has recently undergone extensive renovations and now has a distinct Southwestern motif. They also can now accommodate meeting groups of up to 200.

Their dining room, while small, offers a fine menu. As a guest you may enjoy the convenience of an excellent club, well-appointed rooms with private balconies and the use of their two tennis courts.

This golf course is a bit unusual with a front nine that seems open, offering very little challenge. It may even tend to lull you a bit. It really is not all that tame. When you have finished the back side, it just seems that it was.

But the back nine, which can do everything but turn you loose, will open your eyes wide. Parring at 72, the course stretches 6,784/6,375/5,747 yards. Serving up 56 silica sand traps it also brings hills and ravines into the act. While difficult to navigate, it is also one of the more picturesque golf courses in the area.

Although modest in size, there is a full line pro shop providing all the amenities.

RATES (EP) Rooms: $80/$95. Suites: $115. Green fees: $22/$30, carts $20. Golf package: 2 nights/3 days available midweek only (includes lodging, MAP, unlimited green fees), $185 per person.

ARRIVAL Air: San Diego. Car: from Escondido, I-15 north to Indio/Highway 79, then east.

TORREY PINES INN
11480 North Torrey Pines Road
La Jolla, CA 92037
(619) 453–4420
(800) 448–8355

Torrey Pines Inn has a unique location. It is situated on top of two 18-hole public golf courses (the home of the Andy Williams Open Tournament). Their dining room offers an outstanding view of the rolling golf layouts with the Pacific Ocean forming the backdrop. The Inn has three private meeting rooms and can handle seminar groups on either an EP or MAP basis.

The head professional and staff have their work cut out for them overseeing this extremely busy, 36-hole layout. The South course plays 6,649/6,345 yards with a par of 72/76; the North layout measures 6,317/6,047 with a par of 72/74. I might add, both courses show extremely long yardage for the ladies.

RATES (EP) Rooms: $72/$82. Green fees: $35/$45, carts $20. Golf package: 3 days/2 nights (includes lodging, MAP, 2 rounds of golf), $445 per couple.

ARRIVAL Air: San Diego (25 minutes). Car: I-5 to Genesee, then north on Torrey Pines Road.

WHISPERING PALMS LODGE & COUNTRY CLUB
P.O. Box 3209
Rancho Santa Fe, CA 92067
(619) 756–2471

The lodge, located so close to the San Diego area, opens up a very wide range of activities: a day trip to Tijuana, a visit to the beautiful beaches, an afternoon at Sea World or the magnificent San Diego Zoo are but a few of the things to do and see.

Of course the resort itself provides a variety of activities: golf, tennis, swimming, riding, and a dining room serving outstanding fare. Whispering Palms is, in our opinion, one of the better buys for your vacation dollar to be found.

There are 102 rooms, including suites. The Lodge can also accommodate from 10 to 250 for meetings with both MAP or FAP plans available.

Jim and Jan Mayer, tennis professionals, head up the action to be found on the 11 all-weather tennis courts (two lighted). The 27-hole golf course plays as follows: the North/South measuring 6,346/6,051/5,684 yards pars at 72; the North/East nines combine to 6,141/5,860/5,564 yards with a par of 71; the South/East 18 weighing in at 6,443/6,131/5,776 yards also has a par of 71. The golf operation, along with a very well stocked pro shop, is under the direction of PGA professional, John Combs.

RATES (EP) Rooms: $79. Suites: $132. Green fees: $20/$25, carts $20. Golf package: 2 nights (includes lodging, 2 rounds of golf per person with cart, 2 breakfasts), $280; weekends $295 per couple.

ARRIVAL Car: Between Oceanside and San Diego. East off I-5, on Via DeValle (2½ miles).

PALM SPRINGS—DESERT AREA

The entire area known as the Coachella Valley is comprised of Palm Springs, forming the northwestern boundary, and Coachella on the southeast. There are now several other rapidly growing communities in between—Cathedral City, Palm Desert, Desert Hot Springs, Rancho Mirage, La Quinta, Indian Wells and Indio.

Discovered in the early 20's by Hollywood's elite, it is no longer a group of sleepy little villages. While the area has changed over the years, the one thing which has not been altered is the magnificent clear blue sky, the soft warm days, soaking your body in a warm outdoor pool or playing a round of golf on a manicured course while the rest of the country is slipping and sliding behind a snow plow.

There are enough shopping centers to keep even the most ardent shopper busy. Gift and antique shops as well as photography and artist studios are surpassed in number only by the Carmel/Monterey area. And I'm not sure that is correct.

One could make a profession out of eating in this area with the cuisine ranging from a hamburger or a sumptuous Mexican meal to gourmet and most everything in between.

While the various Chambers of Commerce advise you to bring warmer apparel for evening wear, to use sun glasses and sun screens, all of which is helpful, I am amused by the description of the summer months. "Summer months—June through mid-September—are warmer". Now there is a statement to play with. I have seen the temperature climb well over 125 degrees. I don't care how low the humidity is, when it gets that hot it becomes no place for a human being, much less a golfer, to linger.

Within this area there are over 60 golf courses, 20 or more world class destination golf resorts, plus a few more located a bit further south in the Borrega Springs region. While not as large, the Coachella Valley is rapidly becoming the West Coast version of "The Myrtle Beach" golf scene.

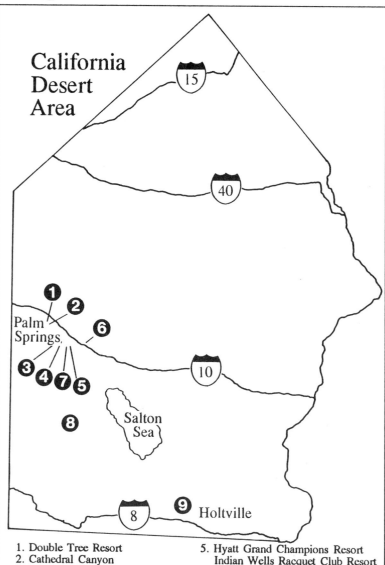

California Desert Area

15

40

1 **2**

Palm Springs

6

3 **4** **7** **5**

10

8

Salton Sea

8

9 Holtville

1. Double Tree Resort
2. Cathedral Canyon
3. Marriott's Rancho Las Palmas
   Resort
4. Avondale Country Club
   Ironwood Country Club
   The Lakes Country Club
   Marriott's Desert Springs Resort
   Monterey Country Club
   Palm Desert Resort &
     Country Club
   Palm Valley Country Club

5. Hyatt Grand Champions Resort
   Indian Wells Racquet Club Resort
   Stouffer's Esmeralda Resort
6. Indian Palm Country Club & Inn
7. La Quinta Resort
   PGA West
8. La Casa del Zorro
   Rams Hill
9. Barbara Worth Country Club

AVONDALE COUNTRY CLUB
75–800 Avondale Drive
Palm Desert, CA 92260
(619) 345–2727

Avondale is basically a private country club rather than a resort hotel. However, for several reasons, we wanted to list it. The course is super, the people are warm and very friendly and they do rent beautiful homes located around the course. For home rentals call (619) 345–7882. Some, by the way, are equipped with a private pool.

The clubhouse is one of the most impressive facilities we have seen. Its basic design, with an expanse of glass walls in the dining area, opens up a panoramic view of the desert and the mountains that is difficult to describe.

As I mentioned, The Avondale Golf Course is one of the better layouts in the desert area. While it is challenging it is also a well-manicured, beautiful course and one that is fun to navigate. Measuring a substantial 6,771/6,386/5,766 yards it pars at 72.

To reach the pro shop, call (619) 345–3712. The extremely well stocked and managed golf shop is under the direction of head professional Fred Scherzer.

RATES 2 bedrooms off-fairway, without heated pool $900, with pool $975, weekly. 2 bedrooms on-fairway $950, with pool $1025, weekly. Green fees: $55/$65 including cart.

ARRIVAL Avondale Drive is off Country Club Drive between Bob Hope Drive and Washington Street.

BARBARA WORTH COUNTRY CLUB
2050 Country Club Drive
Holtville, CA 92250
(619) 356–2806

This 50-room motel overlooks the golf course and offers a heated swimming pool, a whirlpool, driving range, three lighted tennis courts and a dining room.

The course plays at 6,239/5,902 yards, parring at 71/73, and has a pro shop and locker rooms.

RATES (EP) Rooms: $57; weekly $371. Golf package: 2 days/2 nights (includes 2 days golf and cart), weekdays $189—weekends

$200 per couple. Green fees: $18/$20, carts $18. Rates are for November-May.

ARRIVAL Air: El Centro-Imperial. Car: 8 miles east of El Centro, 2 miles from Holtville.

CATHEDRAL CANYON COUNTRY CLUB
68–733 Perez Road.
Cathedral City, CA 92234
(619) 328–8911

The country club's layout consists of a little over 450 acres. The community, surrounded by privacy walls and security gates, includes an 18-hole golf course, ten tennis courts (7 lighted) and a spacious clubhouse with restaurant and lounge. Within this area are numerous swimming pools, therapy pools and slightly over 800 homes.

Accommodations consist of one- and two-bedroom homes (equipped for housekeeping), many with a convertible den. Daily maid service may also be arranged.

The Cathedral Canyon Country Club course plays 6,510/6,193/5,430/5,217 yards with a par of 72/71. With water coming into play on 11 holes plus many very hungry bunkers, it will offer all you can handle. Supported by an excellent pro shop, the entire operation is under the supervision of the Director of Golf, Samuel Howard.

RATES Homes: $135/$185. Weekly: $550/$800. Monthly $1650/$2200. Green fees: $55 including cart. Rates are for December 1-May 31.

ARRIVAL Air: Palm Springs. Car: via I-10, 110 miles from Los Angeles and 5 miles from the Palm Springs Airport.

CATHEDRAL CANYON RESORT HOTEL
34567 Cathedral Canyon Drive
Palm Springs, CA 92264
(619) 321–9000
CA (800) 824–8224
NAT (800) 542–4253

Each of the 162 suites includes a sitting room, dining area, full kitchen and either a balcony or patio. I know the accommodations sound a bit like a condominium complex. I assure you, however, it's a hotel complete with dining room, lounge, a giant, uniquely shaped pool, and a bubbling hot spa.

The Cathedral Canyon Golf & Country Club, adjacent to the hotel, offers tennis on 10 courts (seven lighted), including a stadium court. A resident tennis professional is available for lessons, clinics and to arrange matches. There is also a clubhouse with a restaurant, lounge and pro shop.

For details on the golf course please refer to "Cathedral Canyon Country Club" listed above.

RATES (EP) Suites: $150/$170/$190. Green fees: $55/$65 including cart.

ARRIVAL Air: Palm Springs. Car: from State Highway 111 turn onto Cathedral Canyon Drive. From I-10 drive west on Ramon Road then left on Cathedral Canyon Road.

DOUBLE TREE RESORT
Vista Chino & Landau Boulevard
P.O. Box 1644
Palm Springs, CA 92263
(619) 322–7000
(800) 637–0577

The Double Tree, formerly operating as "The Princess Hotel", is located on 347 acres less than five miles from the center of Palm Springs.

Accommodations consist of 300 rooms in the four-story hotel plus 200, fully equipped one- and two-bedroom condominiums. The resort is well set up to handle meeting groups with its 12 meeting rooms, including two ballrooms, providing 14,600 square feet of function space.

The Promenade is available for casual dining, while the more formal Princess Restaurant features seafood. The Oasis Lounge offers entertainment and dancing nightly and there is the Vista Bar, for a quiet libation.

In addition to golf, recreational amenities include: an outdoor heated pool, a lap pool, two hydrotherapy pools, men's and women's exercise rooms, a massage center, 10 tennis courts (five lighted), two handball courts and two handball/racquetball courts.

The Desert Princess Golf Course, under the direction of professional Dave McKeating, plays 6,636/6,164/5,719/5,326 yards, parring at 72. While basically flat, it brings water into play on 11 holes.

RATES (EP) Rooms: $185/$195/$205. Suites: $280 and up. Condo: 1-bedroom $225. Green fees:$55/$65 including cart.

ARRIVAL Air: Palm Springs International. Car: off 1–10 at the Date Palm exit, turn right on Vista Chino. Travel approximately 1 mile and you have arrived.

HYATT GRAND CHAMPIONS RESORT
44–600 Indian Wells Lane
Indian Wells, CA 92210
(619) 341–1000
(800) 233–1234

The Champions, opened in late 1986, offers a complete change of pace. For openers, the minimum accommodation is a split-level parlor suite. The various penthouses occupy the top floor of the hotel and have private (European-trained) concierge service provided. In total there are 340 suites, 294 split-level parlor suites, 26 private penthouse suites and 20 Italian-style villa suites. I am almost reluctant to mention the one- and two-bedroom Garden Villas for fear you will think I am putting you on. These sumptuous villa suites which are sited around private spas have a butler assigned to each villa court. The meeting facilities are almost as outstanding with a capacity of 350 classroom- or 500 banquet-style.

The four restaurants range from gourmet (Jasmine Room), with the cuisine designed by one of the nation's most celebrated chefs, to less formal and lighter fare (The Trattoria California Restaurant). In addition there is Charlie's Courtside Restaurant overlooking the clubhouse court, offering outside dining, as well as the poolside Bar and Grill for snacks, and sandwiches. The Pianissimo Lounge provides a library-fireplace atmosphere to be enjoyed during the cocktail hour. As a matter of interest the Grand Champions has been awarded the AAA Four Star Award.

Tennis may be played on grass, clay or hard surface courts, with a 10,500-seat stadium court available so your friends may watch your spectacular performance. Additional activities include: a health and fitness center specializing in diet and weight control, four swimming pools, 24 whirlpool spas located throughout the hotel property, supervised walking, hiking and bicycle paths.

The resort is surrounded by two 18-hole public golf courses designed by Ted Robinson. The East layout, with a par of 72, reaches out a substantial 6,686/6,259/5,521 yards. The West 18, also parring at 72, measures a fair 6,478/6,115/5,387 yards. The West Course while shorter offers undulating terrain as well as multi-level greens to keep you honest. At first view it looks easy and open. It is neither. Along with waterfalls, the East course has a par-3 island hole, while the West offers a par-4 island green to shoot for. Each of these layouts comes equipped with a tough dog-leg finishing hole.

RATES (EP) Split-level parlor suite: $250. Penthouse suite: $375. Villas: 1 bedroom $725. Green fees: $55/$85 including cart.

ARRIVAL Air: Palm Springs. Car: from the airport, travel south on Highway 111 (approximately 20 minutes). Resort entrance will be on your left.

INDIAN PALMS COUNTRY CLUB & INN
48–630 Monroe
Indio, CA 92201
(619) 347–0688
CA (800) 426–3458
NAT (800) 327–2669

Accommodations range from rooms at the Inn to condominiums and townhouses of one to three bedrooms. Along with nine tennis courts (five lighted), there are several swimming pools. There is a small pro shop, tennis shop, lounges and dining in the historic clubhouse overlooking the 18th green.

Golf is available on three nine-hole courses making possible (by mixing) three different 18-hole layouts. The yardage is 6,403/6,284/6,279, each parring at 72. Water comes into play on 15 of the 27 holes.

RATES (EP) Inn: $74. 1-bedroom mini-condominium: weekly $475. 2-bedrooms: weekly $500. Monthly golf fee (2 people): $395. Rates November-April. Guests of Inn are offered complimentary green fees and tennis Monday through Thursday. Carts: $20. Weekend green fees: $35 including cart.

ARRIVAL From Palm Springs: east on Highway 111 through Indian Wells. In Indio, turn right on Monroe Street.

INDIAN WELLS RACQUET CLUB RESORT
46–765 Bay Club Drive
Indian Wells, CA 92260
(619) 345–2811

Your vacation home at Indian Wells will be nestled in a cove in the shadow of the majestic Santa Rosa Mountains just 20 minutes from Palm Springs and its many shops and restaurants. Accommodations consist of studios or one-, two- and three-bedroom townhouses which are fully equipped for housekeeping. The resort is also set up to handle meeting groups of up to 100.

Indian Wells Racquet Club Resort clubhouse offers casual dining as well as a cocktail lounge for your pleasure. There is an outstanding view of the Indian Wells Country Club golf course and clubhouse from here. The general area abounds in excellent restaurants.

There are 10 tennis courts along with a group of trained teachers to assist you. For those who prefer a more leisurely pace, there are four private pools located close to your studio or townhouse.

While there are many golf courses to enjoy in this area, the Indian Wells Country Club, adjacent to the racquet club and the home of the Bob Hope Classic, offers 27 holes of outstanding golf. It is a fun layout and one you will long remember. You most certainly will remember it if you should be so unfortunate as to tangle with any of the rock canyon walls. And you can definitely get "involved" should you spray a few shots.

Directly across the road is the Indian Wells 36-hole public golf complex. For details please refer to Hyatt Grand Champions Resort.

RATES (EP) Studio: $140; weekly $840. Studio suite: $150; weekly $900. Deluxe 1-bedroom: $185; weekly $1080. Rates are for December 26-April 30. Green fees: $75/$100, including cart.

ARRIVAL Air: Palm Springs. Car: south on Highway 111 to Indian Wells.

IRONWOOD COUNTRY CLUB
49–200 Mariposa Drive
Palm Desert, CA 92260
(619) 346–0551

Ironwood Country Club is a private club with security gates, impeccably manicured grounds, two lovely golf courses, a very large and beautiful clubhouse and dining room, swimming pools, 14 lighted tennis courts, and a bit more.

Although a private club, rental of privately-owned homes and villas can be arranged through their rental office with a minimum of one week's stay. There is a damage deposit of $250 required, which will be returned after your unit has been vacated and inspected. Maid service is provided once each week. Additional service may be arranged at the prevailing rate.

Golf can be played on either: the North Course, 6,238/5,563 yards parring at 70; or the South, parring at 72. The South layout stretches out 7,286 yards from the masochist tees, or can be played at 6,808/6,518/5,909 yards.

One real plus: the people and the staff are friendly at Ironwood—something you don't always find. Please remember that Ironwood is a private club; thus certain tee times are reserved for members and club events.

RATES (EP) Villas: 1 bedroom $900 per week. Monthly $2400. Homes: 2 Bedrooms $1525 per week. Monthly $4100. Rates are for mid-December through April. Green fees: $60/$75 including cart.

ARRIVAL Air: Palm Springs. From Highway 111 take Portola Drive north. Resort entrance will be on your left.

La CASA DEL ZORRO
Borrego Springs, CA 92004
(619) 767–5323
CA (800) 824–1884
NAT (800) 325–8274

Borrego Valley is nestled against the 8,000-foot-high Santa Rosa mountains with all the beauty these mountains produce as a backdrop. Within this setting is the lovely La Casa del Zorro. While the resort has been in operation for several years it has recently undergone a complete renovation. The rooms have been remodeled with new rugs, new furniture, wall coverings and new bathroom fixtures. Accommodations consist of rooms, suites, deluxe suites and casitas ranging from one to four bedrooms and bath. Some have a fireplace and all have small refrigerators.

Since our first visit here they have added three new buildings (44 guest units), bringing their total to 78. They now also offer meeting facilities and are capable of handling groups of up to 300 people.

The dining and lounge facilities have also been expanded to keep up with the rest of the resort. The food (continental cuisine) is outstanding—as is the service. Jackets are required for dinner except during the summer.

La Casa now offers swimming in three pools as well as lighted tennis courts. The resort has a beauty salon as well as a gift shop.

The Rams Hill 18-hole championship course available for guest play is one of the most beautiful we have had the privilege of playing in this part of the country. For complete details please refer to "Rams Hill" listed in this book.

RATES (EP) Studio: $95. Suites: $125. Deluxe suites: $180. Casitas: (1–4 bedrooms), $180/$450. Green fees: Rams Hill CC $75 including cart.

ARRIVAL Air: (commercial and private aircraft) Borrego Springs (5,000 feet of paved and lighted runway). Phone ahead for courtesy car pick up. Car: from Temecula, take Highway 71 which becomes 79, continue to Montezuma Road, turn southeast.

THE LAKES COUNTRY CLUB
75–375 Country Club Drive
Palm Desert, CA 92260
(619) 568–4321
Reservations (619) 345–5695

While the impressive Santa Rosa Mountains provide a beautiful background for the entire resort, they really set off the magnificent 40,000-square-foot clubhouse. With its massive stone fireplaces, ranch-style atmosphere, large planters and outstanding views of the surrounding area, the clubhouse has become the focal point of The Lakes resort.

The golf shop is on the main level along with a wonderful dining room, and several shops featuring the latest in high fashion. On the lower (ground level) may be found the locker rooms and the Santa Fe Grill.

The resort's name, "The Lakes," is very appropriate. There are a total of 21 lakes covering 25 acres spread throughout the resort complex. The grounds are further enhanced by the presence of over a thousand towering palm trees. Within this setting, accommodations consist of one- to three-bedroom condominiums, each fully equipped for housekeeping. In fact so well equipped that you may not wish to return home. Just to cover a few of the amenities, each condominium has a microwave oven, range, refrigerator (with ice dispenser), washer, dryer, disposal, dishwasher, gas barbecue, and a furnished patio.

In addition to golf, tennis is provided on a grand scale as well. There are 15 courts (eight lighted). A well equipped tennis shop and clubhouse, with its own lounge, overlooks the center stadium court. There is, of course, a professional staff available to assist. They also have a sophisticated video tape system allowing you to review your game. There are swimming pools throughout the grounds, convenient to each condominium grouping.

Golf is an experience on this layout. True to its name, water comes into play on at least nine of the 18 holes. Measuring a modest 6,502/6,130/5,504 yards, the course pars at 72.

Architect Ted Robinson did an outstanding job of blending water, trees, Scottish-style grass bunkers, mixing it with rolling terrain and produced not only a fun course to play but one which will give you all you can handle. In charge of this layout and the superb pro shop is PGA professional, Mike Clifford. For the clubhouse call (619) 568–4321.

RATES (EP) 1 Bedroom $300; with den $310. Green fees: $75 including cart. There are packages, also discounts for length of stay. Rates are for mid-December through April.

ARRIVAL Air: Palm Springs. Car: I-10 to Palm Desert exit.

LA QUINTA RESORT
49–499 Eisenhower Dr. (Box 69)
La Quinta, CA 92253
(619) 564–4111
(800) 854–1271

During Hollywood's heyday La Quinta was the gathering place for many celebrities: Garbo, Davis, Swanson, Chaplin, Gable, Hepburn and many more of the top names in the movie industry. Unfortunately a lot of years have intervened and, while much money has been spent on this resort, it still seems to linger in the past. Sited on 900 acres, lodgings range from rooms and cottage suites to a number of privately owned villas. Tennis can be played on 30 courts. There is a clubhouse complete with dining room and bar, a pro shop, pool and spa. A few of the other activities include: a round of golf or, perhaps, a relaxing day around any of the nine swimming pools.

While there are now three 18-hole golf courses, only one is available to all guests. The Mountain course is restricted to member play. The Citrus course is reserved for select guests. If you push, you may get to play it. This Pete Dye design reaches out a substantial 7,135/6,477/5,932/5,106, parring at 72. While in general I do not like Dye courses, this one is an exception. It is not only beautiful but it's a fair layout as well.

Available to all resort guests, The Dunes plays 6,874/6,307/5,775/5,005 yards, also with a par of 72. While quite long it is very open and appropriately named—it spreads all over the desert.

Private homes on the grounds may be leased. Should you be interested call (619) 564–6098.

RATES (EP) Rooms: $195/$290. Cottage suites: $850/$1800 per night. Green fees: $75 including cart. Rates are December–April.

ARRIVAL Air: Palm Springs. Private aircraft: Thermal (10 minutes). Car: from Palm Springs (19 miles southeast).

MARRIOTT'S DESERT SPRINGS RESORT
74855 Country Club Drive
Palm Desert, CA 92260
(619) 341–2211
(800) 228–9290

Within the spectacular setting of Palm Desert, Marriott has built one of the most magnificent hotels to be found anywhere. The eight-story atrium entrance with water cascading down to a lower level pool, swan and gondola type boats (and all of this is indoor) is so spectacular that on weekends the hotel is crowded with local people wandering around, not really believing what they see—much like country folks at a county fair. Currently rated as a Mobil Four Star resort we predict it will not be very long before it is rated Five Star.

Opened in late 1987, Marriott claims this as one of the largest desert resorts in the nation. Sited on 400 acres, sporting a 30-acre fresh water lake, 892 guest rooms, a 51,000-square-foot separate wing set aside for meetings, 10 restaurants and lounges, it seems their claim may be justified. There are also enough shops of various types to make you feel as if you were living in a department store complex.

The 65 suites range in size from 900 to 3,100 square feet, while the regular guest rooms, featuring mini bars and refrigerators, run 450 square feet.

Just a sample of the activities available include: two swimming pools, 16 tennis courts (eight lighted), a 27,000-square-foot health spa which includes jogging paths, a lap pool, therapy pools, sauna and whirlpools, Swiss showers, a luxurious array of salon and beauty treatments and on and on.

There are two Ted Robinson golf courses. The Palms plays 6,761/6,381/6,143/5,492 yards, parring at 72. Sited on gently rolling terrain giving you a new look on most shots, well trapped, with water coming into play on 10 holes, this course will keep your attention. The newest layout, the Valley Course stretches out 6,713/6,366/6,084/5,348 yards and also pars at 72.

In addition to the tennis pro shop there is, of course, a full-line golf shop and a professional staff under the supervision of the Director of Golf, Tim Skogen.

RATES (EP) Standard: $235/$295. Suites: $350 and up. Green fees: $80 including cart.

ARRIVAL Air: Palm Springs (13 miles). Car: I-10 from Los Angeles (120 miles).

MARRIOTT'S RANCHO LAS PALMAS RESORT
41000 Bob Hope Drive
Rancho Mirage, CA 92270
(619) 568–2727
(800) 228–9290
Condo Rental (619) 345–5695

The structure of Rancho Las Palmas is very impressive, reflecting early California-style architecture with graceful arches, rough textured stucco, exposed wooden beams and red tile roofs. The rich

Spanish-style furnishings as well as the paintings, tapestries and authentic Mexican tile add to its soft and gentle southwestern atmosphere. Lodgings consist of 456 hacienda-style rooms and suites, each with patio or balcony, and all adjacent to the golf course or the various small lakes. This resort, like all Marriott operations, is well set up to accommodate meeting and conference groups.

The dining facilities are outstanding and include The Cabrillo Room featuring French cuisine, The Fountain Court (a bit less formal) and The Sunrise Terrace, which hosts patio dining. Each offers excellent service and a wide menu selection. The Rancho Las Palmas has earned several prestigious awards including The Golden Key, The Pinnacle, The AAA Four Diamond and the Mobil Four Star Award.

Tennis may be enjoyed on 25 courts (eight lighted) with a pro shop and video analysis equipment available. Some of the other amenities include: two swimming pools with companion hydrotherapy pools, a fitness center and once-a-week aerobic classes.

There are 27 holes of golf to be played. The North/South nines measure 6,019/5,716/5,421 yards parring at 71. The West/North combination reaches out 5,558/5,295/4,985 yards and pars at 70. The West/South combination weighs in at 5,569 /5,219/4,886 again with a par of 70. Winding among six small lakes, 80 sand traps and over 1,500 tall palm trees and the condominium structures, they are fun courses to play.

RATES (EP) Rooms: $230/$245. Suites: $430/$665. Green fees: $70 including cart. Rates are for December 26-May 30.

ARRIVAL Air: Palm Springs. Car: I-10 off at Bob Hope Drive.

MONTEREY COUNTRY CLUB
41–500 Monterey Avenue
Palm Desert, CA 92260
(619) 568–9311
Reservations (619) 345–5695

The accommodations at Monterey consist of well set up condominiums and homes, most with fireplaces, wet bars and fully equipped for housekeeping. Within this 360-acre resort complex you will find 19 tennis courts (10 lighted) including a sunken championship court with built-in stadium seating and a 3,000-square-foot tennis clubhouse. There are also several swimming pools scattered throughout the area.

The main clubhouse overlooks the largest on-property lake as well as the 9th and 18th holes. The upper level is the locale of the dining room, while the lower level contains the pro shop, locker rooms and snack shop.

Golf may be played on 27 holes. Using a crossover arrangement you wind up with: the East/West combination, reaching out 6,096/5,798/5,250 yards and parring at 71; the East/South nines at 6,041/5,780/5,242 yards also parring at 71; and finally the West/South combination of nines which runs 6,133/5,838/5,346 yards parring at 72. With water in play on 15 holes, plus some very interesting uphill and downhill fairways, it becomes an intriguing combination of golf holes. For tee times call (619) 340–3885

RATES (EP) 1-bedroom condo with den: $260. 2-bedroom condo: $295. Green fees: $65 including cart. There are discounts for weekly or longer stays. Rates are for mid-December through April.

ARRIVAL Air: Palm Springs.

PALM DESERT RESORT & COUNTRY CLUB
77–333 Country Club Drive
Palm Desert, CA 92260
(619) 345–2781
Reservations (619) 345–8426

The center of the resort is their impressive and well set up clubhouse. It also happens to be the location of the delightful Papagayo Dining Room as well as the golf shop and check in area. Accommodations consist of villas, each with living room, fully equipped kitchen, bedroom, dinette and private patio. The two-bedroom units feature two baths. The Palm Desert Resort can provide a full spectrum of conference and meeting facilities accommodating up to 200 per meeting group.

Tennis, under the supervision of a professional staff, is offered on 17 lighted courts with a 1,000-seat amphitheater as the center court. There are also two indoor racquetball courts and 20 swimming pools scattered throughout the property.

The golf course, parring at 72, plays 6,506/6,202/6,026/5,434 yards. With sand, water and rolling terrain, it is one of the most enjoyable desert courses I have played. That is, until I reached the 9th hole. I was not speechless, but I was unprintable. Suffice to say, it is different and let it go at that.

The pro shop, under the direction of professional Tom Bienek, offers one of the finest selections of equipment and clothing we have seen anywhere in the U.S. In fact it could be referred to as a small department store. The selection not only includes golfing and casual wear but also a choice of bathing apparel.

RATES (EP) Villas: 1-bedroom $150. 1-bedroom plus den: $175. 2 bedrooms: $175. Green fees: $70/$75 including cart. Rates are for January-April.

ARRIVAL Air: Palm Springs. Car: from Los Angeles, I-10 to Washington Street exit, right on Country Club Drive.

PALM VALLEY COUNTRY CLUB
976–200 Country Club Drive
Palm Desert, CA 62260
(619) 345–2737
Reservations (619) 345–5695

Accommodations consist of well equipped homes and condominiums either adjacent to or on the golf course.

The 83,000-square-foot clubhouse presents a magnificent setting for dining. It, of course, performs a much greater function and has become the center of the resort's activities. It is the location of the golf and tennis pro shops, both quite large and offering a wide selection of clothing. On the lower level can be found the spa, racquetball courts, a coed weight room, an aerobics room, saunas, massage and steam rooms, whirlpools, tanning rooms and on and on.

Adjacent to the clubhouse is a 25-meter swimming pool and an outdoor jogging trail. When you add that to the above 19 tennis courts (10 lighted) and include a stadium court I think you will agree there are more than enough activities to keep you occupied.

The South golf course stretches out 6,545/6,105/5,429 yards, parring at 72. With water in play on 12 holes, palm trees all over the place, as well as half the Sahara Desert used as sand traps, this layout will keep your attention. Or perhaps I should say it had better keep your attention. The North course is an executive layout playing 4,245 yards with a par of 63. Both courses as well as the outstanding pro shop are under the direction of Head Professional Scott Walter. For tee times call (619) 345–2742.

RATES (EP) 1 bedroom: $300. 1 bedroom and den: $310. Green fees: $75 including cart. There are discounts for stays of a week or longer. Rates quoted are for mid-December through April.

ARRIVAL Air: Palm Springs.

PGA WEST
55–900 PGA Boulevard
La Quinta, CA 92253
Pro shop (619) 564–7170
Pro shop (619) 564–7429
Reservations (619) 345–5695

The PGA West is, in fact, a resort community. It is on 2,200 acres surrounded by four (eventually to be five) championship golf courses and providing the amenities of a spectacular 63,000-square-foot clubhouse. Accommodations consist of condominiums and homes with future plans for the construction of a world class hotel. Each condo is fully equipped for housekeeping including washer/dryer, a barbecue, patio furniture and an enclosed garage. Daily maid service can be arranged.

Supported by its own tennis club, providing all of the expected amenities, are 19 tennis courts with an exhibition center court offering a seating capacity for 3,000 spectators. You may choose to play on clay, grass or hard surface. Future plans call for a substantial expansion of the tennis complex.

There are now four complete courses. The TPC "Stadium Resort Course" a par-72 Pete Dye design, reaches out 7,271 yards (psychopathic tees). Anyone playing from these tees is either a masochist or in dire need of a session with a very good psychiatrist. To carry on, the remaining tee settings measure 6,821/6,313/5,228. Mr. Dye used the natural undulation of the desert to create a Scottish links type of layout. He also introduced water into play on nine holes. The 17th hole, a par three, is very aptly named "Alcatraz". While only 128 yards from the regular tees, you will find yourself shooting at a green measuring some 28 by 31 yards. The location of the widely telecast Skins Game, it is as rough as the pictures indicated. The course is playable from the white tees but for the average weekend golfer I would suggest staying away from the championship and blue tees.

The Jack Nicklaus Course, available for guest play, measures 7,264/6,671/6,064/5,175 yards, also parring at 72. Bringing water into play on seven holes this is a fun layout to navigate. Something of interest—the 9th and 18th holes share a green, which is very reminiscent of many Scottish layouts.

The other two courses are the Arnold Palmer Private Course and the Jack Nicklaus Private Course. These two layouts are restricted to member play and are not available for guests of the resort. Both of the resort courses are under the supervision of PGA Professional Jeff Walser.

RATES (EP) Condo: (1-bedroom/with den) $300/$310. There are discounts for stays of 5 nights or longer ranging from 17% to 40%. Green fees: $75/$95.

ARRIVAL Air: Palm Springs or Thermal Airports. Car: from Highway 111 travel west on Jefferson Street (about 5 miles).

RAMS HILL
P.O. Box 664
Borrego Springs, CA 92004
(619) 767–5028
CA (800) 524–2800
NAT (800) 732–9200

Few places in the world can match the beauty and grandeur of the Anza-Borrego desert. The surrounding peaks (sometimes snow-capped) reflecting brilliant blues and greens, the desert dusk painting an ever-changing palette of colors, along with the stark silence, combine to produce a state of utter relaxation. There is, however, one drawback to this area. It is remote and a long way from major shopping and dining areas.

Within this setting and located on 3,200 acres, Rams Hill is in the process of building a resort residential community. At the present time there are several homes completed and a very impressive clubhouse and golf course in place. The mix will eventually encompass custom homes, patio homes and casitas.

The restaurant in the clubhouse is outstanding. Featuring French cuisine they also boast the service of a world-renowned chef.

There are rental units now available with either a bedroom or bedroom/living room and kitchen. Eight lighted tennis courts are now in play.

The Rams Hill Golf Course stretches out 7,076/6,328/5,694 yards and pars at 72. Although only a few years old it is in remarkable condition. A few of the hazards include: water on six holes, 56 white sand bunkers and the magnificent views from most of the tees which make it very difficult to keep your mind on the game. Ted Robinson, architect of Rams Hill, took advantage of the natural terrain, creating rises and falls of more than 100 feet on several holes. We found it a most interesting and fun golf course to play. A third nine, also a Robinson design, has just come into play. The course is supported by an excellent and well stocked golf shop. For tee times call (619) 767–5124.

RATES 1 bedroom $165; weekly $895. One bedroom and den: $185; weekly $1035. 2-bedroom home: $210; weekly $1250. Green fees: $65 including cart. Rates are January-May.

ARRIVAL Air: Borrego Springs. Car: from Palm Springs area travel south on Highway 86, then west on State Road 22.

STOUFFER'S ESMERALDA RESORT
44–400 Indian Wells Lane
Indian Wells, CA
(619) 773–4444
(800) 468–3571

The Esmeralda is one of the newer kids on the block. Opening in late 1989 it joined a large number of outstanding resorts in the Coachella Valley.

A great deal of attention and planning went into the resort structure. Consisting of eight multi-storied buildings, there is an eight-story glass-enclosed atrium entrance, a massive dual grand staircase, along with several 40-foot palm trees as well as a stream running through the lobby area.

Situated on 21 acres this massive chateau-like structure offers accommodations in 560 guest rooms including suites. Rooms feature French provincial furnishings and louvered windows rather than curtains. Each has a sitting area, television sets in the bedroom, as well as in the bathroom, and a small balcony.

The meeting facilities are as impressive as the resort. With 33,000 square feet of space devoted to meeting activities, including ballrooms and many smaller breakout rooms, they are exceptionally well qualified to handle large group functions. Along with a series of lounges there are two restaurants serving Mediterranean and Continental cuisine.

A few of the activities provided include: three swimming pools (one featuring a poolside gazebo bar), seven tennis courts (three lighted), two whirlpools and a health and fitness center.

Golf can be played on two layouts adjacent to the hotel. Owned and operated by the city of Indian Wells, the East and the West golf courses have some unusual features. For details on this golf complex refer to "Hyatt Grand Champions Resort".

The Esmeralda and Hyatt Grand Champions hotels are ⅛ of a mile apart and both are located on top of the courses.

RATES (EP) Rooms: $230/$320. Suites: $300/$2000. Green fees: $65/$75 including cart. Golf packages are available.

ARRIVAL Air: Palm Springs. Car: the resort is located on Highway 111 just a few miles south of Palm Desert.

COLORADO

THE BROADMOOR
P.O. Box 1439
Colorado Springs, CO 80901
(303) 634–7711
(800) 634–7711

The warmth of the Broadmoor is felt from the very first moment of your arrival. The stately entrance, often the scene of a great many people coming and going, is under the direction of a group of superb doormen, who tend to sort things out in a gentle and humorous manner.

This is one of the finest resorts in the country. Steeped in tradition since its opening in 1918, the Broadmoor has preserved its glowing past while able to more than keep pace with the present. The original hotel, known as Broadmoor Main, is a unique blend of old world grace and modern convenience. It stands today much as it did originally, showing its magnificent Italian Renaissance decor. It is difficult and very expensive to successfully bring a resort from its luxurious past into the present period. At the Broadmoor it has been accomplished extremely well.

There are, in total, eight restaurants and five lounges not including the Winter House. (Jackets and ties are required in the dining areas after 6 pm).

Three fine restaurants are located in the "Main": the Tavern, with its original Toulouse-Lautrec lithographs; the Garden Room and the stately Main Dining Room. The Broadmoor has won the coveted Mobil Five Star Award each year since 1960. Keep in mind that only 22 hotel/resorts in the United States out of approximately 20,000 facilities have earned this award.

The nine-story Broadmoor South adjacent to the Main, with its Penrose Dining Room and Lounge, offers a spectacular view of the mountains. Broadmoor West, located on the west side of the lake, is a hotel (resort) complete unto itself, presenting outstanding dining, dancing, entertainment and Oriental art dating back to the Ming and T'sing dynasties. If my count was correct there are a little over 550 rooms including suites.

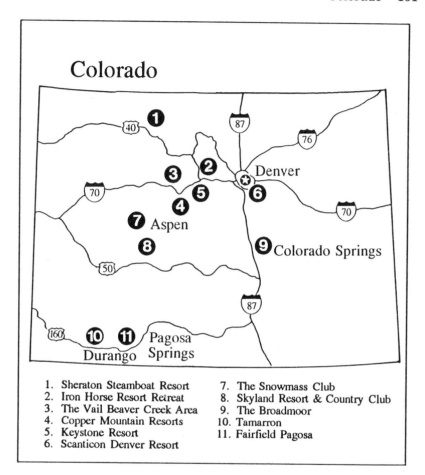

Colorado

1. Sheraton Steamboat Resort
2. Iron Horse Resort Retreat
3. The Vail Beaver Creek Area
4. Copper Mountain Resorts
5. Keystone Resort
6. Scanticon Denver Resort
7. The Snowmass Club
8. Skyland Resort & Country Club
9. The Broadmoor
10. Tamarron
11. Fairfield Pagosa

The Broadmoor is one of the more popular meeting and convention locations in the country, with over 100,000 square feet of meeting and display space.

The younger set has not been forgotten. During the July-August period and in effect Monday through Saturday, the hotel provides a supervised program for children ranging in age from 6 to 12 years of age.

While obviously a well known winter sports location, it has much to offer in the summer: tennis on 16 plexipave all weather courts, under the watchful eye of professional Chet Murphy and staff, swimming, squash, skeet and trap shooting, bicycle rentals, and boating.

Horseback riding can be enjoyed from the Broadmoor's own equestrian center. Tours of this scenic area can also be arranged.

During the winter months skiing and ice skating become king. As a matter of fact, the Broadmoor is world renowned for its ice skating facilities and has hosted the World Figure Skating championships as well as international hockey competition.

Golf, under the supervision of well known professional and Director of Golf, Dow Finsterwald and staff, can be played on three courses. The East Course, designed by Donald Ross in 1918, presents a significant yardage of 7,218/6,555/5,954, with par set at 72/73. The West, a Robert Trent Jones 1965 design, stretches out 6,937/6,109/5,505 yards parring at 72/73. Both courses start from the same pro shop (very well stocked) adjacent to the hotel and are under the direction of head professional Mike Tayler.

And now we come to the South Course, playing 6,781/6,108/5,609/4,834 yards with par set at 72/70. Sounds easy, but this layout is one which can wring your very soul and, as a matter of fact, your tail. On the first nine there is one hole where you are allowed a view of the green from the tee (the eighth). In fact from the third tee it is difficult to determine where the fairway is.

Ed Seay, of the Arnold Palmer organization, designer of the South Course (1976), found a new way to keep everyone awake and alert. On the front nine there are "barrancas" (ravines usually filled with brush) making an appearance on eight holes. On the second nine there are only two barrancas coming into play. I will not describe the 18th hole as it should remain a surprise—something to be long remembered by each golfer. Suffice to say it is a tough closing hole.

The South Course is some distance above the hotel with a view of the surrounding countryside that is something else. As a matter of fact the elevation of this layout is approximately 6,000 feet. Should you get excited about how far you are hitting the ball—remember it is not really you.

The South Golf Course is supported by its own golf shop, under the supervision of professional Hal Douglass, and offers full amenities. There is transportation provided to and from the course.

RATES (EP) Main: $200. South: $210. West: $235. Jr. suites: $295. Deluxe suites: $325 up. Green fees: $55, carts $25.

ARRIVAL Air: Colorado Springs.

COPPER MOUNTAIN RESORTS

P.O. Box 3001
Copper Mountain, CO 80443
(303) 968–2882
(800) 458–8386

The Mountain Resorts are actually a group of five management companies, operating a total of 21 different condominium buildings in one resort area. Included in the list of condominiums are the Copper Mountain Inn, Copper Junction, Copper Valley, Foxpine Inn, Village Point, Anaconda, Bridge End and Snowflake, the latter with its own restaurant.

Mountain Plaza and Village Square, also with their own restaurants, are in the heart of the village, with shops and restaurants readily available. Two new condominiums, the Greens and the Woods, are at the golf course.

The telephone number shown above will give you the reservation department for accommodations. They can arrange lodgings ranging from a studio to a one-bedroom condominium to a penthouse suite with five bedrooms sleeping 24. They now have a meeting/conference center as well.

There are many things to keep you busy: horseback riding, swimming, boating on Lake Dillon, tennis, fishing, Jeep tours, windsurfing, rafting and bicycling.

Golf can now be played on the Pete Dye designed Copper Creek Golf Club. Measuring 6,129/5,742/5,159/4,358 yards with a par of 70, it is an exciting layout. The facilities are complete with clubhouse and pro shop.

RATES (EP) Lodge rooms: $75. Condominiums: 1 bedroom $105/130. Green fees: $45 including cart. Rates are for June-September.

ARRIVAL Air: Denver. Car: I-70 west, exit at 195, approximately 75 miles.

FAIRFIELD PAGOSA

P.O. Box 4040
Pagosa, CO 81157
(303) 731–4141
(800) 523–7704

In the early days of Pagosa, accommodations meant a teepee or lean-to amid towering spruce and ponderosa pine. Today, this is southwest Colorado's showplace, with an inn, luxurious condominiums clustered in communities—but they are still surrounded by the same spruce and ponderosa pine. The 101-room inn offers not only outstanding lodgings but also a view of the lakes and craggy peaks of the magnificent San Juan Mountains. Dining is provided in the South Face, the Great Divide or the Rendezvous Cocktail Lounge.

This family-oriented complex serves up every type of activity you could wish for: bicycle, boat and ice skate rentals, a health spa, indoor swimming, saunas, hydrotherapy pools and game rooms. There is a stable offering horseback riding, chuckwagon cookouts, winter sleighrides and a racquet club (six courts) along with its own pro shop. Baby sitting service is also available.

As you may well have guessed by now, Fairfield Pagosa is quite large. The project itself is 18,000 acres with six lakes and five miles of the San Juan River on site. An additional 2½ million acres of national forest and 226 thousand acres of primitive area border Pagosa.

The Pagosa Pines Club course is now a 27-hole layout. Pine 1/Pine 2 nines weigh in at 6,748/6,282/5,392 yards parring at 71. Pine 1/Meadows, parring at 72, plays an awesome 7,256/6,524/5,380 yards. Finally, The Pine 2/Meadows combination completes the picture, reaching out 6,956/6,154/5,126 yards, also with a par of 72.

The clubhouse provides a full line pro shop and snack bar. During the winter months the golf shop functions as a snowmobile and ski rentals area.

RATES (EP) Inn: $85/$95. Suites: $100/$120. Condos: $120/$150. Green fees: $42 including cart. Golf packages are available.

ARRIVAL Air: Durango. Private aircraft: Pagosa Springs (6,500 foot paved runway). Car: U.S. 160, 3½ miles west of Pagosa Springs.

IRON HORSE RESORT RETREAT
P.O. Box 1286
Winter Park, CO 80482
(303) 726–8851
(800) 621–8190

Of course winter is the time of the premier action in this area. And there are more than enough amenities: 18 lifts, manicured ski runs, sleigh rides, snowmobiling and on and on.

But we are talking about golf and the summer period. Accommodations consist of one-, two- or three-bedroom condominiums. Each is fully equipped for housekeeping, featuring balcony, fireplace, living and dining areas, microwave, dishwasher. Some also provide a private Jacuzzi tub, a wet bar, and a washer/dryer.

The resort can also handle smaller meeting groups and is well set up to do so. The facilities allow groups of from 10 to 100. If you decide not to condo it there is the Rails Bar & Restaurant.

A few of the amenities available include: indoor and outdoor swimming pools, four outdoor hot tubs, weight and exercise rooms, a racquetball court and a steam room.

Golf can be played on the Pole Creek Golf Club course. Parring at 72, it weighs in at a fair 6,882/6,230/4,956 yards. They did not name this Pole Creek just for kicks. The creek meanders throughout the course, forming four lakes. The course features some elevated tees and greens, is very well trapped and enjoys a beautiful setting.

RATES (EP) 1 bedroom: $85. 2 bedrooms, 2 bath $110. Premium: $105/$135. Green fees: $45, carts $20. There are several different packages including golf.

ARRIVAL Air: Denver (90 minutes). Car: from Denver I-70, exit #232 onto I-40, north to the resort.

KEYSTONE RESORT
P.O. Box 38
Keystone, CO 80435
(303) 468–2316
(800) 541–0346 LODGE RENTALS
(800) 222–0188 CONDO RENTALS

The Keystone Resort, 75 miles west of Denver in the 9,300-foot-high Snake River Valley, is one of very few resorts to have earned the AAA Four Diamond Award as well as being a member of Preferred Hotels Worldwide.

The 152-room lodge, along with 900 condominiums and luxury homes, are a part of this four-season resort complex. All condominiums provide fully equipped kitchens and fireplaces. Old Western ambience is experienced in the spacious 50-year-old Ranch House, with its elegant living room, bar, golf shop, dining

and locker rooms. Adjoining the Lodge is a major conference cen
ter, plus 15 rooms. A very recent addition, the 58,000-square-foot
Keystone Resort Conference Center, now has a capacity of up to
1,800 people.

The resort also provides child care and an all-day activities
program.

As for dining, Keystone offers something for everyone: the Bighorn
Steak House, the Garden Room for continental dining, the Edge-
water Cafe for casual family meals and, for special elegance, the
rustic Ranch (open for dinner only during the winter).

Speaking of winter, without getting carried away, this resort is
ideal. Three mountains, Keystone, North Peak and Arapahoe Basin, offer superb skiing on 810 acres with 20 lifts, including the
high-speed gondola.

There are 14 tennis courts (two indoor) with a complete pro shop
and lounge available. Other activities include: backpacking, bicycling, kayaking, sailing, fishing, raft trips, horseback riding and
swimming in several different pools.

Golf is played on a Robert Trent Jones, Jr. course three miles
south of the village. Rimmed by towering peaks it plays 7,090/
6,521/5,720 yards and pars at 72. It is an interesting and beautiful
layout as it passes through the woods, across the meadows and
brings a nine-acre lake and various ponds into play. It is considered by many to be the highest course in the United States with
portions reaching above 9,300 feet.

During the summer months Keystone has started "The Keystone
Music Festival". This concert entertains three days each week and
includes some of the top guest performers in the country.

RATES (EP) Lodge: $140. Condominiums: 1 bedroom $130/$150.
Green fees: $65 including carts.

ARRIVAL Air: Denver. Car: I-70 west to exit 205. East on U.S. 6
for 6 miles.

SCANTICON-DENVER RESORT
200 Inverness Drive West
Englewood, CO 80112
(303) 740-8300
(800) 346-4891

Scanticon is 45 minutes from Denver's Stapleton International Airport. It represents a masterful blending of excellent vacation and superb meeting and conference facilities. A multi-storied hotel, it features a dramatic and beautiful atrium lobby.

Accommodations consist of 302 guest rooms including: queen, king, double queens, parlor as well as executive suites. The rooms are furnished with a large desk, two telephones, remote color TV, and feature either a view of the mountains or of the golf course. You can also select lodgings on the Club Floor. During the week there is a concierge available to assist. There is also a complimentary continental breakfast as well as cocktails and hors d'oeuvres served each evening from 4 to 7 PM.

There are several alternatives for dining. For a touch of French cuisine you might consider the Black Swan (jackets required, ties optional). For less formal dining there is the Garden Terrace and the Copenhagen Restaurant. There are a number of lounges and pubs throughout the hotel complex. JR's Pub offers nightly live entertainment (except Sunday).

The conference and meeting facilities are exceptional. Consisting of 31 meeting rooms and two auditoriums, they are supported by the very latest state-of-the-art audio-visual equipment. The rooms are also soundproof.

In addition to golf, the sporting activities at your disposal include: indoor and outdoor swimming pools, tennis courts, saunas, whirlpools, a fully equipped exercise room and jogging trails nearby.

Golf is available on the Inverness Golf Club course. Designed by Preston Maxwell, it reaches out a substantial 6,948/6,407/5,681 yards with a par of 70/71.

The resort has provided a clubhouse including a pro shop, locker rooms, a clubhouse grill and a snack bar.

RATES (EP) Rooms: $130; 1-bedroom suite: $169. Club floor room: $149; 1-bedroom suite: $209. Green fees: $40, carts $18. Golf packages: (include lodging, Golf Grille breakfast, green fees and cart), $139 per couple.

ARRIVAL Air: Stapleton International. Private aircraft: Centennial Airport (1.5 miles). Car : I-25 to County Line exit—turn left (east). 2nd stoplight is Inverness Road. Turn left to resort.

SHERATON STEAMBOAT RESORT

P.O. Box 774808
Steamboat Springs, CO 80477
(303) 879–2220
CO (800) 848–8877
NAT (800) 848–8878

The nucleus of this resort complex is the Sheraton Village Hotel with 276 guest rooms and its conference center. A few steps away are the 58 luxurious rooms and 75 condominium units of the Sheraton Thunderhead Lodge.

There are three delightful restaurants: Cipriani's, specializing in Italian cuisine; the Soda Creek Cafe for lighter dining; or for something special, Remington's Restaurant. There are also two lounges.

If you are a ski enthusiast, you know about this famous winter resort. Over 300 inches of powder and all the amenities associated with world-class skiing make this one of the best.

Four lighted tennis courts are just steps from the hotel. A sample of the other activities include: whitewater rafting down the Green, Yanpa or Colorado Rivers; sailing and waterskiing on Steamboat Lake; excellent fishing in the 900 miles of rivers, streams or 109 lakes.

Four-legged critters are a big part of Steamboat Springs life, with trail rides, western dinner rides or hayrack rides available.

This Robert Trent Jones, Jr. resort course measures 6,906/6,276/5,647 yards and pars at 72. While you do get some help in the form of the 7,000-foot altitude, the 77 sand traps and seven water holes will bring you quickly back to reality.

RATES (EP) Rooms: Village $79/$89; Suites: $149/$199. Condos: $69/$139. Green fees: $35, carts $20. Golf package: 2 nights (includes room, golf, cart), weekdays $266 per couple. Rates are for June 15-September 30.

ARRIVAL Air: Denver (153 miles) with shuttle flights or private aircraft to Hayden (23 miles from Steamboat Springs). Car: I-70 to U.S. 40.

SKYLAND RESORT & COUNTRY CLUB

P.O. Box 879
Crested Butte, CO 81224
(303) 349–7541

Skyland Resort is in the heart of the majestic Colorado Rocky Mountains. Sited in the beautiful Slate River Valley at the base of the towering Crested Butte Mountain, it offers excellent skiing in the winter and golf during the summer. Accommodations consist of rooms set up for light housekeeping (kitchenettes). They are equipped with small refrigerators and microwave ovens. Some rooms have an additional loft bedroom.

There are restaurants, indoor tennis and racquetball courts, a Jacuzzi and a swimming pool.

Golf can be enjoyed on the Skyland Country Club course. During the summer, the home of the John Jacobs/Shelby Futch "Practical Golf" school, this par-72 layout plays at 7,208/6,635/5,747 yards. The overwhelming stark beauty of this area makes it particularly difficult to keep your mind on the game.

RATES (EP) Rooms: $79/$89. Green fees: $55 including cart. Golf package: 2 nights/2 days (includes lodging, golf and cart, club storage, continental breakfast), $239 per couple. Rates are for July-August.

ARRIVAL Air: Gunnison. Car: north of Gunnison on State Route 135.

THE SNOWMASS CLUB
P.O. Drawer G 2
Snowmass Village, CO 81615
(303) 923–5600
CO (800) 227–5544
NAT (800) 525–0710

Snowmass, in the renowned Snowmass/Aspen valley, is nestled high in the Colorado Rockies. Obviously a mecca for ski enthusiasts, it is now becoming known for its summer activities.

Each spacious guest room or suite, with a private balcony view of the mountains, is warmly decorated. Terrycloth robes for each guest, turndown service and champagne on arrival are but a few of the thoughtful touches offered.

Adjacent to the inn accommodations are available in Club Villas, as well as many different condominiums featuring fireplaces and fully equipped kitchens. These units range from one to three bedrooms. To name just a few: Terracehouse, Litchenhearth, Wood-ridge, Interlude and Snowmass Mountain Condominiums. Snowmass is also able to handle meeting groups in the new Fairway Conference Center with a capacity of 225 theater-style.

While open for all meals, the Four Corners Restaurant is particularly charming for candlelight dining. Then perhaps you might enjoy a nightcap in the Piano Bar Lounge. All in all, Snowmass Club is a lovely and relaxing place.

Physical fitness buffs will have a field day here. The tennis professionals "hold court" on 11 tennis courts (two indoor). The courts are on different levels surrounding the Summerhouse Restaurant and Bar. On the other side of the lodge, swimmers will find the heated lap pool, coed whirlpool and recreation pool with diving area. There are three racquetball courts, squash courts, steam rooms, saunas, whirlpools, a Nautilus gym, massage rooms, lockers and showers. During the summer months guided hiking, horseback riding and fishing expeditions can also be arranged.

Snowmass recently spent over a million dollars in renovating the Club Golf Links. Now playing 6,900/6,055/5,008 yards, it pars at 71. While an open course it is exceptionally well trapped. In playing golf here you must be aware that you are at almost 9,000 feet. If you were not aware, you will be after your very first tee shot.

RATES (EP) Lodge rooms: $150. Suites: $175/$210. Club Villas: 1 bedroom $210. Green fees: $55 including carts. Golf package: (includes lodging, golf, tennis), $99 per night per person. Rates are June-August.

ARRIVAL Air: Aspen. Car: from Aspen, Highway 82 northwest 2 miles to enter Snowmass Village. Now on Brush Creek Road go 3 miles, turn left onto Highline Road. Club limousine available from airport. A car is not needed as on-site shuttle is available.

AN EXTRA: something new has been added to the Snowmass complex. The Silvertree Hotel—featuring a three-story atrium lobby, 250 guest rooms and 12 suites, a Bar and Grill, a Fireside Restaurant and meeting facilities. They offer a bit more in the form of two swimming pools, two whirlpools and saunas. For reservations call NAT (800) 525–9402.

TAMARRON
P.O. Drawer 3131
Durango, CO 81302
(303) 259–2000
(800) 678–1000

In the south-western corner of Colorado, Tamarron is situated in the high mountain valley of the San Juan Mountain Range. The great, hewn timber inn offers a wide variety of accommodations: rooms featuring two queen-size beds, suites with living room/kitchen facilities, Loft Inn suites, townhouses with one to three bedrooms and condominiums. They also provide meeting facilities for groups up to 600.

Dining is outstanding with either Le Canyon for a candlelight affair or the San Juan Club for a more informal dinner.

In the winter this is a ski buff's delight. The slopes of Purgatory average over 200 inches of snow, providing skiing, sleigh rides, tobogganing and ice skating.

During the warmer months a few of the activities include: fishing in Tamarron's private lake and nearby streams, white-water rafting, horseback riding, swimming in both indoor or outdoor pools, tennis on indoor and outdoor courts with a professional staff on deck to assist. There is also a complete health club facility and a supervised children's program.

Tamarron warms into a high country golf resort of unusual beauty during the summer months. Fairways wind amid tall stands of ponderosa pine, age old oaks and aspen. This is some of the most intriguing scenery you will find on any golf course. In fact, one of the most difficult parts of playing here is keeping your mind on the game and not on the scenery or the wildlife.

The Tamarron Golf Course, an Arthur Hill design, plays 6,885/6,340/5,380 yards with a par of 72. The course is supported by a driving range as well as a pro shop offering full facilities.

RATES (EP) Deluxe Room or 1-bedroom townhouse: $116. Green fees: $65 including cart. Golf package: 3 nights/3 days (includes lodging, 3 days golf, cart, club storage), $750 per couple. Rates are for May-October.

ARRIVAL Air: Durango. Car: 18 miles north of Durango on U.S. 550.

VAIL-BEAVER CREEK AREA

For many years the Vail and Beaver Creek areas have been known for their superb ski facilities. The area is also known for its magnificent mountain and forest settings which are virtually un-matched in this country. But, alas, winter does come to an end. The beauty is still there and so are the many restaurants, bars, shops, hotels, condominiums, all representing a huge dollar invest-ment and earning virtually nothing.

The resorts of Colorado have discovered golf. They did not ease into the field but went in under a full head of steam, employing such august names as Jack Nicklaus, Arnold Palmer, Pete Dye, Robert Trent Jones, Jr. and Gary Player to produce some of the finest golf courses to be found anywhere.

Two such areas are Vail Village Resorts and the Beaver Creek Re-sort complex located approximately 10 miles apart. Due to the proximity of one to the other, most of the amenities are available to guests of either.

Within a 20-mile radius there are four first-class championship golf courses. Each course has full pro shop, locker rooms and res-taurants. The Golf season in this area is late June to mid-September.

Both resort areas provide outstanding meeting and convention facilities.

Due to the great number and diversity of accommodations, it is not possible to list their rates. Please understand that the majority of accommodations are very posh and expensive winter lodgings made available at reduced summer rates. There are also golf pack-ages available allowing play on several courses. When making res-ervations request this information.

Oh, yes, there is tennis with over 50 courts in the area.

THE BEAVER CREEK GOLF CLUB, which is now semi-private, was designed by Robert Trent Jones, Jr. With a par of 70 the course measures 6,464/6,026/5,202 yards. The course stretches along Beaver Creek and into the valley with native spruce and as-pen lining the fairways and presenting some very well bunkered greens. For tee times call (303) 949-7123.

EAGLE-VAIL GOLF CLUB lies between Vail Village and Beaver Creek in the residential community of Eagle Vail. The course plays 6,819/6,142/4,856 yards and pars at 72. Considered one of the most challenging in the valley, its 10th hole, a par three plays from 208 to 124 yards. The tee sits 250 feet above the green. Your ball spends so much time in the air you may have to get a permit from NASA. For tee times call (303) 949–5267.

SINGLETREE GOLF LINKS, which is now semi-private, lies west of Beaver Creek at the Berry Creek Ranch. Designed by Jack Nicklaus' company, GOLFORCE, Singletree resembles a Scottish links with its hilly fairways, deep bunkers and natural grass roughs. Parring at 71, this layout stretches out 7,024/6,435/5,907/5,293 yards. It has co-hosted the Gerry Ford 1982 invitational. For tee times call (303) 949–4240.

VAIL GOLF CLUB was Vail's first. Just east of Vail Village, it reaches out a monstrous 7,048/6,282/5,934/5,303 yards with a par of 71/72. Gore Creek winds throughout this 18-hole layout. For tee times call (303) 476–1330.

THE VAIL/BEAVER CREEK RESORT ASSOCIATION
241 East Meadow Drive
Vail, CO 81657
(303) 476–5677
(800) 525–3875

The above number will put you in touch with reservations in Vail as well as the Beaver Creek area. In fact, it will open up accommodations such as lodge rooms, condominiums, townhouses and private residences. Including the many hotels, there are well over 20,000 guest lodgings available.

These full service communities have over 100 restaurants, night-clubs, and bars, more than 300 shops, many heated lodge swimming pools, saunas, whirlpools, drug stores, banks, and other services.

HAWAII

THE ISLAND OF OAHU

Although one of the smaller islands in the chain, Oahu is the population center, the hub of commercial activities and still the location of the largest number of restaurants and night-spots. You will find many wonderful hotels and a few golf resorts here as well. Above all, it is beautiful.

SHERATON MAKAHA RESORT & COUNTRY CLUB
84–626 Makaha Valley Road
Makaha, HI 96792
(808) 695–9511
(800) 325–3535

The Sheraton Makaha, very close to the mountains high in the Makaha Valley, overlooks the famous Makaha surfing beaches.

Accommodations consist of several clusters of two-story cottages offering a total of 200 guest rooms. It is surrounded by beautiful gardens and the fragrance will almost overwhelm you. The resort has set aside 10,000 square feet for meetings and receptions. In the usual Sheraton manner they are well equipped to handle groups of up to 240 banquet- or 300-theater style.

The dining facilities, while informal, are excellent and range from the coffee shop, the Pikaki Cafe, to the elegant Kaala Room. There is also the Lobby Lounge with its outstanding view of the golf course and the ocean beyond—a great place to view a spectacular Hawaiian sunset.

If, on certain days, you tire of loafing on the beach or soaking in the pool, there are many activities open to you: horseback riding along the beach, tennis, surfing, scuba diving, deep sea fishing or perhaps a Hawaiian outrigger canoe ride.

Golf is played on the resort's West Course reaching out 7,090/6,398/6,041 yards, with a par of 72. It is a beautiful layout with more than its share of traps and the most difficult putting greens we have seen. We understand, since our visit, they have added a few "pot hole bunkers". In fact the course has undergone a complete $1.5 million renovation which also included a new irrigation system as well as changes on several of the holes.

Hawaii

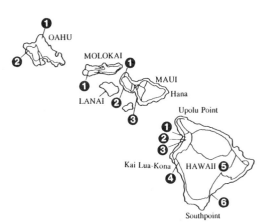

OAHU, HAWAII
1. Turtle Bay Hilton
2. Sheraton Makaha Resort
   & Country Club

HAWAII, HAWAII
1. Mauna Kea Beach Hotel
2. Mauna Lani Bay Hotel
3. Hyatt Regency Waikoloa
4. Keauhou Beach Hotel
   Kona Surf
5. Volcano House Inn &
   Country Club
6. Seamountain at Punalu'u

KAUAI, HAWAII
1. Hanalei Bay Resort
   Sheraton Mirage Princeville
   Princeville Travel Service
   Hawaiian Island Resorts Inc.
   The Cliffs
2. The Westin Kauai
3. Kiahuna Plantation
   Sheraton Kauai Hotel
   Stouffer Waiohai Beach Resort

MAUI, HAWAII
1. Kapalua Bay Hotel
2. The Lahaina-Kaanapali-Kapalua
   Areas
   Hyatt Regency Maui
   Kaanapali Beach Hotel
   Kapalua Bay Hotel
   Maui Marriott Resort
   Royal Lahaina Resort
   Sheraton-Maui Hotel
   The Westin Maui
   Kaanapali Alii
   Kaanapali Plantation
   Kaanapali Royal
   Maui Eldorado
   The Whaler at Kaanapali Beach
3. The Wailea Area
   Grand Hyatt Wailea
   The Maui Inter-Continental Wailea
   Maui Prince Hotel at Makena
   Stouffer Wailea Beach Resort

MOLOKAI, HAWAII
1. Kalua Koi Hotel & Golf Club

RATES (EP) Rooms: $95/$165. Suites: $245 and up. Green fees: $65 including cart.

TURTLE BAY HILTON
Kahuku, Oahu, HI 96731
(808) 293–8811
(800) 445–8667

Located on the northern part of Oahu, this hotel is on a point of land with water on three sides, offering a magnificent view from each room. Because of the way the resort is oriented you cannot see another structure. The secluded beaches serve up the usual tropical tranquility one comes to expect out here.

Tennis may be enjoyed on 10 courts (four lighted) with ball machines. They offer horseback riding and rent equipment for dune cycling along a five-mile stretch of beach.

The golf course, a George Fazio design, is beautiful, but has a few problems. Perhaps I should reword that. In playing it, *I had a few problems.* The course has small greens, lots of sand and what they refer to as an "ocean breeze." I refer to it as WIND. It measures a substantial 7,036/6,366/5,701 yards with par set at 72/74.

RATES (EP) Rooms: $135/$300. Suites: $405 up. Green fees: $65 including cart.

ARRIVAL Air: Honolulu (1 hour). Car: Kamehameha Highway north.

THE ISLAND OF HAWAII

The "Big Island" is one of sharp contrasts, with Hilo on the eastern "wet side" and the warm Kona and Kohala coast areas on the other. There are about 96 road miles between the two, separated by the volcanic mountains of Mauna Loa, at 13,680 feet, Mauna Kea, at 13,796 and Mt. Hualalai, at 8,271 feet.

Although the volcanoes are an obvious attraction, the island is also rich in history, for this was once long ago the home of the kings of Hawaii.

Keauhou-Kona Beach Resort Area

At the heart of the "Big Island's" famed Kona Coast, the Keauho-Kona area is an open door to Hawaii's history, heritage and hospitality.

There are a multitude of things to do and see: visiting century-old churches and tiny villages along the coast, tennis, golf, marlin fishing or just day-dreaming and relaxing.

Although the various resorts offer outstanding dining facilities--if you are visiting for any period of time or should you be staying in a condominium you may wish to choose a "change of pace" dining facility. As a possible alternative I suggest Jamison's By The Sea. Formerly named "Dorians", the name may have changed but the food is still magnificent It is at 77–6452 Alii Drive, Kona. Phone for reservations (808) 329–3195.

As guests of several fine resorts in this area, you may also enjoy golf on the Kona Country Club Course. This Bell designed layout plays 6,814/6,329/5,865 and pars at 72/74. Lava-bordered fairways, a profusion of sand traps and flowering shrubs, along with the wind, make this a tester.

A new nine is now in play. The Mauka Nine, in the hills above the pro shop area, is something else. Playing 3,348/3,082/2,718 yards with a par of 36, it offers some of the most spectacular views we have seen.

The pro shop is situated on a hill with the original 18-hole course falling away to the ocean.

KEAUHOU BEACH HOTEL
78–6740 Alii Drive, Kailua
Kona, HI 96740
(808) 322–3441
(800) 367–6025

When you walk the grounds of this hotel and stroll past ancient rock carvings or the summer home of Hawaiian kings, you feel as if you have stepped back a 1,000 years in history. Although it has undergone extensive remodeling, the "old flavor" has been retained and the hotel remains the same lovely place it has always been.

Just prior to publication we heard that the Keauhou Beach Hotel was to be closed for massive changes and would reopen sometime in late 1990 or possibly in early 1991.

They offer tennis on six courts and have, in addition to a pool, a small sand beach. (There are not many sand beaches on this side of the island).

Guests can play the Kona Country Club golf course described in the "Keauhou-Kona Beach Resort Area."

RATES (EP) Rooms: $77/$135. Suites: $195/$345. Green fees: $65 including cart.

KONA SURF RESORT
Keauhou Bay
Island of Hawaii, HI 96740
(808) 322–3411
(800) 367–8011

The Kona Surf Hotel is sited along the fabled Kona Coast. It is not what one would refer to as a small or intimate affair as it rises some six stories and sits like a castle at the entrance to Keauhou Bay. With the bay on one side, the ocean and golf course on the other, it has a beautiful setting.

Accommodations consist of 535 rooms including suites, with the majority of the rooms offering a view of the Pacific stretched out before them. Rooms are air conditioned and each has a private lanai. They are also equipped with cable TV, refrigerators and individual coffee makers. The Kona Surf is well set up to handle meeting and conference groups with a capacity of 800 schoolroom- and 1,000 banquet-style.

For dining you can choose from the elegant S.S. James Makee or the more casual setting of Pele's Court. For entertainment, there is dancing in the Puka Bar or soft Hawaiian music on the Nalu Terrace.

There is much to do here with a choice of fresh or saltwater pools, deep sea fishing, snorkeling, tennis on three lighted courts with a resident professional to assist and, of course, golf.

Guests can play golf on the Kona Country Club course which overlooks the hotel. For details and a description of the course refer to "Keauhou-Kona Beach Resort Area".

RATES (EP) Rooms: $99/$155. Suites: $375/$525. Green fees: $65 including cart.

The Kohala Coast Area

The Kohala Coast area, stretching north of Kona, is experiencing a rapid growth. With very little rainfall, a number of wonderful golf courses and magnificent hotels, this area has a great deal to offer.

No matter how outstanding a resort's cuisine, if you stay for more than a day or two, you will probably want to try other places to eat as well. In the small town of Kamuela, a few miles from The Mauna Kea Beach Resort, is the Edelweiss restaurant. I promise you won't be disappointed.

HYATT REGENCY WAIKOLOA
Kohala Coast
Island of Hawaii, HI 96743
(808) 885-1234
(800) 233-1234

Opened in early 1989, the Hyatt Regency Waikoloa is, by any standard, not a small resort. Located on 62 ocean-front acres of Waiulua Bay this $360 million hotel presents another alternative for a Hawaiian vacation.

Accommodations (1,244 rooms) are in three low-rise structures: the Ocean Tower, the Palace Tower and the Lagoon Tower. There are extensive tropical gardens, as well as flagstone walkways throughout the grounds and extending along the shoreline. There is also a magnificent lobby featuring a huge grand stairway leading to the lower lagoon. The Regency is also well set up to handle groups with its 19 meeting rooms and two auxiliary ballrooms offering a total of over 29,000 square feet. Remember, you are in Hawaii—you can add another 40,000 square feet of outdoor functional space.

Recreational facilities include: eight tennis courts with an exhibition court (seating 750), four racquetball courts, a 17,500-square-foot health spa complete with Jacuzzis, weight and aerobics rooms, saunas, steam baths, facilities for facials, herbal wraps, loofah scrubs and, of course, massage rooms. There are several swimming pools, with the main one, some 22,000 square feet, sporting waterfalls, slides and a grotto bar.

Nearby can be found horseback riding, deep sea fishing charters, sailing and windsurfing.

Scheduled for future play is the $16 million Morrish/Weiskopf-designed championship golf course. In the meantime, there are two additional courses nearby in the Waikoloa Village. For details on these layouts please refer to the Royal Waikoloan.

RATES (EP) Rooms: $215/$380. 1-bedroom suite: $550. Green fees: $65 including cart.

THE MAUNA KEA BEACH HOTEL
Kohala Coast, HI 96743
(808) 882–7222
(800) 228–3000

The trip across the desert-like terrain makes the first glimpse of magnificent Mauna Kea all the more breathtaking. Surrounded by lush green fairways, tropical gardens and beautiful crescent white sand beaches, this hotel is something very special. Mauna Kea is ranked high among the "Top 25 Golf Resorts" in the United States, Canada and Mexico. I have always believed that Hawaii was more a state of mind than a place, and the Mauna Kea, with its air of solitude, grace and feeling of complete relaxation, enhances this belief.

The open-air architecture allows gentle trade winds to enter the courtyards which are graced with a collection of over 1,600 pieces of priceless Asian and Pacific art. We have taken the time to walk the various levels of the hotel to see the collection of art works, and it was well worth the time.

That Mauna Kea presents an aura of comfort is probably one of the greatest understatements of the decade. I will not attempt to describe the decor of the rooms as this should remain a stunning surprise to be enjoyed on arrival.

Dining here is an experience you will long remember. You may wish to start with breakfast at either the Pavilion, the Garden or perhaps the "19th Hole", adjacent to the pro shop. For an elegant evening (jackets required, ties recommended) there is the Batik Dining Room. As a matter of fact jackets are required during the evening hours in all but the Cafe Terrace. *Gourmet Magazine* reports that "Mauna Kea has the reputation of setting the best table in the Islands".

Of course there is always the choice of candlelight dining on your own private lanai. Mauna Kea is perhaps best known for its bountiful luncheon buffets. The variety and quality of cuisine here is superb.

As a matter of fact if you don't get out of the dining areas, start exercising and stop eating, your doctor may well forbid you to ever come here again.

One of the favorite evening entertainments is watching the giant Pacific Manta Rays as they swirl, almost seeming to dance. There is a lighted viewing area overlooking the ocean. It is a spectacular sight.

The Mauna Kea is capable of handling meeting groups and can accommodate (within the Lloyd Sextan Gallery and their three break-out rooms) up to 200 theater- and 125 classroom-style.

While the resort does provide a beautiful pool, ocean swimming, with one of the finest beaches on the Island, is at its best. Scuba diving from the 58-foot catamaran *Mauna Kea Kai*, horseback riding, tennis on 13 plexipave courts, along with jogging on the two-mile cinder trail, are a few of the activities to be enjoyed. Something new has been added in the form of a complete fitness center along with all of the state-of-the-art equipment.

The tennis complex, under the direction of professional Jay Paulson, has been designated a "Five Star Tennis Resort"

The golf course, a Robert Trent Jones Sr. design acclaimed as one of the best in the nation, is perched on top of a lava flow. Much of the top soil had to be brought in. *What an undertaking it must have been.*

I hate to keep using superlatives but the pro shop, under the supervision of Director of Golf John "J D" Ebersberger, offers a selection of golf and casual attire which surpasses that found in many of the better department stores.

While a great deal has been said and written about the third hole, a par three playing 180 yards from the men's tees and reaching across the Pacific Ocean, our favorite is the spectacular view from the 11th green, looking back at the Mauna Kea Hotel.

The course stretches out 7,114 yards (masochist tees), 6,737 yards (championship), 6,365 (regular tees), with a par of 72. From the ladies' tees the par remains at 72, with the yardage at 5,277. With the traps, lava-bound fairways and occasional gusting wind, you may well find par 72 elusive. Several changes have been made to the Mauna Kea course. The greens which were among the slowest in the country are now being cut lower. While they are still not extremely fast it is a vast improvement. The rough has been cut a bit lower, speeding up play, and they have installed additional tee areas allowing variations on the yardage.

A short time ago, on a return trip to Mauna Kea, we had one of the most memorable visits ever. This lovely resort will always hold a special place in our hearts.

RATES (MAP) Mountain View: $355/$400. Beachfront: $465. Ocean view: $475/$520. Green fees: $55, carts $30. Golf packages are not available during the peak season. Rates are for the peak season mid-December to March 31.

MAUNA LANI BAY HOTEL
P.O. Box 4000
Kohala Coast
Island of Hawaii, HI
(808) 885–6622
HI (800) 992–7987
NAT (800) 367–2323

Mauna Lani, on the edge of the Kohala Coast, is a very modern 351-room structure, with its unique design providing virtually every room an ocean view. Accommodations are equipped with refrigerators and tropical ceiling fans (they are also air-conditioned). While the rooms are larger than normal their nine-foot ceilings make them appear even more spacious.

There are now approximately 116 condominiums available for rent. Ranging from one to two bedrooms (1½ to 2½ baths) they rank among the very best we have seen. Beautifully appointed, they are equipped with the very latest in appliances including microwave ovens and a washer/dryer. Daily maid service is also provided. You have a choice of either an ocean or golf course view. To make reservations call toll free (800) 642–6284 or local (808) 885–5022.

Mauna Lani is well prepared to handle conference groups. With their 4,800-square-foot main ballroom and three, 600-square-foot break-out rooms they can accommodate over 350 classroom-style. You are in Hawaii—the outdoor area adds another dimension.

Dining is offered in the Bay Terrace, the award winning Third Floor Restaurant (located, of course, on the first floor), the Club Restaurant located at the golf course, and the poolside Ocean Grill. There are also several lounges throughout the resort. Jackets are required at both the Third Floor and the Bay Terrace locations. While all of the restaurants are outstanding we particularly enjoyed the relaxed atmosphere and food served up by the Club Restaurant. Make reservations as this one is difficult to get into, but definitely worth the effort.

The Tennis Garden features 10 variable speed courts. There is also a completely supervised health, sports, aerobic and physical fitness center. Other activities available to guests include: deep sea fishing trips, glass-bottom boat cruises, helicopter sightseeing trips, horseback riding, sailing, bicycling, jogging, scuba diving, snorkeling, windsurfing and, of course, swimming. And my favorite sport—sitting in the sun doing absolutely nothing.

There are also many tours available to see this historically rich countryside.

Country Club Golfer magazine referred to Mauna Lani Bay's 18-hole course as "an outstanding golfing experience." We would have to agree with that evaluation. Weighing in at 6,813/6,259/5,275 yards, it pars at 72. It is not only fun to play but is truly a superb layout, offering views rarely found. Virtually sculpted from lava with some "over the ocean" holes you will not soon forget, this course will test not only your skill but your nerve as well. It may also test your vocabulary should you tangle with the many lava outcroppings sprinkled around.

The resort has provided an excellent pro shop and a professional staff headed up by the Director of Golf, Jerry Johnston.

RATES (EP) Rates vary by type of view: $250/$325/$360. Suites: $600. MAP plan is also available. Condo rates: 1-bedroom $215; 2-bedroom $295. Green fees: $65 including cart.

Golf packages are not available during peak season mid-December through mid-April. There are, however, several different golf packages at other times of the year including one for those who choose to stay in the condominiums.

ROYAL WAIKOLOAN HOTEL
Kohala Coast
P.O. Box 5000
Waikoloa, HI 96743
(808) 885–6789
(800) 537–9800

Sited on a half-mile crescent of Anaehoomalu Bay overlooking a serene lagoon, the Royal Waikoloan (formerly a Sheraton) is an outstanding destination resort. The subdued elegance, priceless artifacts, warm old-style Hawaiian atmosphere and welcome extended to guests is most difficult to put into words. The location provides a very large and beautiful white beach, something hard to find on the "Big Island," permitting all manner of water activity.

Each of the 523 rooms and 20 lagoon cabanas has its own private lanai overlooking the bay or the ocean.

There are three restaurants: the open air coffee shop, the intimate Tiare Room with its rich Koa Wood and crystal, specializing in continental cuisine, and the Royal Terrace, overlooking the ocean and offering both Hawaiian and international entertainment. To even things out there are three bars.

By day your activities can be varied and numerous: tennis on six courts with professional guidance available, freshwater swimming pools, horseback riding at nearby Waikoloa stables, ocean action and golf.

The Robert Trent Jones Jr. designed Waikoloa Beach layout opened in 1981. Parring at 70, reaching out 6,404/5,806/5,042 yards, it spreads over 150 acres. Lush with palm trees, bougainvillea, oleander and plumeria, it visually denies the solid lava flow over which it was built.

The older, 18-hole Waikoloa Village championship layout was completed in 1973. Parring at 72 and located a few miles away, it reaches out 6,687/6,142/5,558 yards. Built over a lava flow, it presents a variety of challenges: water holes, sharp doglegs, traps where you do not expect them, trees and shrubs, along with a wind that can whip you without warning. All of the foregoing combine to make this a very interesting golf course to beat your way around.

The clubhouse offers food service, a bar and locker room facilities.

RATES (EP) Rooms: $155/$245. Cabana: $300. Green fees: $65 including cart.

WAIKOLOA VILLAS
Box 3066 Waikoloa Village Station
Kamuela, Hawaii 96743
(808) 883–9588
(800) 367–7042

The Waikoloa Village is 15 miles north of the Kona Airport on Highway 19 and then six miles east of the Highway.

The Villas (104 units) are well furnished condominiums ranging from one to three bedrooms featuring fully equipped kitchens, washer/dryer in each unit and weekly linen service. The Villas are adjacent to the golf course.

Amenities include: two swimming pools, whirlpools, cabanas and a unique gazebo area, tennis courts and horseback riding. The ocean beaches are located a few miles away.

The Club at Waikoloa Village golf course, a Robert Trent Jones Jr. layout, plays 6,687/6,142/5,558 yards with a par of 72. The course is supported by an excellent pro shop and a professional staff under the direction of Head Professional, Randall Carney.

RATES (EP) 1-bedroom condo: $100. 2-bedroom condo: $120. Green fees: $40, carts $25. They offer a monthly green fee schedule. Golf packages are available.

The Ka'u Coast Area

While still on the Big Island we now have shifted to the east side—the home of the startling "black sand beaches". It is the location of one of the most active volcanoes in the world, Kilauea Crater and the home of "Madame Pele", the Hawaiian goddess of volcanoes. It is also the location of two resorts, SeaMountain at Panulu'u and the Volcano House Inn.

SEAMOUNTAIN AT PUNALU'U
P.O. BOX 70
Pahala, HI 96777
(808) 928–8301
(800) 367–8047 (Ext. 145)

In my opinion this resort captures the true essence of the word "Hawaii" and all it represents. On the southeastern side of the Big Island a few miles north of the southern tip, the setting is most unusual—with lush green sugarcane fields behind it, the lovely Pacific Ocean fronting the entire property, and black lava rock and palm-fringed lagoons all about. This is not a hustle, bustle place, but rather one for reflective moments, serene beauty and barefoot quiet. It is more a colony than a resort. If you seek a lot of night life this is not the place.

Accommodations consist of studios and one- to two-bedroom cottage apartments fully equipped for housekeeping with washer / dryers. A store is nearby, so no 20-mile drive for food is required.

Aside from swimming in the lagoons and at the black sand beaches there is a swimming pool, tennis courts nearby and Panalu'u Black Sands Restaurant, open seven days a week, offering continental fare. Something relatively new is the Broiler Restaurant located at the pro shop.

The golf course, parring at 72, reaches out 6,492/6,106/5,663 yards. A Jack Snyder design, with water hazards, traps, pine trees, lava outcroppings, black sand beaches and wind, this can become a very tough and challenging layout. The day we played we were blessed with very little wind and still found it all we could handle. This course, by the way, is the southernmost golf layout in the United States.

RATES (EP) Studio: $73/$83. 1 bedroom: $94/$104. 2 bedrooms: $121/$133. Green fees: $40 including cart. Rates are for mid-December through April. Minimum stay is 2 nights.

THE VOLCANO HOUSE INN & COUNTRY CLUB
Kilauea Crater
Big Island of Hawaii, HI 96718
(808) 967–7321

The Volcano House Inn is one of the few tropical hotels in the world where you will enjoy sitting in front of the lounge's roaring fire. Its old-time Hawaiian charm has delighted visitors for over a century. The setting is extraordinary, with misty ohia and giant fern forests in the midst of volcanic landscapes, active craters, lava tube caverns and steam vents.

The Volcano House was originally a country home, built of lava and perched on the edge of Kilauea Crater. Keep in mind this is an old inn. While the rooms are comfortable, elaborate they are not. The walls of the lounge are lined with the works of world famous artists, drawn here to have their go at painting the enchanting view of the volcano or their vision of Pele, the Hawaiian goddess of volcanoes.

The emerald-green fairways of the Volcano Golf Course are bordered by dark forests of pine and scarlet-blossomed ohia trees, while in the background rise the towering slopes of 13,680-foot Mauna Loa.

The course plays 6,119 yards and pars at 72. At 4,000 feet, watch that you do not overshoot the 15th green or your ball will surely come to rest in the crater.

RATES (EP) Rooms: $69/$79. Green fees: $33, carts $23.

ARRIVAL Air: Hilo (29 miles). You are on the opposite side of the island from Kona.

THE ISLAND OF KAUAI

Justifiably referred to as the Garden Island, Kauai presents a mixture of scenery which must be seen to be believed. Ferns and grottoes to the north, deserts to the west, flowers everywhere and, in the middle, towering mountains with a spectacular "Grand Canyon" some 4,000 feet deep—certainly one of the least accessible places in the world.

Kauai, the northern-most island in the Hawaiian chain, is also the oldest. It is generally accepted that this island was populated between 200 and 300 A.D., some 500 years prior to any of the other Hawaiian Islands. Kauai is rich in history and legends—something for you to dig into on your visit should you be interested.

On the east side of the island is the Westin Kauai; at the northern end is Princeville, the location of Hanalei Bay Resort and The Sheraton Mirage Princeville. On the south side, in the Poipu Beach area, is the Kiahuna Plantation, the Sheraton Kauai Hotel and the Stouffer Waiohai Beach Resort.

The Princeville Mirage Resort Area

Within the 11,000-acre resort community of Princeville may be found 54 holes of golf, including a huge 20,000-square-foot clubhouse, a shopping center, approximately 250 homes, over 20 restaurants, along with a few Polynesian shows located both on the property and nearby. While the restaurants in the area are, for the most part, excellent there is one which we, unfortunately, DO NOT recommend, called the Beachreach.

Various accommodations are available at the Sheraton Mirage Hotel, the Hanalei Bay Resort, as well as many condominiums and rental homes.

Also available within this resort property are: 22 outdoor tennis courts and two fully equipped pro shops along with professionals to assist, a health club, Papillon Helicopter tours, boat tours, scuba diving, snorkeling, kayaking and horseback riding.

Princeville Makai's 54 holes of golf, have been rated in the nation's top 100. They are also the home of the LPGA Kemper Open. The Ocean/Woods combination stretches out 6,778/6,156/5,493 yards; the Woods/Lake combination plays 6,740/6,116/5,339 yards; while the Lake/Ocean nines weigh in at a healthy 6,764/6,076/5,378. All three combinations par at 72. Each of the nines lives up to its name.

Now a new layout has been added—the "Prince Course," a Robert Trent Jones design. It is destined to become one of the finest in the islands (it may well be judged one of the most difficult as well). Perhaps a few of the names used for the different holes will give you a clue as to what you will experience—"Burma Road", "Hazard", "Waterfall" and "Dunkirk". "Dunkirk" is not all that difficult if you can clear the two ravines, stay right of the O.B. stakes, avoid the six deep bunkers and land on the postage stamp size green. If you can do it, this hole is a "piece of cake". I will not attempt to describe the par-six, 604-yard "Burma Road" or the "Eagles Nest" a par-four featuring a 300-foot drop from tee to fairway.

The Princeville Airport, two miles from the Mirage Princeville complex, is served by Aloha Island Airways. Both Hertz and Avis cars may be rented at the airport.

HANALEI BAY RESORT
P.O. Box 220 Hanalei
Kauai, HI 96714
(808) 826–6522
(800) 367–7040

All accommodations consist of condominiums or cottages, each with from one to four bedrooms, fully equipped kitchens including washer/dryer, cable TV and daily maid service.

Dining and cocktails are available in several restaurants: the Princeville Lanai, the Snack Bar (Makai Golf Course clubhouse), Bali Hai (Hanalei Resort). Dancing and entertainment are offered at the Princeville Lanai and the Bali Hai.

Activities available include: tennis on 11 courts, sailing a catamaran beyond the reefs, looking for porpoise, flying fish, or trolling for game fish, horseback riding along the beaches or over the Princeville ranchland.

A word of warning: winter brings dangerous swimming conditions to the north shores of the island. So think before you venture too far out.

Golf can be played on the Princeville complex surrounding this resort. For a more detailed description of the golf facilities refer to "The Princeville Mirage Resort Area".

RATES (EP) Condominiums: 1 bedroom $135; 2 bedrooms $205. Green fees: $65 including cart.

SHERATON MIRAGE PRINCEVILLE
Princeville, Kauai, HI 96714
(808) 826–9644
(800) 826–4400

An interesting bit of trivia: the film "South Pacific" was shot on these magnificent white beaches. I only mention it so you can better comprehend the beauty of the area. The Sheraton Princeville opened here in late 1985.

The resort has 258 rooms, including suites, with many offering a view of beautiful Hanalei Bay. Their meeting facilities are excellent. The 6,786-square-foot Waialeale Ballroom, which can also be divided into four separate meeting rooms, can handle as many as 700 theater- and 450-banquet style.

A real plus, at least to me, is the fact that the Sheraton Mirage has not lost sight of "Hawaii". While the decor is muted and quiet, it truly represents the soft Hawaiian atmosphere and creates the feeling which makes this area so alluring. Last, but by no means least, is the beautiful mood-setting Hawaiian music. They do not overwhelm you with it but you can hear, from time to time, the warm soft strains of classical Hawaiian music in the background.

There are three restaurants: the Cafe Hanalei with its open-air setting overlooking the beautiful Hanalei Bay; the Hale Kapa (Hawaiian for the House of Quilts) with continental cuisine in a most unusual and pleasing setting; and the Nobles, the hotel's signature restaurant, offering some of the finest dining you may ever experience.

A few of the activities, in addition to golf, include: swimming in both pool and the ocean (there is an excellent beach), deep sea fishing, horseback riding along the beach and tennis. Something extra: Papillon Helicopters offers a variety of sightseeing flights presenting views of the rugged canyon area. While expensive, it is a spectacular flight and well worth the time and money.

Guests of the Sheraton have playing privileges as well as a reduced rate on the 54 holes of the Princeville courses. For details on these golf layouts refer to "The Princeville Mirage Resort Area".

RATES (EP) Rooms: $175/$265. Suites: $500. Green fees: $65 including cart. Golf packages are available.

ARRIVAL Air: Lihue Airport. Commuter flights are also available to and from the Princeville Airport.

Condominium Lodgings—Princeville Area

For condominium-type lodgings and reservations in the Mirage Princeville Resort complex, as well as the Hanalei Bay Resort (which is listed in this book), call the following numbers:

PRINCEVILLE TRAVEL SERVICE
P.O. Box 990 Hanalei Kauai, HI 96714
(808) 826–9661
(800) 445–6253
(800) 367–8047 ext 211

HAWAIIAN ISLANDS RESORTS INC.
P.O. Box 212 Honolulu, HI 96810
(808) 531–7595
(800) 367–7042

THE CLIFFS
P.O. Box 1005 Hanalei, HI 96714
(808) 826–6219

The East Side of Kauai

This part of Kauai, the location of the Westin Kauai, is less than two miles from the major airport of Kauai and the town of Lihue.

THE WESTIN KAUAI
Kalapaki Beach
Kauai, HI 96754
(808) 245–5050
(800) 228–3000

In 1986, the Kauai Surf Hotel was acquired by Westin Hotels. Although already a lovely resort, Westin invested $350 million to produce a world class-affair. It opened in late 1987.

Guests are transported to the hotel via a posh stretch Cadillac limousine. This drive is taken along the resorts "private road" from the airport. Enroute you will see a portion of the 200-plus acres of botanical gardens and lawns. Upon entering the resort you take an escalator to the lower level. There you are greeted by the sight of a huge two-acre reflecting pool complete with various species of swan and ducks. Finally (if you are lucky) you may arrive at the main lobby.

On route to your accommodations you will see the main swimming area. You may have noticed I said "area" rather than pool. There is no way you could call these 26,000 square feet of water anything but an area. It is huge.

Accommodations consist of the Beach Tower, fronting Kalapaki Beach and Surf Tower, a 10-story structure. Additional accommodations are available in the four-story Bay Tower, the 10-story Ocean Tower (286 rooms) and so on, for a total of 847 guest rooms.

For meetings and conferences the resort has set aside 41,000 square feet of space including a 17,200-square-foot ballroom.

There are many restaurants and lounges (some 15 or more) scattered throughout the complex—ranging from informal (swim wear acceptable) to casual, to one where jackets are required (in Hawaii that is formal). By all means attempt to dine at the Inn on the Cliffs Restaurant. It is best described as SUPERB. Not only is the food outstanding but getting there is an adventure. You may elect to arrive via a magnificent motor launch and return in a carriage drawn by massive Clydesdales. A great way to wind up a Hawaiian evening. There is also nightly entertainment, and so much more available—*YES IT IS LARGE*. But then read on.

Just a sample of the other amenities and activities include: eight tennis courts, supported by a separate tennis shop and a professional staff to assist. They also sport a central stadium court seating 1,000. The tennis/golf shop area is also the location of two additional, and outstanding, dining facilities. The Terrace, features breakfast and lunch (what they do to a tuna sandwich I will leave for you to discover and enjoy). The other restaurant is The Masters a world-class dining room, open for dinner six nights a week.

Within the Lagoons Golf & Racquet Club there is a complete European health spa, including Jacuzzi massage, body buffs, herbal wraps, facials, saunas, and steam baths. There is also a regulation-size swimming pool.

We are not done yet. There are 35 carriages to transport guests along an eight-mile carriage road with over 100 horses (Clydesdales, Belgians and Percherons). 1,400 feet of beach runs along Kalapaki inlet. There is also an inland waterway system with 90 outrigger canoes and 40 "taxi boats." There are a total of 70 shops with some located in the hotel and others in the two shopping villages on the lagoon. They really do seem to have thought of everything—there is a 1,000-square-foot chapel by the sea. I understand it is kept very busy performing marriages.

Although both golf courses are Jack Nicklaus designed layouts, the Kauai Lagoons spreading over 190 acres is principally intended for the recreational golfer. It shows a yardage of 6,942/6,545/6,108/5,607 with a par of 72. The 262-acre Kiele Lagoons layout is a tournament class affair, complete with substantial gallery areas. This course weighs in at 7,070/6,637/6,164/5,417 yards and also pars at 72.

The golf shop under the supervision of Mark Spandoni and the Director of Golf, Kim Worrel, is one of the most beautiful we have visited.

RATES (EP) Rooms $195/$400. Suites: $400/$1500. Green fees: Kauai Lagoons Course, $75 including cart; the Kiele Championship Course, $105 including cart.

The Southeast "Poipu Beach" Area

Stay with us as. We are still on Kauai. This area of the island is conceded to be the "dry" side. There are three outstanding resorts, the Kiahuna Plantation, the Sheraton Kauai Hotel and the Stouffer Waiohai Beach Resort. The Sheraton and the Stouffer offer hotel rooms, while lodgings at the Kiahuna Plantation consist of fully equipped condominiums.

A short distance away from each of these resorts is the Kiahuna Golf Club. A Robert Trent Jones Jr. design, it is a beautiful layout. Parring at 70, it stretches out 6,380/5,669/4,901 yards. While only a modest amount of water comes into play (on six holes) it seems to be just where it should not be. The course is supported by a well stocked pro shop and is under the direction of PGA Golf Professional Charlie Ortega. Carts are mandatory and must keep on the cart paths at all times.

Also a part of the clubhouse is the outstanding Waiohai Terrace Restaurant, home of Kauai's most famous Sunday Champagne Brunch.

KIAHUNA PLANTATION
RR #1 Box 73
Koloa, Kauai, HI 96756
(808) 742–6411
CANADA (800) 268–1734
U.S. (800) 367–7052

At one time this 35-acre site was part of the oldest sugar cane plantations in Hawaii. This resort offers an almost perfect blend of the "old legendary Hawaii" (quiet and peaceful) and an almost endless list of activities to choose from.

Accommodations consist of 253 well equipped condominiums. Ranging from one- to two-bedroom units, they feature a separate living and dining area, lanais and fully equipped kitchens. They also are equipped with ceiling fans, rattan furniture and cable T.V. Although there are no washer/dryers in the units, coin operated facilities are available. The resort provides daily maid service, 24-hour front desk telephone, a baby sitting service, plus rental car arrangements.

Even though you have the equipment to prepare your own meals you might well find the dining facilities here irresistible. They range from casual lagoon-side barbecue pits and picnic tables to the Courtside Bar & Grill and the Clubhouse Restaurant. And finally to one of the island's award-winning dining facilities, The Plantation Gardens. The grounds are filled with fruit trees, tropical flower gardens and lily ponds—truly a beautiful setting.

Activities at your disposal include: swimming from one of the best beaches in the islands or pool swimming, snorkeling, surfing, sailing, tennis on 10 courts with a professional to assist, deep sea fishing, helicopter tours and trips to the Waimea Canyon (some 4,000 feet deep), historic Hanalei and, of course, golf.

Before we get into golf, I think you might be interested in the activities planned for the younger set. You won't have to be concerned with their keeping busy. They will be pretty tied up with arts & crafts, shell collecting, lagoon fishing, lei-making, basket weaving and hula lessons to say nothing of swimming.

The Kiahuna Golf Club, less than ½ mile away, is a beautiful layout. For complete details refer to "The Southeast Poipu Beach Area".

RATES (EP) 1-bedroom condo (1–4 people): $150/$170/$210/$280. Rates are for high season mid-Dec to mid-April. Lower at other times. Green fees: $55 including cart. Golf packages are available.

ARRIVAL Air: Liuhie Airport (15 miles). Car: from the airport take Highway 50 west (signs will say to Poipu Beach). Turn off onto Highway 520 and follow signs to Piopu Beach.

SHERATON KAUAI HOTEL
RR #1 Box 303
Koloa Kauai, HI 96756
(808) 742–1661
(800) 325–3535

The Sheraton Kauai, with its 456 guest rooms and suites, fronts along one of the better beach areas to be found in Hawaii. The hotel itself consists of three low-rise buildings, the garden wing, the lawn and the ocean vista units. All rooms are air-conditioned and have a private lanai.

Recently refurbished, the Drum Lounge is a favorite spot for viewing the spectacular Hawaiian sunsets. For dining the hotel offers the Outrigger Room or the Lanai Terrace Restaurant. In addition there is the Breakers specializing in steak and seafood, the Naniwa featuring Japanese selections and a Polynesian revue, offered every Wednesday and Sunday evening. For lighter fare there is the Poolside Cafe and the Makihana Snackshop & Bar.

The hotel has set aside 6,717 square feet for meeting groups. This space is supplemented by an additional 17,230 square feet of outdoor area. Depending on the weather they can handle up to 1,200.

There are, of course, many activities to be enjoyed: three tennis courts, swimming at either the ocean front or garden swimming pools, whirlpool spa, snorkeling, sailing or perhaps just soaking up the sun with an occasional dip in the calm blue waters of the ocean.

For details on the golf course, refer to "The Southeast Poipu Beach Area".

RATES (EP) Rooms: $140/$250. Suites: $275 and up. Green fees: $55 including cart.

ARRIVAL Air: Liuhie Airport (15 miles). Car: from Liuhie take Highway 50 west (signs will say to Poipu Beach). Turn off onto Highway 520 and follow signs to Poipu Beach.

STOUFFER WAIOHAI BEACH RESORT
2249 Poipu Road, Box 174
Koloa, Kauai, HI 96756
(808) 742-9511
(800) 426-4122

The Waiohai Resort is on the southern tip of Kauai's Poipu Beach area. Accommodations consist of 430 guest rooms, including 21 suites all featuring wet bars, refrigerators and private lanais. The suites have a separate living room. Their meeting facilities can accommodate up to 900 banquet-style, less than that classroom-style.

For dining you can select from the Waiohai Terrace (breakfast and dinner), or the Tamarind Restaurant featuring contemporary cuisine. There is also the Beach Bar & Grill located poolside for lighter fare. Do not fear—they also have several lounges.

The magnificent sand beaches in this area make possible all manner of water sports: surfboards, catamarans, windsurfing, snorkeling and on and on. There are, in addition, three fresh-water swimming pools, six tennis courts, a fitness center and massage facilities.

For details on the golf course refer to "The Southeast Poipu Beach Area".

RATES (EP) Rooms: $140/250/$325. Suites: $375/$850. Green fees: $55 including cart.

THE ISLAND OF MAUI

Many years ago, when the only method of reaching the Hawaiian Islands was by ship, Oahu was the ultimate destination. Then along came aircraft and some of the heartier souls ventured to the outer islands. Not too many. After growling along 2,600 miles from the West Coast on a piston driven aircraft, with the knowledge that you would grind your way back, you usually settled for the beauty and relaxation provided by Waikiki. But two things happened at this point: first, the advent of the jet, turning the islands into a reachable destination for most of the U.S.; second, with the sudden flood of new *Haoles* the islanders felt they had been overrun. Seeking to rediscover the "Old Hawaii," they started a retreat to the outlying areas.

The rest is history. The development of Maui has been rapid and, although not nearly as congested as Oahu, it is gaining. It is a place of beautiful beaches, magnificent hotels, condominiums, and golf courses by the ton. It is also the location of Lahaina, the first capital of the islands, and of Mt. Haleakala, a dormant volcano rising to almost 10,000 feet.

The Wailea Area of Maui

Wailea is on the southwest coast of the island, only a 35 minute drive (via a new limited access highway) from Kahului Airport. Dominating the area from the southeast is Haleakala (House of the Sun), the world's largest dormant volcanic crater. Its slopes embrace 500 square miles of tropical rain forest, arid deserts, lush cattle ranches and some of the most spectacular scenery to be found anywhere on this planet.

Golf, which may be played by guests of the various hotels or condominiums of Wailea, is available on two 18-hole layouts. Each of these two courses will provide not only a real test of your skill but views which make it difficult to keep your mind on the game.

The Wailea Blue Course, reaching out 6,743/6,152/5,686 yards, pars at 72. The Orange Course also with a par of 72 measures a healthy 6,810/6,304/5,644 yards. While both are beautiful layouts, the Orange must be considered the more difficult of the two.

Now to get back to Wailea: in addition to the golf courses, there is a picturesque hillside tennis complex offering 14 courts (11 hard and three grass), a pro shop and an exhibition stadium seating 1,200.

Hotel accommodations are available at the Maui Inter-Continental Wailea and The Stouffer Wailea. There are also a great many individually owned condominiums for rent (approximately 150), ranging from one to three bedrooms and featuring private lanais, living room and kitchen.

These extremely well equipped units (micro-wave, disposal, dish-washer, washer/dryer ice maker), are located across from the Blue Course and front directly on the ocean. Within the complex there are two swimming pools as well as one of the better beaches on the island at your disposal.

A couple of nice extras: there is a 24-hour security gate entrance, a small library at the manager's office, a mail service on premises and a barbecue facility adjacent to each of the swimming pools. Maid service is provided once each week. However, arrangements can be made (at additional cost) for daily service. Most important of all, personnel go out of their way to be helpful and are ex-tremely friendly.

Should you be interested, write Wailea Elua Village Rentals, 3600 Alanui Drive, Kihei, Maui, HI 96753 or call (808) 879–4726 or toll free (800) 231–0611.

Although the food and service at the resorts is excellent, should you desire a change of pace we suggest The Wailea Steakhouse Restaurant, adjacent to the Blue Course at Wailea on 100 Wailea Ike Drive. You will find it outstanding. For reservations call (808) 879–2875.

GRAND HYATT WAILEA
Wailea Beach
Kihei, Maui, HI 96753
(808) 923–1234
(800) 233–1234

Opening early in 1990 the Grand Hyatt seems determined to live up to its name "Grand". A massive eight-story resort (787 rooms including 53 suites), it is perched along the south Maui shore. The target was to create a spectacular destination resort and spectac-ular it is.

A 2,000-foot-long river pool, 15,000 square feet of pool and deck area, a huge lobby bar, Japanese gardens throughout the property, hot tubs, swim-in caves, a bubbling spring and a swim-up bar are some of the "spectacular" features of the Hyatt Wailea.

The meeting and conference facilities are also in the grand style. The main ballroom is some 28,000 square feet and, including 17 meeting rooms, the total area devoted to groups is 55,000 square feet.

There are several dining areas including the main dining room, a coffee shop, a lobby bar and, of course, the various restaurants located in the general area.

Guests of the Hyatt can play golf on the Wailea golf courses as well as the 14 tennis courts. For details please refer to "The Wailea Area of Maui."

RATES (EP) Rooms: $185/$350. Suites: $600 and up. Green fees: $60 including cart.

THE MAUI INTER-CONTINENTAL WAILEA

P.O. Box 779 Wailea
Maui, HI 96753
(808) 879–1922
From Oahu 537–5589
(800) 367–2960

Prior to actual construction, two years of research were involved to site the structure. This extraordinary move was made in order to take maximum advantage of the incredible location. As a result, 80% of the rooms offer an ocean view.

Six restaurants provide a wide selection of cuisine, running the gamut from the coffee shop, the Wet Spot (the pool area), the Lanai Terrace offering its magnificent view of the Pacific Ocean, the Kiawe Broiler to the Holiday-award-winning La Perouse Restaurant (open for dinner only), featuring outstanding seafood. Then perhaps a visit to the Inu Inu Piano Bar & Lounge to watch the sun go down as it can only be seen in Hawaii—maybe for a slight libation and dancing. Inu Inu means "Drink Drink". I LOVE THESE HAWAIIANS—THEY DON'T FOOL AROUND.

The Inter-Continental is exceptionally well equipped to handle meeting groups with its 13 break-out rooms in addition to the ballroom and can accommodate 300 classroom- and 500 banquet-style.

There are, in addition to golf, many other activities: snorkeling, sailing, surfing, catamaran sailing, deep sea fishing, swimming (two swimming pools), as well as ocean swimming. They offer tennis on 11 courts (three lighted) backed up by a professional staff to assist. You may also elect to put the body down on the beach and just unwind. During the winter months whale watching can be added to the list of activities.

The resort is situated almost on top of two of the better courses on this island. For details refer to "The Wailea Area of Maui". Golf can also be enjoyed at the Makena course three miles south of the hotel. For details on this course refer to the "Maui Prince Hotel at Makena".

RATES (EP) Rooms: $185/$210/$295. Suites: $350 and up. Golf packages are not available during peak season. Green fees: $55 including cart.

MAUI PRINCE HOTEL at MAKENA
5400 Makena Alanui
Kihei, Maui, HI 96753
(808) 874–1111
From Oahu 531–0305
(800) 321–6284

The Maui Prince Hotel opened in August of 1986. Just three miles south of Wailea, this lovely 300-room six-story resort, situated on 1,800 acres, can offer almost every Hawaiian amenity and recreation facility you could wish for.

All rooms and suites are air-conditioned and are equipped with remote controlled TV and refrigerators. The Prince resort is well qualified to handle modest size meeting groups. With their four meeting rooms they can handle 50 classroom- and 300 banquet-style. A very thoughtful extra—upon check-in you will find a fruit basket as well as a small flower arrangement in your room.

There are three dining areas: the Prince Court featuring American Cuisine; the Cafe Kiowai, with a magnificent garden setting; and the Hakone, an authentic Japanese restaurant. All are backed up by 24-hour room service. There is, of course, the Molokini Lounge with a variety of nightly entertainment.

For just a moment I would like to return to the indoor/outdoor Cafe Kiowai and attempt to describe the beautiful 30,000-square-foot courtyard adjacent to it. An Eden of cascading waterfalls, rock gardens, sparkling fish ponds, a meandering stream, with typical Japanese foot bridges—all softly packaged in hushed harmony with an understated oriental theme—it truly is a stunning addition.

A sample of available activities includes: the tennis complex (six courts, two lighted) with a professional staff on deck to assist, swimming (two pools and the beautiful beach), sailing or perhaps just loafing and sunning. During the winter months a favorite pastime is watching the humpback whales as they cavort along the coast of Maui.

A Robert Trent Jones, Jr. design, the Makena Resort golf course plays right along the Pacific Ocean. Parring at 72, it measures 6,739/6,210/5,441 yards. While water is brought into play on only three holes, there are 64 traps to avoid. Be sure to bring a camera as the golf course and ocean views, particularly on the back nine, are such that you will be angry with yourself if you can't get a few pictures.

Currently underway, and due to come into play by 1991, is a second 18-hole championship course.

The golf club provides the amenities of a very large (4,000-square-foot) clubhouse and pro shop. Hidden from view, behind the pro shop, is an excellent restaurant and lounge.

RATES (EP) Rooms: $180/$290. Suites: $350/$700. Green fees: $60 including cart. There are package plans available at various times of the year.

ARRIVAL Air: Maui's Kahului Airport. Car: from Kahului Airport drive south to Wailea. Continue on for approximately 3 more miles.

STOUFFER WAILEA BEACH RESORT
Wailea, Maui, HI 96753
(808) 879–4900
(800) 992–4532

A multi-story structure (347 rooms including suites), the Stouffer Wailea is 35 minutes from the Kahului airport. The hotel is on a knoll with the lawns sloping down to the beach area. With the landscaped gardens and many waterfalls, it is a serene setting.

In addition to accommodations in the main buildings there are lodgings in the Makapu Beach Club, offering the ultimate in seclusion and luxury. All rooms are equipped with T.V. (HBO as well) and individual air conditioning controls. A very nice extra that we wish all hotels offered—there are laundry facilities in each wing.

Stouffer Wailea is well set up to handle meeting groups and has a capacity for 280 indoor and as many as 700 outdoor banquet-style.

The dining facilities are excellent with the Raffles Restaurant (Travel/Holiday award), the Palm Court for less formal dining or the Maui Onion for cocktails and/or a light repast by the pool. They claim their "Raffles" outdoes its namesake in Singapore. Unfortunately we did not get the opportunity to test this claim. But the Stouffer Resort has been awarded the AAA Five Diamond Award for seven consecutive years.

In addition to its many other amenities the resort has two large swimming pools. All of the usual beach activities are available including: windsurfing, scuba and snorkel charters, sunset sails, horseback riding (located nearby), tennis at the Wailea complex as well as golf. For details on golf and tennis please refer to "The Wailea Area of Maui".

RATES (EP) Rooms: $185/$350. Green fees: $60 including cart. Golf package: 3 nights/3 days EP [includes ocean view room, rental car, 2 rounds golf and cart), $849 per couple. Rates are for December-April.

The Lahaina-Kaanapali-Kapalua Areas

This large stretch of beach on the northwest side of Maui sports many world-class hotels, several luxury condominium complexes, over 150 shops, 60 restaurants and an outdoor whaling museum. In addition there are a dozen dinner and lounge shows, 28 tennis courts, 36 holes of golf (if you include Kapalua there are 72 holes) and all the beach activities you come to expect in the islands: snorkeling, surfing, outriggers, deep sea fishing, and so on. Each of the hotels is well equipped to handle meeting groups.

The Royal Kaanapali courses are available for play by guests of the various hotels and condominiums. The two courses are: the South, playing 6,758/6,250/5,658 yards; and the North, reaching out 7,179/6,305/5,577 yards from the white tees. The South pars at 72 while the North has a par of 72/73.

The older of the two, the North, a Robert Trent Jones design and developed in 1961, starts at the ocean and winds its way up the lower reaches of the mountain. It presents some beautiful views enroute. The South, originally an executive layout and redesigned by A. J. Snyder, although flat, brings into play palms, monkey pod trees, banyans and brilliant bougainvillea. Both courses operate out of the same excellent pro shop. There are a few places on the back nine of the South course where, if you were to hook just right, you could very easily find yourself in the lobby of one of the hotels. Green fees: $70 including cart.

For information on the Kapalua courses refer to the Kapalua Bay Hotel & Villas.

HYATT REGENCY MAUI
200 Nohea Kai Drive,
Lahaina, Maui, HI 96761
(800) 233–1234

The Regency is on 18-plus acres of tropical forest complete with lagoons, waterfalls and grottoes. The 815 rooms offer outstanding views of either the ocean, mountains or the Royal Kaanapali golf course. Meeting and convention groups are accommodated in the Lahaina Wing of the hotel providing 25,000 square feet of banquet and meeting space.

For dining, they offer the elegant Swan Court, the Spats II restaurant, specializing in Italian cuisine, the Lahaina Provision Company for steak lovers and, for dinner shows, the Sunset Terrace.

Whatever your favorite libation may be you will find it available at any of the three lounges, the Atrium Lobby, the secluded Grotto Bar or the Weeping Banyan.

A WORD OF WARNING!! One of the island's favorite drinks is called a "Fog Cutter". *Should you dive too deeply into a "Fog Cutter" you may well wind up emulating a "Weeping Banyan".*

All of the amenities indicated under "The Lahaina-Kaanapali-Kapalua Area" are available to guests of this resort.

RATES (EP) Rooms: $195/235/$375.

KAANAPALI BEACH HOTEL
P.O. Box 696,
Lahaina, Maui, HI 96761
(808) 945–6121
(800) 657–7700

This hotel's spacious rooms are arranged in a semicircle, creating an enclosed courtyard that opens onto the beach and those famous Maui sunsets. The soft, gentle, tropical air allows dining and cocktails to be served in the open court and dancing under the stars.

All amenities described under "The Lahaina-Kaanapali-Kapalua Area" are available to guests of this resort.

RATES (EP) Rooms: $135/$185. Suites: $525.

KAPALUA BAY HOTEL
1 Bay Drive
Maui, HI 96761
(808) 669–5656
From Oahu 537–2311
(800) 367–8000

A bit north of the Kaanapali complex of resorts, the Kapalua Bay Hotel is situated within the 23,000-acre Kapalua Plantation property on its own 750 acres. The resort is nestled between the coastline and the rolling hills of a lush pineapple plantation.

Accommodations consist of rooms (194 including suites) in the very lovely hotel plus 180 villas, some offering bay exposure, others a golf course view. Each room is equipped with a refrigerator along with cable TV, providing a separate sitting area and a private terrace. The villas feature fully equipped kitchens, washer/dryer and daily maid service.

The resort is well set up to accommodate meeting groups and can handle gatherings of up to 200 classroom- and 350 theater-style.

There is a wide range of dining facilities to choose from. The relatively new and very nice Pool Terrace for casual dining and cocktails, the Garden Restaurant and Lounge (jackets required), the Plantation Veranda or for gourmet dining the Bay Club. There is also a delightful restaurant adjacent to the main pro shop of the Bay Course called The Grille & Bar. Not only is the food and the service outstanding, but it is a wonderful place for people watching. Make reservations early as it is one busy place.

As to outdoor activities, you can enjoy swimming in several fresh water pools (between the hotel and the villas there are about 10), tennis on 10 private courts (four lighted), with a professional and staff available.

It takes just minutes by shuttle to three golden sand beaches offering up snorkeling, scuba, surfing, sailing, or deep-sea fishing. Conversely, these secluded coves, coral reefs and clear water bays make *doing nothing* a welcome option.

The two golf courses are Arnold Palmer designs. The Bay, parring at 72, stretches 6,761/6,151/5,274 yards. The Village Links reaches out 6,611/5,981/5,134 yards with a par of 71. Both courses take full advantage of the natural terrain, rolling hills, lava outcroppings and the spectacular views offered from elevations of up to 750 feet above the sea.

While the pro shop for the Village course is quite modest the golf shop at The Bay layout is outstanding. Both are under the supervision of the Director of Golf, Gary Planos.

RATES (EP) Hotel: garden view $205/$250; ocean view $295/$340; ocean front $385. 1-bedroom villas: $275/$375. 2-bedroom units: $315/$435. Green fees: $55 including cart. Rates are for the peak season mid-December to mid-April. MAP rates are also available.

MAUI MARRIOTT RESORT
100 Nohea Kai Drive
Lahaina, Maui, HI 96761
(808) 667–1200
(800) 228–9290

The Maui Marriott is directly across from the Royal Kaanapali golf course and features 720 rooms and two nine-story towers, with a four-story lobby between. They present a variety of dining areas ranging from a Japanese steak house to the rustic atmosphere of old Lahaina Town.

The resort offers the use of five lighted tennis courts, a pro shop and a special electronics game room for the younger set. All of the amenities and activities indicated under "The Lahaina-Kaanapali-Kapalua Area" are available to guests of this resort.

RATES (EP) Rooms: $185/$280. Suites: $400 and up.

ROYAL LAHAINA RESORT
2780 Kekass Drive,
Lahaina, Maui, HI 96761
(808) 661–3611
(800) 447–6925

The Royal Lahaina is probably one of the most complete resorts on Maui. Sited on 27 acres it offers a wide variety of accommodations. Ranging from luxurious private cottages to charming guest rooms, each of the 514 guest accommodations features air-conditioning and refrigerators.

Amenities include: three swimming pools, three excellent restaurants as well as a nightly luau. There are also three cocktail lounges. This resort happens to be the location of the Royal Lahaina Tennis Ranch with its 11 courts.

Guests may take advantage of all the other amenities described under "The Lahaina-Kaanapali-Kapalua Area".

RATES (EP) Rooms: $150/$225. Suites: $300 and up.

SHERATON-MAUI HOTEL
2605 Kaanapali Parkway,
Lahaina, Maui, HI 96761
(808) 661–0031
(800) 325–2525

Wrapped around a splendid black rock promontory, this is the hotel that started it all at Kaanapali. Occupying the broadest expanse of Kaanapali Beach, the Sheraton-Maui provides some of the finest snorkeling, sailing and surfing to be found. You have a wide choice of accommodations: rooms, suites and deluxe oceanfront cottages.

There are enough restaurants to satisfy any gourmet, ranging from superb breakfast to candlelight dining.

Two freshwater pools and three lighted tennis courts are also at your disposal.

Guests can use all the amenities indicated under "The Lahaina-Kaanapali-Kapalua Area".

RATES Rooms: $165/$255. Suites $550.

THE WESTIN MAUI
2365 Kaanapali Parkway,
Lahaina, Maui, HI 96761
(808) 667–2525
(800) 228–3000

Originally it was the Maui Surf, and I once described this beautiful resort as bright, comfortable and casually elegant. Acquired by Westin Hotel in 1986 and reopened in late 1987 they have spent $155 million to produce a world-class destination. The change has been massive. The multi-million dollar art collection, displayed throughout the hotel, represents items gathered from China, Hong Kong, Bangkok and Indonesia.

Immediately upon entering the hotel you are confronted by a lagoon and waterfalls gracing the front entrance and the lobby area. The inhabitants of this lagoon are an international group, ranging from graceful Siberian mute white swans, to North American wood ducks, mandarin ducks, and South American whistling tree ducks. I do believe there might even have been a couple of just plain ducks in there somewhere.

Accommodations consist of the 11-story Ocean Tower and the 11-story Beach Tower. All rooms are air-conditioned and equipped with remote control TV, mini-bar and a small private balcony. Each room or suite has a view of either the ocean or the Royal Kaanapali golf course. There are also 37 posh rooms available at the Royal Beach Club, bringing the total of guest rooms to 854.

The Westin Maui has set aside 31,000 square feet of space to accommodate meeting and conference groups. With their 8,820-square-foot Valley Isle ballroom and many break-out rooms they can handle groups of from 11 to 1,100.

There are eight restaurants and lounges, so if you hunger or thirst here you have a problem of choice only. Live entertainment and music are offered in several of the restaurants and lounges.

The Westin offers what is recognized as possibly the best stretch of Kaanapali Beach for swimming, snorkeling, surfing and sunning. The resort virtually revolves around almost 55,000 square feet of pools, waterfalls and meandering streams. There are five free-form swimming pools on various levels. Three of the pools are joined by two waterslides ranging in length from 20 to 150 feet. It looked like fun (we didn't test out the waterslide). There is also a coed health club.

Guests have playing privileges on the nearby 18-hole Royal Kaanapali golf course as well as The Royal Lahaina Tennis Ranch with its 11 courts. The hotel provides complimentary shuttle service to each location.

For detailed information on the golf courses refer to "The Lahaina-Kaanapali-Kapalua Area".

RATES (EP) Courtyard views: $185. Ocean views: $285. Royal Beach Club: $375. Suites range from $600 to $1600. Green fees: $75 including cart. Golf package: 3 nights (includes lodging, 3 rounds of golf per couple, with cart), $1100/$1,200 per couple. This package is offered only in the "Off Season," mid-April through mid-December.

Lahaina-Kaanapali Area Condominiums

KAANAPALI ALII
50 Nohea Kai Drive
Lahaina, Maui, HI 96761
(808) 667–1400
(800) 642–6284

This 11-story resort is on the beach directly across from the Royal Kaanapali golf complex.

Accommodations consist of one- to three-bedroom condominiums. Each unit has a fully equipped kitchen and features two baths, a living room and washer/dryer. The one-bedroom units are 1,500, two bedrooms are 1,800 square feet. A few additional amenities include: VHS recorder and twice-daily maid service. Through their concierge service such extras as baby sitting can be arranged.

While the resort does not have a restaurant of its own, specialized room service menus are available from several nearby establishments.

There are three tennis courts as well as a swimming pool in addition to the beach.

RATES 1-bedroom condo: $205/$215/$250. 2-bedroom unit: $235/$270/$395.

KAANAPALI PLANTATION
150 Puukolii Road,
Lahaina, Maui, HI 96761
(808) 661–4446

These are modern condominium apartments (one to three bedrooms) completely equipped for family-style living with full electric kitchens, washer/dryers and daily maid service. Each unit, by the way, features a private entrance.

While not right on the beach, they are within easy walking distance. They offer a pool, tennis courts and, of course, guests have access to all the amenities indicated under "The Lahaina-Kaanapali-Kapalual Area".

RATES (EP) 1-bedroom: $125. 2 bedrooms (up to 4 people): $210.

KAANAPALI ROYAL
2560 Kekaa Drive,
Lahaina, Maui, HI 96761
(808) 667–7200
(800) 367–7040

These condominiums, bordering right on the golf course, are two-bedroom, two-bath units with fully equipped kitchens and washer/dryers. They are unusually spacious with sunken living rooms and nine-foot ceilings.

There are two tennis courts, swimming pool, sauna and Jacuzzis.

Guests have access to all the amenities listed under "The Lahaina-Kaanapali-Kapalua Area".

RATES (EP) 1-bedroom: $160/$180.

MAUI ELDORADO
Kaanapali Beach
Maui, HI 96761
(808) 661–0021
(800) 367–2967
Canada (800) 663–1118

A luxury low-rise hideaway in a lush garden setting, the Maui Eldorado is surrounded by mountains, the golf course and the Pacific Ocean.

Each of the two-story apartments has living room, dining area, fully equipped kitchen, including dishwashers and icemakers.

Units are one and two bedrooms (750 to 1,800 square feet) and offer the use of three swimming pools. They also provide their own private beach cabana.

Guests have access to all the amenities described under "The Lahaina-Kaanapali-Kapalua Area".

RATES (EP) Studio: $124/$139. 1-bedroom: $149/$169. 2 bed-rooms: (up to 4 people) $195/$219.

THE WHALER AT KAANAPALI BEACH
2481 Kaanapali Parkway, Lahaina
Maui, HI 96761
(808) 661–4861
(800) 367–7052

The Whaler consists of two large condominium complexes featuring 360 units fronting right on the beach. The units are one- to two-bedroom suites equipped for living, not just sleeping.

Fully equipped kitchens, large lanais, a mini-market and underground parking are a few of the basics. An oceanside pool, paddle tennis, four tennis courts, saunas and exercise rooms complete the facilities.

Guests have access to all of the amenities described under "The Lahaina-Kaanapali-Kapalua Area".

RATES Studio: $160/$180. 1 bedroom: $195/$230. Rates are for mid-December through April.

THE ISLAND OF MOLOKAI

Ah! Molokai. Long the favorite of the Hawaiians, an island unspoiled, innocent, secluded and beautiful.

KALUA KOI HOTEL & GOLF CLUB
P.O. Box 1977
Maunaloa, HI 96770
(808) 552–2555
(800) 367–6046

For many years this resort operated as the "Sheraton Molokai." Now the Kalua Koi, there have really been very few changes. The original builders were wise enough to blend the hotel structure into the general fabric of the island. Consisting of 33 buildings, the tallest being two stories, the hotel has been constructed in a rambling rustic Polynesian style. All 290 rooms and suites have high beamed ceilings, tropical fans and rattan furnishings.

Meander down the garden walkway to the Ohia Lodge, a superb restaurant, where cocktails and Molokai music form that special atmosphere so unique to the islands.

You can choose to swim in the pool or in the sparkling Pacific, or take a picnic lunch from the hotel and tour the island, or perhaps play a set of tennis with a professional available to assist. Tennis is, by the way, complimentary for guests.

Golf is offered on the hotel's Kalua Koi course—playing 6,618/6,211/5,437 yards and parring at 72. Designed by Ted Robinson, it features some water, along with ingeniously placed trees and traps. A full-line pro shop offering complete facilities is available.

RATES (EP) Rooms: $100/$135. Cottages: $180. Green fees: $55 including cart.

ARRIVAL Shuttle service is available from the airport to the hotel.

IDAHO

KETCHUM-SUN VALLEY AREA

Since so many articles have been written and so many photographs released about this area, perhaps a little history is in order.

In 1935, Averell Harriman, then Chairman of the Board of Union Pacific Railroad and a long-time avid ski buff, sought means to increase traffic from the east to the west via his railroad (and in the process create a ski facility he would enjoy). After much searching he happened on Ketchum. Count Felix Schaffgotsch, commissioned by Harriman to locate the ideal spot for a resort, felt this location superior to any he had seen—in fact, potentially better than any in Europe. The 4,300 acres were purchased and in December of 1935 "Sun Valley," the first complete ski resort in the United States, came into being.

The idea was that a visit to this resort area was to be a "roughing it" outing. That is, roughing it Hollywood style—glass-enclosed swimming pools, exquisite food, impeccable service and orchestras performing nightly. At a later date, the Sun Valley Center for Arts and Humanities and many other amenities were added, thus transforming it into an all-season operation rather than just a winter ski resort.

It is, in reality, a large, self-contained village, with an opera house (movies), its own lake (rowing and paddleboat rentals), swimming pools, horseback riding, skeet and trap shooting, whitewater raft trips on the Salmon River and fishing. Within the valley itself there are a total of 85 tennis courts and in Hailey, (13 miles away) there are several indoor lighted courts. Of course, you can also choose to just relax.

Additional services available include: a drug store, barber and beauty shop, post office, several clothing stores, a florist, bank, hospital, taxi service, excellent meeting and convention facilities and so many restaurants I could not name them all. During the summer months there are a great many activities to be enjoyed including: a jazz festival, motorcycle and bicycle races, flower and musical festivals, a backcountry run, a Mexican Fiesta Grande, ballet performances, parades, a rodeo and many more activities.

The Sun Valley-Ketchum area is big, it is lovely and there is almost no end to the activities to be enjoyed.

Today there are two major resorts in Sun Valley—The Elkhorn Lodge & Condominiums and The Sun Valley Lodge, Inn & Condominiums. Each resort has its own championship golf course and provides excellent winter ski facilities.

For a wide selection of possible accommodations in the area, call the Sun Valley-Ketchum Chamber of Commerce's new toll free reservations number, (800) 634-3347.

ELKHORN RESORT
P.O. Box 6009
Sun Valley, ID 83354
(208) 622-4511
ID (800) 632-4101
NAT (800) 635-9356

Accommodations at Elkhorn consist of 135 guest rooms in the Lodge and 140 condominiums fully equipped for housekeeping. In fact you can request the condo be stocked prior to your arrival, a nice touch and much better than last-minute shopping after a tough day of travel.

Should you elect to dine out there are four excellent restaurants: Tequila Joe's featuring Mexican food; Papa Dino's for pasta and pizza; Jesse's for fish and beef; and for breakfast and lunch, the Clubhouse Cafe.

Elkhorn has outstanding meeting and conference facilities and can handle groups of up to 350.

A great many activities await your pleasure: tennis on 18 Laykold courts with another three indoor courts nearby, seven spas, five swimming pools (two Olympic size), hiking in the most incredible area in the United States—Sawtooth National Recreation Area, with elk, deer, moose and bighorn sheep to be studied. A few additional attractions include: horseback riding, hayrides, folk art and music festivals, water skiing, windsurfing, biking, balloon and glider flights or even bar hopping in nearby Ketchum. And then there is golf.

The Elkhorn layout, like the Sun Valley course, is a Robert Trent Jones Jr. design. Stretching out 7,160/6,610/5,701 yards, the course

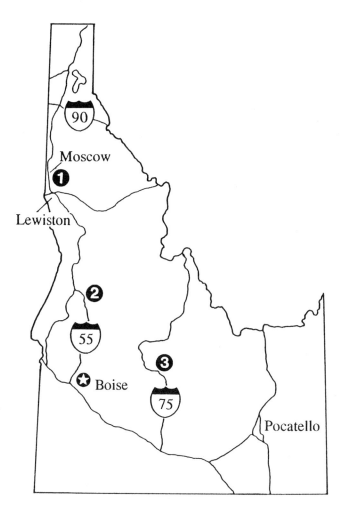

Idaho

Moscow

Lewiston

Boise

Pocatello

1. Twin Lakes Village
2. Kimberland Meadows
3. Elkhorn Resort
   Sun Valley

pars at 72. With elevation changes from 6,150 feet to 5,750 feet on the front nine and Willow Creek becoming a nuisance on the back side, it is not only a tester but a fun layout to play as well. There is a full-line pro shop under the direction of PGA Professional, Jeff Steury, and staff.

Once more a word of caution: you are playing golf at 6,000 feet above sea level. If you play from the blue tees you will feel as if you are playing about 6,400 yards not 7,100. Your ball gets that much extra carry. Don't, however, try to make the same shots when you return to the beach area or you are going to be embarrassed.

During the winter months when the snow starts coating the ground the ski season moves into high gear. With transportation provided every 30 minutes to Mount Baldy and lifts for Dollar Mountain virtually at your door you have 16 lifts and 64 runs ranging from gentle to hair raising. With this number of lifts you will rarely encounter a line or have to wait. There are also cross country trails as well as helicopter lifts available, not to mention sleigh rides and ice skating.

RATES (EP) Lodge rooms: $78/$138. Suites: $158/$248. Studio condo: (kitchenette) $100/$108. Fully equipped 1-bedroom condo: $158. Green fees: $34/$38, carts $24. Rates quoted are for the summer season.

ARRIVAL Air: Salt Lake City or Boise, Idaho with flight connections to Sun Valley. Car: State Highway 75, approximately 80 miles from Twin Falls, Idaho.

SUN VALLEY LODGE & INN
Sun Valley, ID 83353
(208) 622–4111
ID (800) 632–4104
NAT (800) 635–8261

Accommodations are provided in the original and beautiful Lodge (which has been updated) and at the Inn. In addition there are eight large groupings of condominiums which are fully equipped for housekeeping.

While there are a number of fine restaurants (as well as intriguing shops) in the Sun Valley Village, you need go no further than the Lodge itself. The Lodge Dining Room (for many years called

The Duchin Room) is superb. While the food and service are outstanding, the entertainment (dance music) is in a class by itself. Jackets are required, ties are optional.

On the main level and available for all three meals is Gretchen's. Again the selection, preparation and manner of presentation is outstanding. The lovely Duchin Lounge has become a favorite gathering place in the evening.

Sun Valley Lodge offers a play school program, designed to offer the children six and under a fun vacation while you do "whatever". They also provide a "Young Summer" program for the 7-to-11 age group and a Teen Summer program for ages 12 to 18. All the programs are under the supervision of trained professionals and include activities such as tennis, fishing, skin diving, horseback riding, archery, indoor and outdoor ice skating (available year round) golfing, shooting, sailing, kayaking, hayrides and hiking. A few of the adult activities offered by the Lodge include: bowling, game rooms, horseback riding, tennis on 18 courts and the use of three swimming pools.

During the winter months Sun Valley Lodge becomes a skier's paradise. Known as "the grand dame of American ski resorts", it offers downhill and cross country courses (vertical rises of up to 3,144 feet), as well as the assistance of 160 certified instructors. With the new high-speed lifts in place (installed in 1989), they are now capable of lifting some 1,500 skiers per hour to the very top of Mt. Baldy within 10 minutes. I could go on and on but I think the following brings into focus the scope of their facilities. Baldy has 12 lifts, 57 runs, 3,400 vertical feet of drop, with a summit at 9,140 feet. Dollar Mountain has four lifts, 13 runs, 628 feet of vertical drop and a summit elevation of 6,638 feet.

A few of the other winter activities include sleigh rides and ice skating. As a matter of fact the traditional Sun Valley Lodge Terrace hosts elaborate ice shows featuring world-class skaters. Starting in mid-June and terminating in September, these performances take place each Saturday evening, on one of two Olympic-size rinks.

Golf may be enjoyed on the Robert Trent Jones, Jr. designed Sun Valley Resort course. Reaching out 6,565/6,057/5,241 yards, the men's par is set at 72 and the ladies' at 73. Trail Creek, which wanders all over the place, tight fairways and trees make this no run-of-the-mill resort course. While very much a manicured layout the Sun Valley course will present you with some extremely interesting and challenging shots. There are, for example, a couple of par-threes which may well produce a hard swallow. Not only is the course well bunkered but the beauty has been further enhanced by the use of brilliant "Petersburg White" sand.

The pro shop is under the direction of PGA professional Bill Butterfield and provides a luncheon terrace.

RATES (EP) Lodge: $85/$135. Inn: $72/$112. Condo: 1-bedroom $115; 2-bedroom, $220. Green fees: $45, carts $24. Golf package: 2 nights/2 days (includes golf and lodging) $148 per person. Rates are for June-September.

ARRIVAL Air: Salt Lake City or Boise with flight connections to Hailey Airport (14 miles). Car: State Highway 75 (Twin Falls is 81 miles).

KIMBERLAND MEADOWS
P.O. Drawer C
New Meadows, Idaho 83654
(208) 347–2163
ID(800) 632–1244

The Kimberland Meadows Resort is 132 miles south of Lewiston and 120 miles north of Boise in Idaho's heartland. Accommodations are available in well appointed townhouses. The units, which can house up to six, are fully equipped for housekeeping and feature fireplaces and oversized Jacuzzi tubs. There are also a few private homes available for rental with a capacity of from six to ten people.

In the event you tire of "condo" fare you might well consider dining at the main Hawk Valley Lodge. The recipient of the AAA Four Diamond Award, the restaurant presents a varied menu.

While the visual and recreational focal point of the resort is the golf course, other activities available include: tennis on three courts, an equestrian center providing trail rides into the adjacent forest and, depending on the time of year, buggy or sleigh rides.

Fishing is outstanding on the Little Salmon River, which runs through the property, as well as in the five-acre stocked lake at the park entrance. The 35-mile stretch of river running north from the Meadows Valley is famous for its salmon and steelhead runs. Payette Lake in McCall (12 miles away) opens up another choice of activities including sailing and swimming, water skiing and fishing.

The golf course, designed by Bob Baldock, plays 6,966/6,515/5,934 yards with a par of 72/74. Although water comes into play on seven holes it is not an overwhelming factor. While a bit on the difficult side (slope rating from the men's regular tees is 131), it is a fun layout to play.

RATES (EP) Townhouses: 1-bedroom $95; 2-bedroom/2-bath $125. Homes: $140/$190. Green fees: $15/$18, carts $16.

ARRIVAL Air: McCall airport (12 miles) has a 5,000 foot runway and rental cars. Private aircraft: 2,450-foot strip in New Meadows (maintained during summer and fall only). Car: on U.S. 95, 3 miles north of New Meadow.

TWIN LAKES VILLAGE
Route 4, Box P-551
Rathdrum, ID 83858
(208) 687–1311

Twin Lakes, an intimate village-type complex, is situated on 160 acres. Accommodations are offered in some of the nicest condominiums (one to three bedrooms) we have stayed in. They are well furnished, featuring completely equipped kitchens, living rooms and fireplaces. The hub of activity is the clubhouse, site of the dining room, lounge, Jacuzzi, meeting rooms and, on the lower level, the pro shop.

The proximity of the village to Twin Lakes provides immediate access to fishing, boating and sandy beaches, with several swimming pools and tennis courts at various locations within the grounds.

Golf is played on a full-size, 18-hole course measuring 6,158/5,836/5,362 yards with a par of 71/72. A second nine was recently added. It is a beautiful layout, taking advantage of the lush terrain and magnificent trees which surround the entire area.

Twin Lakes has a small, but well equipped golf shop with PGA professional Mark Gardner on deck to lend assistance.

RATES (EP) Suites: 1-bedroom $75 per night, $385 per week; 2-bedrooms $90 per night, $470 per week. Rates are for June-August; a minimum stay of one week is required. Green fees: $18, carts $16.

ARRIVAL Air: Spokane (30 miles) or Coeur d'Alene (20 miles). Car: from Rathdrum, 5 miles north on 41.

ILLINOIS

EAGLE RIDGE INN & RESORT
P.O. Box 777 Highway 20 West
Galena, IL 61036
(815) 777–2444
IL (800) 892–2269
Limited Area (800) 323–8421

The tradition of the country inn has long been cherished by travelers wherein, at the end of a long day on the road weary guests would gather round a cozy fire with their tankard of ale and relax before enjoying a hearty meal, served by the bustling innkeeper.

Here in the northwest corner of Illinois, perched on a ridge overlooking Lake Galena, the welcome extended by Eagle Ridge Inn brings back that warmth and tradition. The scene really comes into focus when you see the antique furnishings, dormer windows, fireplaces and quilt-covered beds. The Inn can also handle modest-size meeting groups of up to 100.

Dining here does nothing to detract from the ambience with a selection which can only be described as excellent.

Recreational facilities include: indoor swimming, a sauna, whirlpool, tennis, horseback riding, sailing, fishing and water skiing.

Golf can be played on the Eagle Ridge Golf Club North course, reaching out a hefty 7,012/6,527/5,665 yards and parring at 72. The terrain is hilly with small creeks running throughout and it is very well trapped. The second 18, the South course, plays 6,785/6,410/5,356 yards, also with a par of 72. Both layouts are supported by a large and well equipped pro shop.

RATES (EP) Inn: $95/$195. Townhouses: 1 bedroom $165. Green fees: $50 including cart. Golf package: 2 nights/3 days (includes lodging, MAP, golf, cart, bag storage and taxes), $770 per couple.

ARRIVAL Air: Dubuque. Car: Route 20, 6 miles east of Galena, Illinois.

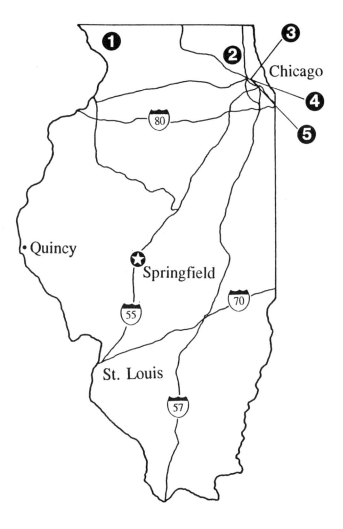

Illinois

- ❶ Eagle Ridge Inn & Resort
- ❷ Marriott's Lincolnshire Resort
- ❸ Nordic Hills Resort
- ❹ Indian Lakes Resort
- ❺ Pheasant Run Resort

1. Eagle Ridge Inn & Resort
2. Marriott's Lincolnshire Resort
3. Nordic Hills Resort
4. Indian Lakes Resort
5. Pheasant Run Resort

INDIAN LAKES RESORT
250 West Schick Road
Bloomingdale, IL 60108
(312) 529–0200
(800) 334–3417

To refer to this resort's structure as "Ultra Modern" is a definite understatement. Its six-story atrium lobby, with sunlight filtering through the many hexagonal skylights, touching the profusion of tropical trees and plants, is a most unusual and pleasing sight. The resort, by the way, recently underwent a multi-million dollar renovation. The 308 guest rooms, 23 suites and 28 meeting and banquet rooms, (not to mention its proximity to O'Hare Airport) make it an excellent choice for meetings and conventions. They have a meeting capacity of 12 to 1,200. The resort is actually a little over 30 minutes from O'Hare International and under an hour to downtown Chicago.

Three excellent restaurants, four lounges, a health club, indoor and outdoor swimming pools, six tennis courts and two 18-hole golf courses complete the list of facilities.

Golf can be played on the Iroquois Trail 18, playing 6,580/6,239 yards, parring at 72, or the Sioux Trail layout, again with only two tee settings playing 6,564/6,225 yards and also with a par 72. With only two tee settings that yardage gets a little much for the ladies.

RATES (EP) Rooms: $135/$145. Suites: $235/$375. Green fees: $24, carts $22.

ARRIVAL Air: O'Hare Airport. Car: between Bloomingdale Road and Gary Avenue on Schick Road.

NORDIC HILLS RESORT
Nordic Road
Itasca, IL 60143
(312) 773–2750
(800) 334–3417

Approximately 30 minutes from O'Hare Airport, this resort makes an excellent meeting place. In addition to the 22 meeting rooms, there are 220 guest rooms and six luxurious penthouse suites.

Dining is offered in the Scandinavian Room or the less formal Vulcan's Forge, with cocktails and entertainment available in the Skoal Lounge or the Playroom Bar.

Activities include: eight indoor racquetball courts, six bowling lanes, five outdoor tennis courts (three lighted), indoor and outdoor swimming pools and a full health club with exercise equipment.

The resort has its own 18-hole, 5,897-yard, par-71/73 course. Playing privileges are also extended at the nearby Indian Lakes Resort and its two championship layouts.

RATES (EP) Rooms: $125/$135. Suites: $160/$400. Green fees: $24, carts $22.

ARRIVAL Air: Chicago. Car: the resort is on Old 53 Rohlwing Road and Nordic Road, off Highway 20.

MARRIOTT'S LINCOLNSHIRE RESORT
Marriott Lane
Lincolnshire, IL 60015
(312) 634–0100
(800) 228–9290

The Lincolnshire offers over 400 rooms, plus six restaurants and lounges. There are, in addition, 17 meeting rooms, with a capacity of 1,800 theater- and 1,000 banquet-style. Additional amenities include: legitimate theater presentations, game rooms, the use of canoes or paddleboats on the private resort lake, tennis on five indoor courts, four racquetball courts, and a health spa.

You may tee it up on the resort's course, playing 6,600/6,6315/5,795 yards with a par of 71. A Fazio design, you know you are going to look at raised, and often small, greens. While the general terrain is flat, the course is made interesting by water on five or six holes.

RATES (EP) Rooms: $159. Suites: $300. Green fees: $55 including cart. Golf package: 2 nights/3 days (includes lodging, breakfast, green fees, cart, bag storage), $299 per couple.

ARRIVAL Air: Chicago. Car: on Route 21.

PHEASANT RUN RESORT
P.O. Box 64
St. Charles, IL 60174
(312) 584–6300

Pheasant Run resort, on 200 acres in the Fox River Valley, is about 45 minutes from Chicago. Consisting of 550 rooms and a new convention center with 12,320 square feet of meeting space (a capacity of from 20 to 1,250), this is certainly no roadside motel.

An outstanding and varied choice of dining facilities includes: the Smuggler's Cove, the Baker's Wife Steak House and the dinner-theater, featuring Broadway hits. For musical entertainment and dancing there is the Baker's Wife Lounge and Bourbon Street, jumping with New Orleans style, Dixieland music.

After you have destroyed yourself *weight wise* with the above, you might try the complete health spa, tennis on the nine outdoor courts, a swim in the indoor or outdoor pools or perhaps a round of golf. Pheasant Run offers not only a super pro shop but an interesting golf course as well. The Challenge takes the form of five lakes, sloping greens and too many traps. It plays at 6,315/5,955 / 5,472 yards and pars at 71/73.

RATES (EP) Rooms: $89. Tower rooms: $109. Green fees: $35, carts $22. Golf package: 2 nights/2 days (includes lodging, MAP, with 1 night a dinner show, green fees), $356 per couple.

ARRIVAL Air: Chicago. Private aircraft: DuPage County, paralleling the golf course. Car: on Route 64, 3 miles east of St. Charles.

INDIANA

FRENCH LICK SPRINGS
French Lick, IN 47432
(812) 935–9381
IN (800) 742–4095
NAT (800) 457–4042

French Lick Springs Golf & Tennis Resort is in a quiet corner of southern Indiana. The first hotel, built in 1837, was destroyed by fire in 1897 and rebuilt, at a later date, to its present format. In order to entice guests, they even constructed a railroad line running from Chicago to their front door. It was a popular place during the 20's and 30's—gambling was a large part of the attraction.

On 2,600 acres with densely wooded hillsides (butternut and oak trees), footpaths and lovely gardens, the resort is in a beautiful setting. While large (500 rooms), French Lick Resort still retains its original charm and elegance.

They offer all of the amenities normally found in a hotel of this size. There is outstanding dining in Normans. La Bistro (for a quick breakfast) and the Hoosier Rib Room are also available. Nightly entertainment is offered in the Convention Hall. Their meeting facilities are also exceptional—in fact an entire wing is set aside to handle meeting and conference groups.

The tennis complex consists of 25 courts (12 indoor/13 lighted outdoor) and USPTA professional Mike O'Connell is available to assist your ailing game. Other activities at your disposal: two swimming pools, one outdoor and one indoor, four bowling lanes, skeet and trap shooting, two golf courses, a health spa and horseback riding from the resort's own stables.

The golf course adjacent to the hotel is called the Valley course—a par-70/71 playing 6,003/5,687 yards.

The Country Club course, three miles away, is under the direction of PGA Professional Dave Harner. Reaching out 6,629/6,291/5,781 yards it pars at 71/73. Designed by architect Donald Ross, it uses hilly terrain, with trees along holes six, seven and eight, a little water on three holes, and traps to keep you alert. I will not describe the 18th green other than to say one look at it will keep your

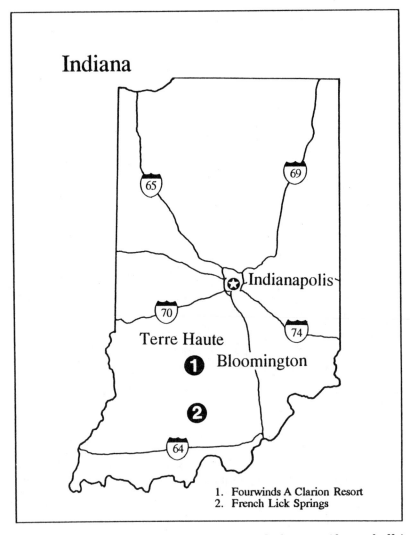

Indiana

1. Fourwinds A Clarion Resort
2. French Lick Springs

your full attention. This will most definitely be true if your ball is on the upper level of the green and the pin is on the lower part.

RATES (MAP) Rooms: $159/$179 per couple. Green fees: Valley course $16; Country Club course $28, carts $22. Golf package: 2 nights/3 days (includes MAP, lodging, green fees and cart), $396 per couple. Rates are April-October.

ARRIVAL Air: Louisville (75 minutes). Car: Highway 150 to 145.

FOURWINDS, A CLARION RESORT
Lake Monroe, P.O. Box 160
Bloomington, IN 47402
(812) 824–9904
(800) 252–7466

The resort's location, on the shores of Indiana's Lake Monroe, opens up many activities. Accommodations consist of 126 rooms, all equipped with private steam baths, *a nice way to wind up the day*. The nine-room meeting and conference facility has a capacity of 250.

Classic French and American dishes are featured in the Tradewinds or, for a slight libation, try the Windjammer Lounge.

They claim their marina is the largest inland facility of its type in the United States. This could well be true, as it is huge. You are invited to bring your own craft or, if you prefer, rent a pontoon boat for a tour of the lake or a little fishing. There are tennis courts, an indoor/outdoor pool, Jacuzzi and saunas.

Golf is played on The Pointe championship course. Ranked among the best in the country, it measures 6,639/6,131/5,252 yards and pars at 71.

RATES (EP) Rooms: $105. Suites: 1-bedroom $205 and up. Green fees: $35, carts $22. Golf packages are available.

ARRIVAL Air: Bloomington (10 miles). Car: from Bloomington, take Highway 37 south, Harrodsburg exit, east to Fairfax Road, then south to the resort.

LOUISIANA

TORO HILLS RESORT
P.O. Box 369
Florien LA 71429
(318) 586–4661
(800) 533–5031

This large resort hotel, the only one of its kind in Louisiana, was built around two large swimming pools, a children's pool and lighted tennis courts. In addition to the hotel accommodations they now can offer lodgings in over 23 fully equipped condominiums as well. Toro Hills offers outstanding meeting facilities separated from the hotel, with rooms that may be divided to accommodate groups of up to 200 banquet- or 300 theater-style.

Unfortunately the resort suffered very serious fire damage a short time back. By the time you read this, however, the new office and restaurant complex will be in operation.

Golf is played on the Toro Hills course, virtually surrounding the property. With its lush, tree-lined fairways, and water coming into play on five holes, it is a fun layout to navigate. Playing 6,548/6,307/5,329 yards, it pars at 72.

The resort provides a full-line pro shop and a clubhouse, with the 19th hole for a quick libation.

RATES (EP) Rooms: $50. Condominiums: 2 bedrooms, kitchen, 2 baths $125. Green Fees: $14/$16. Carts: $16/$18. Golf package: 2 nights/3 days (includes lodging, green fees, cart, taxes), $183 per couple; weekends $194 per couple. Lodging in a condo: $224/$264 per couple. Rates are March-September.

ARRIVAL Air: Shreveport (2½ hours). Private aircraft: Hodges Garden, 2,200-foot strip. Car: U.S. 171 between Many and Leesville.

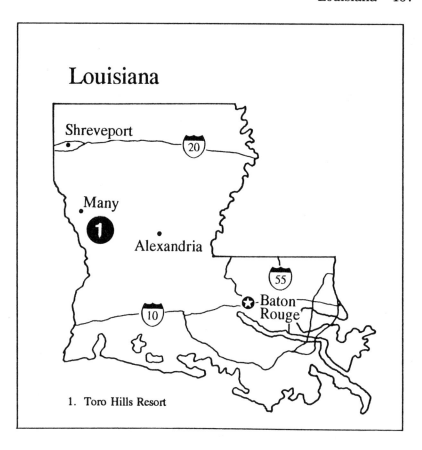

Louisiana

Shreveport

20

Many

1

Alexandria

55

10

★-Baton Rouge

1. Toro Hills Resort

MICHIGAN

BAY VALLEY INN
2470 Old Bridge Road
Bay City, MI 48706
(517) 686–3500

Bay Valley, with its 150 guest rooms, offers a comfortable country-inn type atmosphere. Dining is provided in the outstanding Heatherfield Restaurant overlooking the golf course, or in the intimate English Room. The delightful Players Lounge is available for dancing in the evening. The resort is a natural for meetings with a capacity of 310 theater-style and 210 for banquets.

A resident tennis director is on deck to supervise activities on the six indoor and six outdoor tennis courts. Other amenities include: swimming pools, a sauna and a Jacuzzi/whirlpool bath.

Designed by Desmond Muirhead/Jack Nicklaus, the resort's championship course is reminiscent of many of the Scottish layouts. Parring at 71, this beautiful and challenging course plays 6,610/6,113/5,587/5,151 yards. Apparently the Scots liked water, as the course has over 60 acres of the stuff—unfortunately not in just one place, but seemingly coming into play wherever you look. When you add the well-placed traps and trees, it becomes a challenge.

RATES (EP) Inn: weekdays $90/$102; weekends $93/$106. Green fees: $45/$50, including cart. Golf packages are available. Rates are for mid-June to mid-September.

ARRIVAL Air: Tri-City Airport. Car: I-75, take M-84 Saginaw Road exit. Turn right, go 1 block, then at Standard Station right again.

BOYNE HIGHLANDS
Harbor Springs, MI 49740
(616) 526–2171
(800) 462–6963

Situated in northern Michigan, Boyne Highlands is just four miles from Lake Michigan. Long recognized as a premier winter resort,

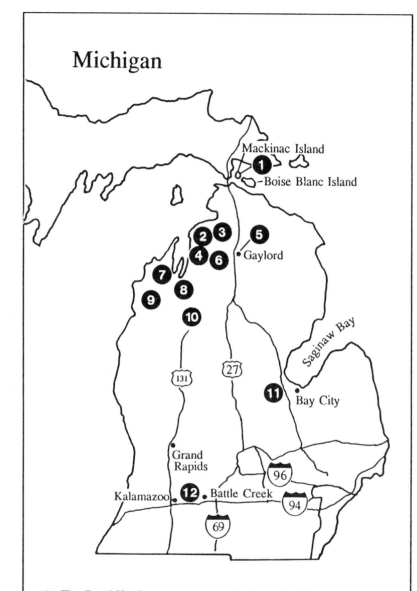

Michigan

Mackinac Island
Boise Blanc Island
Gaylord
Saginaw Bay
131
27
Bay City
Grand Rapids
Kalamazoo
Battle Creek
96
94
69

1. The Grand Hotel
2. Boyne Highlands
3. Boyne Mountain
4. Shanty Creek/Schuss Mountain Resort
5. Hidden Valley Club Resort
6. Schuss Mountain Resort
7. Sugar Loaf Resort
8. Grand Traverse Resort Village
9. Crystal Mountain
10. McGuire's Motor Lodge & Resort
11. Bay Valley Inn
12. Gull Lake View Golf Club

it has also moved into prominence as a summer destination. Lodgings are provided at the Highland Inn (165 rooms) as well as the new Heather Highlands Inn Condo Hotel (72 units). Including the many privately-owned condominiums (available for rental), the resort can handle over 800 guests. Each unit features a fireplace, fully equipped kitchen and balcony. The Highlands, with its remodeled conference center, is well set up to handle meeting groups.

Two swimming pools, saunas, fishing, tennis on four courts and golf, with horseback riding nearby, are some of the activities available. There is also a children's program as well as a baby sitting service.

If it is golf you want, it is golf you will get. There are now three regulation courses, plus a nine-hole par-three affair on premises. You can also play on the two at Boyne Mountain, some 26 miles away. For details on the golf facilities, see Boyne Mountain Resort. The Moor Course, parring at 72, plays a monstrous 7,179/6,521/6,032/5,459 yards. The Heather links weigh in at an even more generous 7,218//6,554/6,090/5,263 yards, also parring at 72.

Due to the general terrain of heavily wooded hills and lots of water, these layouts provide a wide variety of possible shots and a great deal of challenge. There is a well stocked pro shop, a putting green and driving range.

And now an exciting addition: coming into play in July of 1989 was the Donald Ross Memorial Course. They have selected 18 of the best holes designed by Mr. Ross, one of the world's finest golf architects, and have duplicated them, as closely as is possible. Examples are from Pinehurst Course #2, Scioto, Oakland Hills, Royal Dornoch, Seminole and many others. To say the very least it has produced a unique and intriguing golf adventure. With a par of 72 the Ross Memorial Course plays 6,840/6,308/4,977 yards. This new golf facility is supported by a 17,000-square-foot clubhouse, complete with two restaurants, lounges, tennis as well as a golf shop and locker rooms.

RATES (EP) Hotel room: $100/$125. Condos: $150/$180. Green fees: $50/$70, including cart Golf package: 2 nights/2 days (includes dinner each night, lodging, green fees, cart), weekdays $440, weekends $500 per couple.

ARRIVAL Air: Emmett County Airport (11 miles from Boyne Highlands).

BOYNE MOUNTAIN
Boyne Falls, MI 49713
(616) 549–2441
(800) 462–6963

Boyne Mountain, bounded by Deer Lake and U.S. 131 has long been recognized as a top notch winter sports complex. Recently, it has gained wide acceptance as a summer destination as well.

Accommodations consist of over 400 rooms including hotel rooms; the Deer Lake Beach Villas, each with private suites, full kitchens and room for four; the Mountain Villa condominium complex; Edelweiss Lodge; Boynehof Lodge; the Cliff Dweller; and the Main Lodges. Boyne Mountain Resort is an ideal place for meeting groups. There are a variety of dining rooms and lounges also available.

Many activities are at your disposal, including: three swimming pools, saunas, fishing, sailing, the Beach Club, a tennis complex with a total of 14 courts and golf.

The Alpine Links, with four tee settings, plays 7,017/ 6,546/6,014/ 4,986 yards and pars at 72. A recent addition, which we have not seen, is the Boyne Monument Championship Course. Opened to play in early 1986, it stretches out 7,086/ 6,377/5,744/4,904 yards, also parring at 72. Boyne Mountain offers the facilities of two driving ranges, a pro shop and golf on a par-three executive course.

RATES (EP) Rooms: $100. Villas: 1-bedroom $120. Green fees: $50/$70 including cart. Golf package: 2 nights/2 days (includes lodging, MAP, green fees and cart), weekdays $380, weekends $440/$580 per couple.

ARRIVAL Air: Traverse City. Private aircraft: Boyne Mountain, 4,200-foot lighted runway. Car: off U.S. 131, 1 mile south of Boyne Falls.

CRYSTAL MOUNTAIN
Thompsonville, MI 49683
(616) 378–2911
Limited area (800) 321–4637

The resort, while small enough to allow individual attention, has all the amenities of a larger facility. Accommodations are varied and include: one- or two-bedroom condominiums, some overlooking the 18th green; the Hamlet's 36 poolside rooms each featuring a whirlpool (built for two) and The Colony rooms, each with a private Jacuzzi/whirlpool bath. Some also have a fully equipped kitchen as well as a fireplace. Within easy walking distance of the Lodge and pool are found the Village Chalets and Resort Homes— each fully equipped for housekeeping.

If you do not care to "condo it," superb dining is available in the main dining room along with dancing and entertainment. Of course there is always the whirlpool *tub for two,* standard equipment in the Hamlet rooms.

Additional possibilities include: swimming, tennis on two courts, jogging, biking trails, boating, charter fishing and miles of canoeing available on the Betsie and the Platte Rivers. During the winter their slopes are set up for nighttime skiing.

Golf is offered on a course selected by *Travel Weekly* as one of the "Par Excellence" resort layouts in the United States. The Crystal Mountain golf course offers three possible tee settings. Parring at 72 it stretches out 6,873/6,266/5,773/5,178 yards. With water coming into play on three of the first nine holes and seven on the second nine, undulating terrain, trees and very well trapped greens, it will give all you want. A recent agreement was reached which allows guests playing privileges at the Crystal Golf Club, in Beulah 12 miles away.

RATES (EP) Lodge: $105 weekdays, $129 weekends. Chalets: $149 weekdays, $169 weekends. Green fees: $35, carts $20. Golf packages are available.

ARRIVAL Air: Traverse City or Cadillac (36 miles). Car: north on U.S. 31, turn east on County Road 602, 6 miles north of Bearlake.

GRAND HOTEL
Mackinac Island, MI 49757
(906) 847–3331
(800) 334–7263

Your adventure starts when you leave the ferry or air taxi and step into the gleaming hotel carriage. Attended by an immaculately clad coachman, resplendent in his hunting pinks and complete with top hat, you will travel to the Grand. On the ride to the hotel you will glimpse the quiet wilderness of the island, with a view of both passing ships and departing guests. Your first sight of the Grand is breathtaking: pristine white and lovely, it sits on a high bluff overlooking the Straits of Mackinac, where Lakes Huron and Michigan touch.

A dowager Queen, over 103 years of age, the Grand Hotel is beautifully preserved and vibrantly alive. The spell does not break when you arrive and step into the Grand Hotel parlor and enter a world where the tradition of demitasse and after dinner cordials, evening concerts and dressing for dinner is still in vogue. Jackets and ties are required after 6 PM. Indulge in the proud tradition of high tea, complete with sandwiches, freshly baked cakes and tortes, or request a picnic basket prepared for bikers, strollers, golfers or horseback riders.

Accommodations do nothing to dispel the setting with their excellent furnishings. The meeting facilities are outstanding with accommodations for up to 1,200.

The fact that automobiles are not allowed on the island adds to the atmosphere of tranquility.

There are many activities to enjoy: bicycling through the hills, swimming in the great Serpentine Pool, tennis and shuffleboard or enjoying the 500 acres of gardens.

Golf is available on a nine-hole executive course. Playing it twice the yardage is 4,670/4,488/4,106.

RATES (MAP) Bedroom: $120/$225 per person. Green fees: (18 holes) $24, carts $20. The resort is open May through November.

ARRIVAL Air: Pellston Airport. Car: park at Mackinac City or St. Ignace. It is a 30-minute ferry ride across the Straits to the Island.

GRAND TRAVERSE RESORT VILLAGE
6300 North U.S. 31,
Grand Traverse Village MI 49610
(616) 938–2100
(800) 748–0303

Much of Michigan's lower peninsula is covered by thick pine and hardwood forests, lush cherry orchards, deep lakes and fish-filled streams. Traverse Bay washes ashore here at the gateway to the Great Lakes. This resort has undergone a giant transformation in recent years. The village now encompasses 850 acres, including a half a mile of shoreline along East Bay. There are over 345 condominiums and 244 hotel rooms. The new 15-story, 186-room Tower has two floors consisting of over 20,000 square feet of shopping space. Also within the Tower is the 15th floor cabaret-style restaurant and lounge. The Beach Club, adjacent to East Grand Traverse Bay, provides additional accommodations in the form of 150 studio and one-bedroom villas. Many of the rooms are equipped with two-person whirlpools *(don't knock it if you have never tried one)*.

The resort is well set up to handle meetings. With the various meeting rooms and ballrooms, they can accommodate groups of up to 1,100.

Your evenings can vary from pizza with the children, to candlelight dining over French cuisine, to lounges with entertainment and dancing. There are four restaurants and five lounges.

Year-round activities in the $4 million sports complex, attached to the hotel, include: weight rooms, aerobic classes, tennis on indoor and outdoor courts with a resident professional staff available to assist, racquetball, indoor and outdoor pools, saunas and whirlpools. You are also just minutes from deep-water fishing, canoeing, hunting and waterskiing.

The original golf course, home of the 1983 Michigan Open Championship, is a par-72, reaching out 6,899/6,295/5,387 yards. It brings water into play on 11 holes and is very well trapped. The newer course is a Jack Nicklaus designed tournament layout. The par 72-Bear Course measures 7,177/6,440/5,423 yards. Anyone who wants to play from the blue tee setting on this layout needs the assistance of a psychiatrist. The Bear Course comes complete with four lakes and water hazards on 10 holes.

Some food for thought—the score card says, "attention golfers, beware of deep bunkers and terraced fairways". I suggest you pay attention to those words.

RATES (EP) Hotel: $140. Tower: $185/$195. Condos: $110/$275. Green fees: Bear Course $75 including cart; Resort Course $45. There are a variety of package plans available. Rates are for June-August.

ARRIVAL Air: Traverse City. Car: U.S. 31, 6 miles north of Traverse City.

GULL LAKE VIEW GOLF CLUB
7417 M-89
Richland, MI 49083
(616) 731–4148

The resort, in the heart of Michigan's lake region, is adjacent to Gull Lake. The new Fairway Villas, 24 two-bedroom, two-bath units with kitchen and living room, can be rented as described, or a one-bedroom, one-bath portion may be requested.

The recently remodeled clubhouse has banquet facilities for 200 and provides the 19th hole lounge for cocktails and sandwiches.

There are now four golf courses to navigate. The West measures 6,300/6,058/5,216 yards and pars at 71/72. The first nine is fairly open while the back side brings water into play on six holes and sports many trees. The East course, the newer of the two, while shorter, plays 6,002/5,546/4,918 yards and pars at 70. It provides its own stimulation with water coming on 10 holes, tree-lined fairways and small greens. The Bedford course, parring at 72, gets a little exciting with its rather long yardage of 6,890/6,554/6,076/5,106. This one has been the host of the Michigan Open for several years. The newest of the lot is the Stonehedge course. On rolling, wooded terrain, it reaches out 6,656/6,234/5,775/5,191 yards and again pars at 72.

RATES (EP) Villas: $125. Green fees: $20/$24, carts $22. Golf package: 2 nights/3 days (includes lodging in a villa, green fees), $299 per couple.

ARRIVAL Air: Kalamazoo. Car: I-94, exit 85.

HIDDEN VALLEY CLUB & RESORT
P.O. Box 556
Gaylord, MI 49735
(517) 732–5181

This resort is in the northern region of the Michigan peninsula. Each of the nine lodges has its own unique charm and European alpine decor. Both dining rooms in the Main Lodge offer outstanding views and a menu selection ranging from the lighter side to fine dining. There are also two lounges. While ties are not required, after 6 PM jackets are requested. They are able to handle meetings, conferences and banquet groups.

Hiking trails, a private lake, swimming in a heated pool, canoeing, fishing, four tennis courts, even a private wooded picnic area, are a few of the activities to be enjoyed.

Golf is played on the Hidden Valley Club course, a William H. Diddel design layout. Playing 6,305/6,115/5,591 yards, it pars at 71/73. There is a clubhouse and a very well stocked golf shop.

RATES (MAP) Rooms: $78/$89 per person. Green fees: $35/$45 including cart. Golf package: 2 nights/2 days (includes lodging, MAP, 2 rounds of golf, cart, taxes and gratuities), weekdays $325/$436; weekends $425/$525 per couple.

ARRIVAL Air: Detroit. Private aircraft: Oresgo Airport. Car: 1 mile east of Gaylord on M-32.

McGUIRE'S MOTOR LODGE & RESORT
Mackinaw Trail
Cadillac, MI 49601
(616) 775–9947
(800) 632–7302

On 320 acres overlooking Lake Cadillac, McGuire's now features 123 well appointed, air-conditioned guest rooms. The resort is well set up to handle modest-size meeting groups and can supply the audio/visual aids which may be required.

Dining in the Terrace Room with both a menu selection and, on Saturday evening, a smorgasbord may be followed by dancing in the Irish Pub, a charming place to unwind.

Added attractions include: a heated indoor pool, a sauna, whirlpool spa and two game rooms. Tennis is available on two outdoor courts with additional courts available in Cadillac. Across the street are a total of 14 racquetball courts along with a complete athletic club including weight rooms.

As for golf there are 27 holes: the Norway, a 9-hole affair playing 2,792 yards, parring at 36; and the Spruce course, stretching out 6,601/6,202/5,217 yards, with a par of 71. Professional, Bill Snider, and staff are on deck to assist.

RATES (EP) Rooms: $60/$95. Suites $170. Green fees: $30 including cart. Golf package: weekdays only 2 night/2 day (includes 2 breakfast, 1 dinner per person, green fees), $328 per couple.

ARRIVAL Air: Cadillac. Car: 1 mile south of Cadillac on Highway 131.

SCHUSS MOUNTAIN RESORT
Schuss Mountain Road
Mancelona, MI 49659
(616) 587–9162
(800) 632–7118

Long ago Chippewa Indian Chief Megissee and his people hunted abundant game, fished the trout streams, canoed the rivers and swam these beautiful blue lakes. The resort is on 2,200 acres of rolling, wooded hills within this beautiful setting. The focal point of the resort is the Schuss Village, composed of the Main Lodge, the Ivanhof Supper Club (a two-story restaurant), gift shops and the meeting center.

Accommodations in the Village Square consist of fully equipped condominiums. A short distance away can be found the Sudendorf Condos and Schuss Mountain Chalets with various sleeping arrangements of from two to six.

Dining is provided in two fine restaurants. The Ivanhof serves breakfast and lunch and, in the evening, transforms itself into the "Supper Club." And what a supper club it is, featuring the "Schus-sycats," 11 collegiate waiters and waitresses singing the hits of the 40's through the 80's.

For a change of pace you can arrange a luncheon cruise aboard the *Star of Charlevoix,* a custom-made dining vessel operating on Lake Charlevoix.

Just a few of the many activities available during summer include: an outdoor swimming pool, a six-court tennis complex, bicycling, volleyball and, on nearby Torch Lake, sailing, canoeing, snorkeling and wind-surfing.

While we are concerned with summer activities, I cannot completely pass over the outstanding facilities they provide in the winter. The Shanty Creek and Schuss Mountain resorts unite in offering their guests some of the finest skiing facilities found in the area.

Golf is played at the Schuss Mountain Golf Club, with the course stretching out a rather substantial 6,922/6,394/5,423 yards and parring at 72. An interesting affair, it presents large greens, tree-lined fairways, some strategic water holes and traps which seem to blend with the terrain.

RATES (EP) Village room: $105/$125. Sudendorf 1-bedroom condominiums: $145. Golf packages are available. Green fees: $42 including cart.

ARRIVAL Air: Traverse City. Private aircraft: Bellaire. Car: 6 miles west of Mancelona, on Highway 88.

SHANTY CREEK/SCHUSS MOUNTAIN RESORT
Shanty Creek Road
Bellaire, MI 49615
(616) 533–8621
(800) 632–7118

The Inn is located in the beautiful north-woods of Michigan and offers the best of both worlds. It has all the traditional amenities of a fine resort, along with an outstanding meeting/conference center, yet in a peaceful and picturesque atmosphere. While this is a difficult balance to attain, Shanty Creek has been successful.

Accommodations consist of rooms and suites in the Main Lodge, the Trapper Lodge, the Timberline Studio Apartments, as well as many one- to three-bedroom condominiums. Some accommodations are equipped with whirlpool baths and are about as well appointed and furnished as we have seen.

The only problem with dining here is deciding where to eat: the Main Dining Room, the pro shop Snack Bar, the Cafeteria or, located in the village, La Bodega Deli. The cozy Lounge offers top flight entertainment. (Jackets are required in the evening). Speaking of jackets, while it is pleasant during the day it can get nippy in the evening. I suggest you bring a warm jacket.

There are so many things to do here it is difficult to list them all. Fishing, tennis, golf, bicycling, bowling, horseback riding, water skiing on Torch Lake, canoeing, swimming (two indoor and two outdoor pools or the lake), racquetball, skeet shooting and a one-mile exercise course are a sample of the activities at your disposal. A resident tennis professional is available to assist with lessons or setting up tournaments on the four all-weather courts.

Golf is offered on the resort's Deskin course. A Bill Diddle design, it weighs in at 6,559/6,197/5,285 yards, parring at 72/74. This layout presents undulating fairways, 35 traps, as well as very tough greens, to keep your attention. It is fairly wide open and has water on only one hole.

The Legend, the newest course, is an Arnold Palmer design. Also parring at 72, it measures 6,764/6,269/5,801/4,943 yards. Many say this may well be Palmer's best effort. If you expect a flat country look think again. The first hole has a 175-foot drop from the tee area to the green while number five hole gives you a 180-foot elevation change.

Tee times can also be arranged at any of six different courses in the area including Schuss Mountain Resort in Mancelona (three miles away). There is a resident professional and staff available to assist in setting up tournaments or arranging lessons.

RATES (EP) Inn: $105/$125. 1-bedroom condo: $145. Green fees: $42 including cart; the Legend course, $70 including cart. Golf packages are available. Rates are for June-August.

ARRIVAL Air: Cherry Capital. Private aircraft: Antrim County Airport (5,000-foot surfaced and lighted, 2 miles) Car: from Mancelona take Route 88 west.

SUGAR LOAF RESORT
Route One
Cedar, MI 49621
(616) 228–5461
(800) 632–9802

Sugar Loaf Resort, nestled at the base of the mountain, is surrounded by rolling countryside, sparkling lakes and the peaceful beauty one expects from the Leelanau Peninsula.

Over 150 guest rooms are available in the lodge, with additional accommodations offered in the two- to four-bedroom townhouses.

Business and pleasure mix well here as the resort's meeting facilities can accommodate up to 600.

The Four Seasons Dining Room provides a spectacular view of the mountains with Lake Michigan beyond, while the Lobby Bar serves up nightly entertainment.

Their tennis complex features five outdoor courts, along with three swimming pools (one indoor, two outdoor), a weight room and a sauna. Of course, nearby Lake Michigan provides all manner of water activities as well.

Golf is served up on the Sugar Loaf Golf Club course which can be stretched out a fair 6,813/6,124/5,134 yards. The men's par is 72, ladies' is set at 74.

Their 8th hole will make a believer out of you: a 360-yard par-four, running between two ponds and featuring five traps between the ponds and the green. *It calls for a fast exit to the 19th hole.*

RATES (EP) Lodge rooms: $89. Townhouse: $145/$230. Green fees: $40, carts $24. Golf package: 1 night/1 day (includes lodging, MAP, 1 round of golf), $158 per couple. Rates are for July-August.

ARRIVAL Air: Traverse City. Private aircraft: 3,500-foot, lighted strip, located at the resort. Car: 18 miles northwest of Traverse City on Route 651.

SYLVAN RESORT
3962 Wilkinson Road
Gaylord, MI 49735
(517) 732–6711
(800) 444–6711

This year-round resort is centrally located in the upper part of the lower peninsula of Michigan. Accommodations range from 172 hotel rooms and suites to individual chalets with kitchenettes. Dining as well as nightly entertainment are served up in the Ale House Dining Room and Lounge.

The resort also has excellent meeting and conference facilities with rooms designed for small groups of from 25 to 90 and others set up to handle as many as 200 people

There are many enjoyable activities offered: indoor and outdoor swimming pools, an indoor and an outdoor whirlpool-spa, two saunas, exercise rooms, tennis courts, hiking trails, volleyball, putting greens and of course golf.

During the winter months you can add cross country skiing, ice skating, night cross country as well as downhill skiing (225-foot vertical drop, 11 slopes, a triple and double chair lift and rope tows).

The Treetop Links is a Robert Trent Jones, Sr. layout. With a par of 71, it plays 7,046/6,399/5,817/4,972 yards. The course is sited on undulating terrain with tree-lined fairways and some of the most interesting water hazards we have seen. While the wet stuff comes into play on only five holes the eighth green with its water setting will get your attention. It is a beautiful layout and, while not a back breaker, it will require your attention and patience. There is an excellent pro shop and a staff directed by head professional Rick Smith.

RATES (EP) Lodge rooms: $84/$135. 2-room suite: $170. Green fees: $55 including cart. Golf package: 1 night/1 day (includes Inn lodgings, MAP, cart, 1 round of golf, taxes), $228 per couple.

ARRIVAL Air: Mackinaw City (55 miles). Private aircraft: Otesego Country Airport. Car: from Lansing, travel State 27 intersecting I-75 approximately 170 miles north.

MINNESOTA

BIRCHMONT RUTTGER RESORT-O-TEL

530 Birchmont Beach Road
Bemidji, MN 56601
(218) 751–1630

This family-style resort is on the north shores of Lake Bemidji. Accommodations consist of rooms or suites in the main lodge, or one- to four-bedroom cottages with living room and fireplace. The resort can accommodate meeting groups of from 20 to 250. They have two separate dining rooms and cocktail lounges to handle such gatherings. The Lakefront dining room prepares its own pastries daily. *I defy you to pass on these.*

Children, as well as adults, will find the 1,600 feet of sandy beach, two heated pools, the playground, recreation rooms, paddle boats, kayaks, canoes, sailboats, water skiing, four tennis courts and the supervised recreation program a great deal of fun and all they can handle.

Golf can be played on two 18-hole courses: the Bemidji Town & Country Club, site of the annual Birchmont International Golf Tournament; or the Castle Highlands. The Bemidji T. & C. C. course measures 6,385/6,198/5,489 and pars at 72/74. The Castle Highlands, also an 18-hole layout, is seven miles away.

RATES (MAP) 1-bedroom housekeeping cottages: $59/$185 per person. Green fees: $20/$25, carts $22. EP plan is also available.

ARRIVAL Air: Bemidji. Car: 5 miles north of Bemidji on old U.S. 71.

BREEZY POINT RESORT

HCR 2 Box 70
Breezy Point, MN 56472
(218) 562–7811
MN (800) 432–3777
NAT (800) 328–2284

Breezy Point, on Pelican Lake not far from the Mississippi River, is only 140 miles north of the Minneapolis-St. Paul Airport. The 250-plus, guest accommodations range from Lodge Apartments, Pinewood Cabanas, and Executive Beach Houses, to Beachside

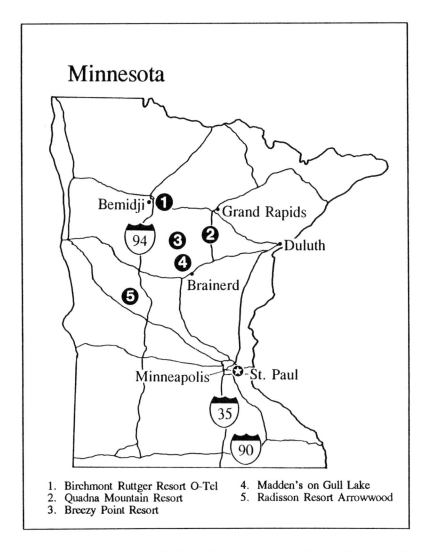

Minnesota

1. Birchmont Ruttger Resort O-Tel
2. Quadna Mountain Resort
3. Breezy Point Resort
4. Madden's on Gull Lake
5. Radisson Resort Arrowwood

Apartments. Recently added to this mix are 32 Point Place condominiums ranging from one- to two-bedroom units. All units feature a fully equipped kitchen, dishwasher, micro oven, and a washer/dryer. A nice extra—the resort can arrange baby sitting service.

The Breezy Point Center, with 18,000 square feet of space, including 14 break-out rooms, is capable of handling meeting groups of 750 banquet-style.

Dining facilities include the Marina Restaurant, overlooking Breezy Bay, the Captain's Cove at the Breezy Center, and Charlie's, located just minutes outside the main gate, featuring live entertainment, steaks and barbecued ribs.

Tennis on four Laykold courts with a professional on deck to assist, swimming in indoor and outdoor pools, horseback riding from stables nearby and bicycling are a few of the activities at your disposal. If you walk down to their marina you can add: fishing, canoeing, powerboating, and sailing.

Golf is played on the Breezy Point course. Called "Traditional," it plays 5,192/5,127 with a par of 68/72. Very good news: a championship 18-hole layout came into play in 1989. Named "Excellence," it has a yardage of 6,601/6,602/5,718 with a par of 72 / 76. The resort also provides a golf shop and a driving range.

RATES (EP) 1-bedroom unit: $55/$99/$169. Green fees: $23, carts $22. Rates are for the summer season. There are many different package plans available.

ARRIVAL Air: Minneapolis-St. Paul. Private aircraft and some commercial: Brainerd Airport. Car: I-94 north to Monticello; take a right to Highway 371. Turn left (north) on 371 going beyond Brainerd to Pequot Lakes. At this point take a right (east) and continue on to resort.

MADDEN'S ON GULL LAKE
Box 387
Brainerd, MN 56401
(218) 829–2811
MN (800) 642–5363
NAT (800) 233–2934

They laugh now, but they certainly did not on opening night, May 29, 1942, when Madden's had a crowd of two guests for the night. From that inauspicious beginning, three resorts now thrive: Madden Lodge, where it all began; Madden Inn & Golf Club, with its view of Gull Lake; and Madden Pine Portage, perched on a pine-clad ridge near the waters of Wilson Bay.

Dining facilities include The Prime Rib Room, the Coffee Shop and the O'Madden Pub, with dancing offered each Saturday evening in the Wanigan Room. In 1986 the resort completed a new conference center allowing them to handle meeting groups of 750 theater- or 450 schoolroom-style.

Tennis can be played under the direction of a tennis professional. The resort has a tennis shop and also croquet facilities.

A few of the activities possible include: indoor and outdoor swimming pools, saunas, whirlpools, game rooms and, in season, a children's program. The lake offers the opportunity for sailing, water skiing and fishing or—relaxing on one of the three lovely beaches.

Golf is played on one regulation 18-hole course, an executive layout, as well as a par-three nine-hole affair. Recently having undergone extensive renovation, the Pine Beach East course plays 5,920/5,526 yards and pars at 72. The Pine Beach West, an executive layout, measures 5,014/4,884 with a par of 67/69.

RATES (EP) Inn room: $75/$95. Inn cottage: (EP) $89/$99. Villas: $105/$135. MAP plan is also available. Package plans including golf, tennis and children's supervised programs are available. Green fees: $25, carts $22. Rates are for July-August.

ARRIVAL Air: Brainerd. Private aircraft: East Gull Lake. Car: from Brainerd, 4.5 miles on 371, left on 77 for 7.5 miles.

QUADNA MOUNTAIN RESORT
100 Quadna Road
Hill City, MN 55748
(218) 697–8444
(800) 422–6649

Quadna is a Chippewa word meaning "Lake at the Foot of the Mountains." The name only begins to describe the beauty and solitude of this northwoods resort, with its blend of rustic atmosphere, comfort and modern living. Accommodations vary from a full-service camp ground, an economical roadside inn, a massive, rustic Main Lodge, to townhouses and villas fully equipped for housekeeping with dishwasher and fireplaces. They have excellent meeting facilities and can handle groups of from 10 to 500.

You can dine in the Harvester Restaurant overlooking Hill Lake with nightly dancing and entertainment available. Then there is the bar named the "Loose Moose Saloon" *I didn't name it, they did.*

Starting in November, snowmaking equipment assures outstanding conditions for use of the 15 varied slopes, four-person chair lifts and 500 miles of groomed snowmobile trails. An indoor swimming pool and saunas complete the list of possible activities. During summer, the use of four outdoor tennis courts, two outdoor swimming pools, hunting, fishing, canoeing, paddleboating, water skiing and lawn games add to the fun.

There is a recreational director in charge of golf and tennis. The golf course is actually a nine-hole layout with a total (if played twice) of 6,130 yards and a par of 70. A second nine is now in the planning stage.

RATES (EP) Lodge: $70. Motel: $50. Villas: $100/$150. Townhouses: (1 bedroom) $115. Green fees: $20 (18 holes), carts $22.

ARRIVAL Air: Duluth (60 miles). Car: U.S. 169 north, turn in at Quadna Motel.

RADISSON RESORT ARROWWOOD
P.O. Box 639
Alexandria, MN 56308
(612) 762–1124
(800) 333–3333

Some 130 miles northwest of the twin cities, the Arrowwood Resort enjoys the setting and beauty of rolling grassland and gentle forests. The lodgings consist of 170 rooms, including special feature rooms, some with lake views, others overlooking the golf course. They also provide two floors of meeting rooms and can accommodate groups of 15 to 750.

The dining room, which overlooks the lake, specializes in fish delicacies and steaks.

While we are concerned with golf and summer activities, they also have a winter program.

Due to the proximity of Lake Darling, they are able to provide sailing, motor boats, canoes and swimming. Tennis is played on four courts, with horseback riding, and a variety of indoor amenities such as a heated pool, whirlpools and saunas also available.

Golf is on an executive layout. Located adjacent to the lake, it plays 5,350 yards with a par of 68.

RATES (EP) Rooms: $115/$140. Rates are for July-September.

ARRIVAL Air: Alexandria Airport (5 miles). Car: from Minneapolis, off I-94 (130 miles).

MISSOURI

THE LAKE OF THE OZARKS

The lure of The Lake of the Ozarks with its hundreds of coves and inlets, together with its proximity to both Kansas City and St. Louis, has made this area a favorite year-round recreational site. First developed with the construction of Bagnell Dam on the Osage River in 1933, the 140-mile-long lake has 1,400 miles of shoreline. With its tree-studded rolling terrain bordering the lake it provides all manner of water activity. While already offering a perfect location for resorts, the setting was further enhanced by the construction of seven golf courses.

Three resorts, Dogwood Hills, the Lodge of the Four Seasons and Marriott's Tan-Tar-A, are described on the following pages.

DOGWOOD HILLS GOLF CLUB & RESORT INN
Route 1 Box 219 State Road KK
Osage Beach, MO 65065
(314) 348–1735
(800) 528–1234

Accommodations consist of 45 rooms overlooking the golf course. There are also Fairway Villas with from one to four bedrooms, complete with fully equipped kitchens, fireplaces, living and dining rooms.

Because of the location, adjacent to the lake, they are able to offer their guests a variety of things to do, including fishing, boating, swimming in the lake or in their own heated pool and use of a Jacuzzi.

The Dogwood Hills Golf Course shows a yardage of 6,105/5,893/5,262, parring at 71/73. The restaurant and lounge are in the clubhouse. They offer not only a driving range but a practice sand trap—something not found on many courses.

RATES (EP) Rooms: $74/$79. Villas (2 bedrooms) $176. Green fees: $20/$23, carts $22. Golf package: 2 nights/3 days (includes lodging, 3 days green fees, cart for 36 holes, club storage, one night dinner), $459 per couple.

ARRIVAL Air: Lee C. Fine Airport (25 minutes).

THE LODGE OF THE FOUR SEASONS
Lake Road HH
Lake Ozark, MO 65049
(314) 365–3000
MO (800) 843–3010
NAT (800) 843–5253

The Lodge of the Four Seasons is tucked away in a unique show-case of Japanese gardens and cascading waterfalls—truly a beautiful setting. The resort offers a selection of accommodations ranging from lakeside rooms and suites, to water edge-condominiums and villas. The Lodge is well equipped to handle meeting groups with various room capacities ranging from 10 to 1,500.

Dining at the award-winning Four Seasons is an exceptional treat. The Toledo Room presents French cuisine while HK's, overlooking the golf course, has a relaxed country-club atmosphere. If that is not enough there is the Fish Market or Roseberry's Restaurant. Together they can destroy your will to stay trim. I almost forgot—there is another restaurant at the Racquet Club.

You may wish to take advantage of the complete health spa program or swimming in any or all of the five indoor and outdoor pools. If that does not do it, perhaps water skiing, horseback riding, sailing, fishing, trap shooting, or bowling will get you back in shape—it's all available.

The new Racquet Club, a bit over a mile away, offers 13 outdoor and four indoor tennis courts as well as two racquetball courts. It is the home of the famous Dennis Van der Meer Tennis University and is rated one of the top 50 tennis resort facilities in the United States. There is also a lap swim pool and a health assessment program.

Robert Trent Jones, Sr, who designed the Four Seasons USA Driftwood Golf Course, used every inch of Mother Nature's work to mold it into a thing of beauty and challenge. With a par of 71, it plays 6,346/5,772/5,289 yards. Shortly after its opening in 1974, the 13th hole was recognized as the apex of the course. It is bisected by an inlet of the lake, and you will need all the cunning (or skill) you possess to avoid the water and the five hungry traps guarding the green.

When we played it in the spring of the year, the dogwoods were in bloom—combining the views of the lake, trees and streams. We had not only a most enjoyable round but a difficult time keeping our minds on the game.

Missouri

1. Dogwood Hills Golf Club & Resort Inn
   The Lodge of the Four Seasons
   Marriott's Tan-Tar-A Resort

A PGA professional, Jack Coyle and staff, are ready to assist.

RATES (EP) Rooms: $94/$144. Condominiums: $140/$290. Green fees: $33/$35, carts $22. Golf package: (EP) 2 night/2 day (includes standard room, green fees, cart club storage), weekdays $318, weekends $346 per couple. Rates are for June-August.

ARRIVAL Air: Jefferson City. Car: U.S. 54 to Bagnell Dam, exit to Lake Road HH, follow to resort.

MARRIOTT'S TAN-TAR-A RESORT
State Road KK
Osage Beach, MO 65065
(314) 348–3131
Limited area (800) 392–5304
NAT (800) 228–9290

In 1977, Marriott purchased this magnificently sited resort and began extensive renovations. Spending in excess of $17 million, they transformed it into an outstanding 1000-room facility (including villas). Its sophisticated yet casual atmosphere, complemented by its rustic decor, blends well with the natural setting.

Accommodations consist of rooms or suites in the hotel, as well as villas or "estate"-style homes. The majority of the villas feature fully equipped kitchens and range from one to five bedrooms. The resort, with its convention center and 47 separate break-out rooms, is well qualified to handle meeting groups of 20 to 3,000. A baby sitting service is also available.

For dining, there are eight different locations from which to choose. To name a few: the Cliff Room; the Windrose, at the marina (closed in the winter); the Happy House; the Oaks for casual dining; and at the golf course, the Grille. Market Lane, one floor above the lobby, offers various shops and boutiques. The selection ranges from cheeses and sausages to gifts, souvenirs, sports equipment, and designer clothing.

For recreation, there is tennis on six outdoor and two indoor courts under the direction of a professional staff. There are also four indoor racquetball courts, five swimming pools, bowling and a health spa with all of the associated amenities.

You have a choice of several different types of boats to rent, ranging from waterskiing or trolling boats, to canoes. A tip—fishing in this lake provides a shot at some very feisty bass.

The Oaks golf course, a beautifully sculptured layout designed by Van Hagge and Bruce Devlin, had some severe problems to overcome: rocky terrain, little or no top soil and an ineffective means of irrigation. But all of these problems have been corrected. The Oaks 18 reaches out a respectable 6,442/5,952/5,329/3,943 yards and pars at 71. Accuracy rather than distance is the prime requirement on this layout. Watch the seventh hole, a par-three, from an elevated tee. Looking down, all you can see is water with the green guarded by three sand traps.

The resort has a well run and well stocked pro shop, complete with restaurant, lounge and locker rooms.

Since our visit, a third nine, the Hidden Lakes, has been put together. It plays 3,015/2,705 yards with a par of 35 from the men's tees and 2,232 yards parring at 36 for the ladies. It also has its own pro shop.

RATES (EP) Rooms: $125/$145. Suites: $205/$235. Green fees: $30, carts $28. Golf package: 2 nights/3 days (includes lodging, green fees, cart and club storage), $435 per couple.

ARRIVAL Air: Lee C. Fine Airport (20 minutes). Private aircraft: Grand Glaize. Car: from Kansas City, I-70 to Route 5, to Camdenton. East on Highway 54, 10 miles to Lake Road KK, then a left, drive 2 miles.

MONTANA

BIG SKY
P.O. Box 1
Big Sky, MT 59716
(406) 995–4211
MT (800) 824–7767
NAT (800) 548–4486

Long a dream of the late Chet Huntley, Big Sky Resort opened in 1974. Unfortunately, just three days prior the opening, he was taken by cancer. His dream envisioned creating an outstanding resort while being sure it remained in harmony with the fabulous natural environment. Although a tall order, it was accomplished.

The drive to this area, 44 miles from Bozeman, is something you will long recall. The highway winds its way along the Gallatin River as it tumbles down from Lone Mountain (11,166 feet) and the high country. You may occasionally spot elk or moose and pools which cry to be fished. Judged by any standards, this must be considered magnificent country. Big Sky also happens to be only 48 miles north of West Yellowstone National Park. The entire complex is actually spread over a wide mountain valley with Meadow Village at the lower end. Seven miles further up the valley, at the base of Lone Mountain, is the Huntley Lodge.

Accommodations consist of 204 rooms in the main lodge, plus over 194 condominiums, featuring all electric kitchens and fireplaces, with many sporting private Jacuzzis. They have recently added a seven story condominium complex. Adjacent to the Huntly Lodge, each unit is fully equipped for housekeeping. A very nice extra located at the lodge is a small guest laundry.

While the Huntley Lodge provides two outstanding restaurants and a saloon (Chet's Bar), the resort complex offers an additional selection of places to eat as well as music for dancing. The new convention center is capable of handling groups of up to 750 banquet-style and can provide all of the audio/visual aids which might be required.

A few of the activities which can be enjoyed include: swimming pools, saunas, Jacuzzis, a health club, live entertainment, tennis courts, hayrides, and horseback riding. Of course there is also

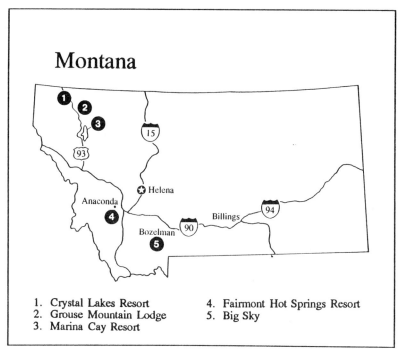

Montana

○ Helena

Anaconda

Billings

Bozelman

1. Crystal Lakes Resort
2. Grouse Mountain Lodge
3. Marina Cay Resort

4. Fairmont Hot Springs Resort
5. Big Sky

stream and lake fishing as well as white water rafting. The Adventures Big Sky Company offers a choice of half- or full-day trips on the Yellowstone, the Madison or the Gallatin Rivers. There are even two- or three-day trips featuring fishing as well as "rafting". You can also arrange (for the less adventurous) a scenic float trip on calmer stretches of the Gallatin—my kind of trip.

To give you some idea of the size and complexity of the ski facilities: there are 35 miles of slopes, four-passenger gondola lifts, as well as double and triple chair lifts. Located at the base of the ski area are seven restaurants, two ski rental and repair shops, clothing stores, a drug store and several gift shops. Big Sky offers an International Ski School staffed by highly qualified ski instructors gathered from the United States and Europe.

Golf is played on the Arnold Palmer designed 18-hole course located in the Meadow Village area. Parring at 72, this layout stretches 6,748/6,115/5,374 yards. The altitude of some 6,500 feet above sea level creates some interesting conditions for play. While relatively flat and open it has mountain streams and ponds coming into contention on six holes.

RATES (EP) Huntley Lodge, including breakfast: $85/$106. Condominium villas: 1–3 bedrooms $75/$265. Green fees: $24, carts $20. Golf packages are available.

ARRIVAL Air: Bozeman. Car: Route 191. South from Bozeman (44 miles), then turn right at the Conoco station.

CRYSTAL LAKES RESORT
P.O. Box 255
Fortine, MT 59918
(406) 882–4455

The Crystal Lakes Resort is in northern Montana. On 1,400 acres, adjacent to Crystal Lake and with the Canadian Rockies as a backdrop, it most certainly enjoys a magnificent setting. Accommodations consist of approximately 40 condominiums and townhouses. Ranging from one to two bedroom, each is fully equipped for housekeeping. Each contains a washer dryer, fireplace and dining area.

Meeting groups of up to 120 can be accommodated. Dining facilities consist of the Crystal Lakes Dining Room and lounge as well as a snack bar at the golf course.

Tennis, volleyball, hiking, lake fishing and, of course, golf are a few of the activities. The Crystal Lakes course, opening in 1987, plays 6,500/6,202/5,643 yards and pars at 71/72. Extremely well trapped and tree-lined it takes full advantage of the general rolling terrain. There is a professional staff available to assist as well as a fully stocked golf shop.

RATES (EP) Studio: $50. Condominiums: $125. Green fees: $25, carts $20.

ARRIVAL Air: Glazier International (Kalispell 48 miles). Private aircraft: 5,200-foot paved strip located on property.

FAIRMONT HOT SPRINGS RESORT
Anaconda, MT 59711
(406) 797–3241
MT (800) 332–3272
NAT (800) 443–2381

Fairmont Hot Springs is nestled at the foot of the Pintlar range. The resort has 151 guest rooms, and saunas to help wipe out the travel aches, *or perhaps a slight libation in the bar or lounge will do the trick.*

Dining is provided in either the main dining room or in the coffee shop. The resort is well set up to handle meeting groups from 20 to 300. Fairmont is open year-round and also has excellent winter facilities.

During summer there is a wide choice of activities: trail riding (with experienced guides), fishing for some of the fightingest brook, brown, rainbow and native cutthroat trout found anywhere, or swimming in four pools. There are two indoor and two larger than Olympic-size pools with the mineral waters maintained at a temperature ranging from 80 to 108 degrees.

Golf is played on a 6,732-yard, par-72 course. The women's tees are set at a long 6,193 yards, parring at 74. They must grow'em healthy in this area as that is a long reach for ladies. There is a full-line pro shop and snack bar.

Pro shop manager Sparky McClean is on deck to sort things out.

RATES (EP) Rooms: $65. Rates include use of mineral water pools and saunas. Green fees: $22, carts $20.

ARRIVAL Air: Butte (15 miles). Car: I-90 exit 211 south approximately 3 miles.

GROUSE MOUNTAIN LODGE
1205 Highway 93W
Whitefish, MT 59937
(406) 862–3000
MT (800) 621–1802
NAT (800) 321–8822

Opening in mid-1984 Grouse Mountain Lodge is just 27 miles from Glacier National Park. On seven acres, the setting is in one of the most beautiful parts of Montana.

The resort features 145 guest rooms plus meeting rooms with a capacity for 300. Some special features include ten loft rooms with kitchenettes, two guest laundry facilities, a card room, a video arcade room and a gift/sundry shop.

Dining is available in the 100-seat Logan's Bar and Grill. While Whitefish is only one mile away and provides a wide selection of excellent restaurants, Logan's is, in our opinion, one of the better choices.

The Lodge has an indoor swimming pool and sauna, an indoor and two outdoor spas, with tennis available across the road.

Of possible interest to fishing buffs, the Lodge can arrange a fishing package including a one-day float on the North Fork of the Flathead. White water rafting is also available.

Only eight miles from the fabulous ski area of Big Mountain, and with transportation provided by the Lodge, many other activities open up during the winter months.

Golf is played on the 27-hole Whitefish Lake Golf Club. The Woods/Mountain nines reach out for a total of 6,548/6,322/5,593 yards with a par of 72/73.

The Mountain/Lake combination weighs in at 6,458/6,200/5,489 yards, also parring at 72/73; while the Woods/Lake layout plays 6,460/6,302/5,590 yards and pars at 72.

While not exhibiting extremely narrow or tight fairways these layouts are tree-lined and bring water into play on a total of only six holes.

The course and pro shop (including a small restaurant) are directly across the road from The Grouse Mountain Lodge. The PGA Head Professional is Mike Dowaliby.

RATES (EP) Rooms: $80. Loft-kitchenette units: $100. Deluxe suites: $125. Green fees: $25, carts $18. There are golf packages available. Rates are for May 30-September 7th.

ARRIVAL Air: Glacier International (20 minutes with pickup by Lodge). Car: one mile west of Whitefish on Highway 93W.

MARINA CAY RESORT
P.O. Box 663
Bigfork, MT 59911
(406) 837–5861
(800) 433–6516

Although the great majority of Montana is truly beautiful, this portion—the Flathead Lake area—has few equals in the United States.

Marina Cay offers nicely appointed vacation mini/suites with wet-bar or condominium suites including fully equipped kitchens. They are, indeed, a far cry from the traditional "rustic" lakeside retreats. The condominium suites, ranging from one to three bedrooms, have been professionally decorated and are fully equipped for housekeeping. There are also laundry facilities available.

A few steps from your lodging is the Bay Club, offering a smorgasbord of amenities: the lounge and restaurant, the swimming pool and, nearby, the marina. While the resort is outstanding, we unfortunately found the restaurant much less than outstanding and the service even worse. We have since been informed that the restaurant is under new management and the problems have been corrected.

The "Village" (a short walk away), offers a variety of shops, galleries and restaurants. If you enjoy excellent service and outstanding food, the Big Fork Inn in the Village is a must. Another rather quaint restaurant, in an old bank building, is the Backstage Bar & Grill.

The resort property is on Bigfork Bay, a delightful and picturesque inlet of scenic Flathead Lake, reputedly the largest fresh water lake west of the Mississippi. I understand the fishing is something else here. During the summer months, all manner of water sports are supported by the resort's full service marina. Boating activities range from water skiing and windsurfing, to sunset cruises aboard the *Red Eagle*. The cruise boat, *Far West,* is also available for convention groups of up to 200. In addition trips on the *Questa,* a world-class 51-foot racing sloop, may also be arranged.

During the winter months some of the best downhill skiing to be found anywhere is at nearby Big Mountain. There are also many miles of cross country ski trails.

Less than two miles away is the Eagle Bend Golf Club. A public course, it is open to play by guests of the Marina Cay Resort. Designed by William Hull & Associates this beautifully manicured layout plays 6,758/6,237/5,398 yards and pars at 72. A well trapped layout, with aspen, birch and pine trees becoming an occasional nuisance, it brings water into play on eight holes.

The very new clubhouse, which equals many of the more luxurious private club layouts, sports an excellent restaurant, lounge and pro shop.

RATES (EP) Mini-Suites: (bedroom and sitting room) $73. 1-bedroom condo/suite: $140. Green fees: $28, carts $25. Rates are mid-July to late-August.

ARRIVAL Air: Kalispell (15 miles). Car: U.S. 93 south to the intersection of State Road 82. Turn east to Bigfork.

NEVADA

DESERT INN HOTEL & CASINO
3145 Las Vegas Boulevard South
Las Vegas, NV 89109
(702) 733-4444
(800) 634-6906

It is awfully tough to keep your mind on golf in Las Vegas. While you may be losing the farm on the course, your mind keeps reverting to all that action going on back in the casinos, where you could well be winning a newer and bigger farm. *Of course you could become one of those unfortunate souls who arrives in a $30,000 car and returns home in a $300,000 bus.*

The Desert Inn is a beautiful high-rise structure offering some of the finest cuisine to be found in the area: La Promenade off the lobby, the Monte Carlo Room offering French gourmet dining, Portofino, featuring Northern Italian fare, and the lavish Crystal Room presenting some of the top names in show business. A recent addition is Ho Wan featuring Chinese Mandarin, Szechuan and Cantonese cuisine. There is also the grill room at the country club.

Accommodations are outstanding. Some rooms are equipped with Hydrowhirl baths and wet bars. The resort has recently undergone a multi-million dollar renovation and the rooms have been completely redone. The meeting facilities are excellent with a capacity for groups from 10 to over 900.

In addition to five lighted tennis courts there is also an Olympic-size swimming pool and 10 outdoor Hydrowhirl pools. A health spa, completed in 1985, added a new dimension to the Inn. It is some 16,000 square feet, with men's and women's facilities in the form of a gym, hydrotherapy and thermotherapy pools, herbal wraps, massage and five additional tennis courts.

Golf is served up on the resort's own course. It is, by the way, the home of the Las Vegas Panasonic and the Las Vegas Senior Classic. Stretching out a rather awesome 7,111/6,633/5,809 yards, it pars at 72.

The greens, which are fairly large (many rebuilt and improved) are very well guarded by bunkers. Tree-lined fairways and water

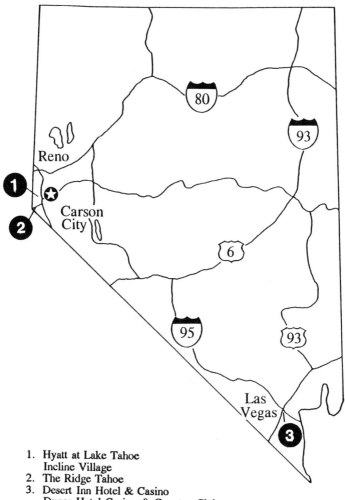

Nevada

1. Hyatt at Lake Tahoe
   Incline Village
2. The Ridge Tahoe
3. Desert Inn Hotel & Casino
   Dunes Hotel Casino & Country Club
   Showboat Hotel & Country Club
   Tropicana Resort & Casino

coming into play on six holes combine to produce a lush and beautiful desert layout.

RATES (EP) Rooms: $90/$175. Suites: $250/$750. Green fees: $75/$100, including cart. Due to the extreme summer heat in this area, golf is best played in the spring or fall.

ARRIVAL Air: Las Vegas (10 minutes from the airport).

DUNES HOTEL CASINO & COUNTRY CLUB
3650 Las Vegas Boulevard South
Las Vegas, NV 89109
(702) 737–4110
NAT & CANADIAN (800) 777–7777

I am not sure why the resorts in Las Vegas insist on building multi-storied hotels when they have millions of acres in the Nevada desert to work with, but they do. The Dunes is another one. It happens to be, however, one of the best we have seen, providing enough eating places to accommodate a medium-sized city. Accommodations consist of 1200 guest rooms divided between the twin towers and the remodeled Garden Rooms.

The Top of the Dunes offers dining, entertainment, and dancing. The restaurants include: the Dome of The Sea for a superb selection of seafoods; the Chinese Kitchen serving Cantonese dishes; the Terrace Buffet; the Sultan's Table; and the Dunes Casino Theater presenting lavish shows nightly. *I may well have missed a few restaurants, but then I probably spent too much time in the casino.*

At present there are five tennis courts (two lighted), a health club and Solaria (facilities for men and women) on the 24th floor, with a whirlpool, gym, steam, sauna and massage facilities. Plans are underway for an entire sports complex, including many more tennis courts and an enlarged health/exercise facility.

The Dunes Golf Course, parring at 72, shows a massive mileage of 7,240/6,571/5,982 yards. While flat, it does provide more than its share of surprises with water, trees and bunkers. There is a full-line pro shop and clubhouse.

RATES (EP) Rooms: $55/$85. Suites: $230/$250. Green fees: $60/$72, including cart and club storage. Due to summer heat the best time for golf is spring and fall.

ARRIVAL Air: Las Vegas (10 minutes).

HYATT AT LAKE TAHOE
P.O. Box 3239
Country Club Dr. & Lakeshore Rd.
Incline Village, NV 89450
(702) 831–1111
(800) 233–1234

The High Sierras with their towering pines are the setting for this beautiful hotel. Accommodations consist of 460 guest rooms and suites. Some of the suites are equipped with fireplaces.

They offer many possible activities: water skiing, boating and use of the beach (no swimming, unless you have polar bear blood, as Lake Tahoe is deep and very, very cold), three tennis courts (a total of 42 nearby), an indoor health spa, an outdoor heated pool and, located nearby, horseback riding.

Dining facilities include: Hugo's Rotisserie, Alpine Jack's or The Pines. The Hyatt Lake Casino is open 24 hours—after all this is Nevada.

Golf can be played on the two Robert Trent Jones courses at Incline Village, One is an executive par-58, playing 3,450/2,800 yards. Do not let the mileage fool you as this little stinker is not easy and can easily embarrass you. The second course is a par-72 championship layout, playing 6,910/6,446/5,327 yards. For a more complete description of these courses, refer to "Incline Village" in this book.

RATES (EP) Rooms: $159/$249. Suites: 1-bedroom $400. Villas: $650. Green fees: $75, including cart. Executive course: $40, including cart.

ARRIVAL Air: Reno. Car: U.S. 395, south of Reno, turn off southwest on Highway 431.

INCLINE VILLAGE
c/o B.R.A.T Reality Co.
P.O. Box 7107
Incline Village, NV 89450
(702) 831–3318
(800) 468–2463 Ext BRAT

This resort area, established in 1960 on the north shores of Lake Tahoe 39 miles from Reno, has a number of homes, condominiums and several casino/hotel complexes. The area not only provides outstanding beauty and clear mountain air, but offers a variety of activities: horseback riding, backpacking, tennis and the full gamut of water sports on Lake Tahoe. A word of warning: *THIS IS ONE EXTREMELY COLD LAKE.*

There are two courses adjacent to Incline Village which are well worth playing. Surprisingly enough, one is an executive par-58, 3,450/2,800 yard course. *It is absolutely not a pushover.* Negotiating very rugged terrain, this Robert Trent Jones design has embarrassed some very fine golfers looking for an easy conquest. The Championship golf course, also a Jones design, plays 6,910/6,448/5,327 yards and pars at 72. With mean fairway traps, a stream seemingly without a home as it wanders all over the place, some ponds and towering pines, this is a fun but very difficult layout.

Since there are so many different choices of accommodations it is not possible to quote exact rates. One-bedroom condos range from $120 to $175. Contact the above address for reservations. If using the toll free number you must ask for the B.R.A.T. Realty Company extension. Green fees: Incline Championship Course, $75 including cart; Executive Course, $40 including cart.

ARRIVAL Air: Reno. Car: U.S. 395, south of Reno, turn off southwest on Highway 431.

THE RIDGE TAHOE
P.O. Box 5790
Stateline, NV 89449
(702) 588–3553
(800) 648–3391

Accommodations at the Ridge Tahoe consist of suites set up to handle from two to six people. They feature a fireplace, wet bar, a stereo/television center, a fully equipped kitchen and gas barbecue on the patio deck.

The multi-million dollar, "Five Star Award" Ridge Club is the centerpiece for The Ridge Tahoe. It is staffed with health fitness professionals and backed by the latest in equipment. While this is basically a time-share operation there are a few rentals available. They are currently building more units which should free things up a bit.

Swimming in the indoor/outdoor pool, racquetball, aerobics, steam and sauna rooms, tennis indoor or out, are but a few of the activities available. Sailing and fishing in Lake Tahoe during the summer as well as skiing, tobogganing and sleigh rides in the winter, are additional activities to be enjoyed.

If you prefer dining out, there is the Ridge Tahoe Restaurant and the piano lounge, or you can elect to visit Stateline, just six miles away, for an evening of casino action. The Ridge is also well set up to handle group meetings or conventions.

Golf can be played on the Edgewood Lake Tahoe Golf Course. This beautiful layout with towering pines and more water than you might like, plays at 7,725 yards (gold,masochist tees). From the tee settings used by earthlings the yardage is 7,030/6,444/5,667 with a par of 72/73. From time to time it can be a bit difficult to secure desirable tee times. There are, however, several other courses in the area.

RATES (EP) Hotel room: $115. Studio: $130. 1-bedroom suite: $170. 2-bedroom suites: $265. Green fees: $60, including cart. Golf packages are available.

ARRIVAL Air: Reno International (65 miles away) or Lake Tahoe Airport (11 miles away and served by Aircal). Car: from Stateline take Highway 50 to Kingsbury Grade. Turn right (east) and travel for 3 miles to Tramway. Take Tramway heading south to Quaking Aspen Lane. Turn left onto Quaking Aspen Lane which will take you to the entrance gates of Ridge Tahoe.

SHOWBOAT HOTEL & COUNTRY CLUB
2800 East Fremont Street
Las Vegas, NV 89104
(702) 385–9123
(800) 826–2800

The Showboat is a large hotel complex with 500 rooms, a meeting capacity from 25 to over 3,000 people, a 106-lane bowling facility (THE LARGEST SUCH FACILITY IN THE U.S.). Of course it has a great deal more to offer: casino gambling, professional boxing and wrestling events held in the 45,000-square-foot arena with a seating capacity of 4,500. The various dining areas and the coffee shop offer a wide selection of dishes ranging from foreign to American cuisine.

The Showboat Country Club golf course is in Green Valley, about eight miles away, with regular transportation provided from the hotel. Parring at 72, this layout measures 7,149/6,389/5,524 yards.

The clubhouse sports an Olympic-size swimming pool, two tennis courts, a complete pro shop, coffee shop and a men's sauna.

RATES (EP) Rooms: $45/$55/$60 per couple. Suites: $90/$120. Green fees: $55 including cart.

ARRIVAL Air: Las Vegas.

TROPICANA RESORT & CASINO
3801 Las Vegas Boulevard
Las Vegas, NV
(706) 739–2222
(800) 634–4000

Sprawling across 137 acres of Nevada desert, this resort has been turned into a lush tropical setting. With the completion of the second tower in 1986 the hotel offers 1900 rooms, including 500 low-rise terrace rooms with spectacular views of the inner gardens. There are three large swimming pools, one of which is among the largest in the world, joined by 30 water falls, various lagoons and a huge water slide.

The resort now offers a selection of eight restaurants with the variety of cuisine ranging from Oriental to American and everything in between. The Tropicana, well known for its lavish shows, is probably most famous for its "Folies Bergere" revue presenting one of the finest chorus lines in Las Vegas. They also rank as one of the better equipped hotels in the country to handle meetings or conventions, with over 105,000 square feet of space set aside for exhibit or convention activity.

Because of the topography, most of the desert golf courses are flat and, therefore, depend on monster yardage and/or lots of water to spice up the action. While there is some water on the Tropicana Country Club course (five holes), it is oriented to finesse rather then length. The Tropicana course plays 6,481/6,109/5,787 yards with a par of 70/72. It is a golf course which will make you think, but should not destroy you. Again, due to the climate, golf is best enjoyed in the spring and fall.

RATES (EP) Rooms: $49/$85. Tower rooms: $99/$129. Suites: 1 bedroom $225. Green fees: $60—including cart. Golf package are available.

ARRIVAL Air: Las Vegas Airport—about a mile away.

NEW MEXICO

ANGEL FIRE
P.O. Drawer B
Angel Fire, NM 87710
(505) 377–6401
(800) 633–7463

Moreno Valley, almost 35 miles long, is the home of two magnificent lakes: Eagle Nest, in the center of the valley, and Monte Verde Lake at the 22,000-acre Angel Fire resort. This valley is, by the way, a little over 8,000 feet above sea level. Lodgings are available at the 157-room Legend Hotel. The older Starfire Lodge has been converted to a time-share arrangement. There are also fully equipped condominiums (approximately 200), featuring dining and living rooms and kitchens.

The resort can host meeting groups of up to 250 people, theater-style.

A word of warning, while the days are bright and warm, the evenings can get cool. Bring jackets or sweaters.

Aside from golf there is much to do here: tennis, swimming (indoor pool) and horseback riding. If you have never visited Taos (26 miles away), by all means make the effort. It is enchanting. Perhaps a little trout fishing would be just the thing, or sailing or paddle-boating might be more to your liking.

Golf is served up on the resort's own layout of 6,624/6,349/5,356 yards and parring at 72. This course introduces you to water on 10 holes, very hilly terrain and trees. And then more trees. If you should be an early morning addict, you may well run across the added distraction of elk.

Keep in mind, at 8,000 feet you have not gotten better, the ball just flies farther. Should you get too excited about your game, the resident professional, Chris Stewart, will bring you back to reality.

RATES (EP) Lodge rooms: $60. Condominiums: $70. Green fees: $35, carts $20. Golf package: 2 nights/2 days (includes lodging, green fees, cart), lodge room $198 per couple, condominium $234 per couple. Rates are for summer season July-September.

ARRIVAL Air: Albuquerque (150 miles). Private aircraft: Angel Fire 8,900 foot paved runway. Car: Route 64 to New Mexico State Highway 434.

DOUBLE EAGLE COUNTRY CLUB & RESORT
10035 Country Club Lane NW
Albuquerque, NM 87114
(505) 898–0960

This is a small 12-room lodge 11 miles northwest of Albuquerque. As a guest of the lodge, you are considered a "Guest Member" of the beautiful Paradise Hills Country Club. If you wish to charge back to your club, be sure to bring a "Letter of Good Standing" from your club manager. The clubhouse provides a dining room, swimming pool, four tennis courts and meeting/conference facilities.

Golf is played on the Paradise Hills Course. Parring at 72/74, it stretches out 6,895/6,629/6,098 yards. The surrounding terrain is flat. There is an excellent pro shop and a professional staff to assist.

RATES (EP) Lodge: $50/$56. Green fees: $22, carts $20. Golf packages are available.

ARRIVAL Air: Albuquerque. Car: I-40 west to Route 448 (Coors Road), go north and follow signs.

INN OF THE MOUNTAIN GODS
P.O. Box 269
Mescalero, NM 88340
(505) 257–5141
(800) 545–9011

This Mescalero Indian Reservation was established in 1873 in a very remote section of south central New Mexico. The resort itself was the dream of Tribal Chief Mr. Wendell Chino, who chose the site so that it viewed the sacred Indian grounds. After many years of political and administrative maneuvering, The Inn of The Mountain Gods became a reality in 1975.

The primary objective of the Mescalero Apache Tribe was that the resort function as a training ground and job center for their people. The ultimate goal is for the Inn to be completely staffed by tribal members.

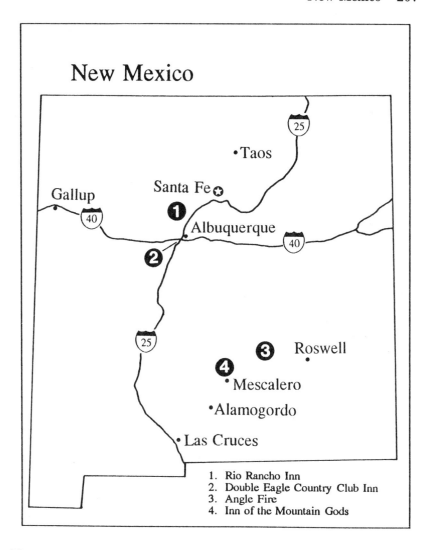

New Mexico

1. Rio Rancho Inn
2. Double Eagle Country Club Inn
3. Angle Fire
4. Inn of the Mountain Gods

The original rooms and suites (134 in number) are spacious and afford sweeping views of the lakes and mountains. A five-story complex with an additional 116 rooms was opened in 1982.

In the evening, a special charm may be found in the three restaurants and four cocktail lounges providing dancing, entertainment and excellent food. The Inn has facilities for seminars and meeting groups of 800. In fact there is a large conference center, adjacent to the golf course, specifically set up to handle large meeting groups.

There are a variety of recreational opportunities, ranging from absolute relaxation to hunting mule deer and elk. A few of the other activities include: trap and skeet shooting, fishing, archery, bicycling and canoeing. There is also tennis available on two indoor and six outdoor courts with resident professional. There is no better way to experience the beauty of this area than on horseback. Trail horses are provided for all ages and riding abilities.

A few years back the Tribe purchased Ski Apache Ski Area 17 miles away. It has become one of the most popular winter activity locations in New Mexico. This ski complex is situated entirely within the 460,000-acre reservation as is the Inn of the Mountain Gods. It offers eight ski lifts, five triple chairs, a four-passenger gondola, 25 miles of ski trails and the services of 100 certified ski instructors. Transportation is provided from the Inn to the ski area.

The Ted Robinson designed golf course, nestled among the pines, is as outstanding as the Inn. Due to the terrain, many of the holes have elevated tees or greens and most enjoy a panoramic view of the Sierra Blanca Mountains. The 18th hole calls for a very well placed shot across Lake Mescalero, while the 10th requires a shot to an island and then to the green. Parring at 72, it stretches out a substantial 6,819/6,416/5,459 yards. At an elevation of 7,200 feet, it is one heck of a course.

The clubhouse includes the amenities of a restaurant, a 19th watering hole and men's and women's locker rooms.

RATES (EP) Rooms: $115. Suites: $120/$130. Green fees: $35, carts $22. Golf package: 3 nights/3 days (includes lodging, 3 rounds of golf with cart, breakfast each day, all taxes), $595 per couple.

ARRIVAL Air: El Paso (124 miles); Alamagordo (45 miles). Private & commercial aircraft: Sierra Blanca Regional Airport (21 miles). Car: 3½ miles out of Ruidoso.

RIO RANCHO INN
1465 Rio Rancho Drive
Rio Ranch, NM 87124
(505) 892–1700
(800) 528–1234

Rio Rancho is an 80-room, motel-type resort. Some of rooms feature kitchenettes. If you prefer condominium accommodations, fully equipped for housekeeping, call the Country Club Villas in New Mexico, (505) 892–9200 or (800) 545–8316.

There is dining in the Aspen Room, as well as a lounge offering nightly dancing. The resort, by the way, has meeting facilities for groups from 20 to 200.

Activities open to guests include: swimming in the Inn's very large pool; a visit to the nearby Sandia Mountains to fish, hunt, or picnic; or perhaps a visit to Old Albuquerque to enjoy the Spanish charm would interest you.

While there is no course at the Rancho, they do provide playing privileges for their guests at the Rio Rancho Country Club less than a mile away. The course measures out a healthy 7,045/6,408/ 5,593 yards and pars at 72. To be sure you stay awake, there are lakes on six holes, along with cottonwoods, pinion and juniper trees bordering the fairways.

In addition to the pro shop the clubhouse has six lighted tennis courts, a pool, lounge and dining room.

RATES (EP) Inn: $48. Kitchenette: $59. Free pick up at airport. Green fees: $20, carts $18.

ARRIVAL Air: Albuquerque. Car: located on New Mexico Route 528 (Rio Rancho Drive) just north of Rio Rancho City.

OKLAHOMA

ARROWHEAD RESORT & HOTEL
HC 67 Box 5
Canadian, OK 74425
(918) 339–2711
OK (800) 445–2711
NAT (800) 422–2711

A few years ago this entire property was a part of the Oklahoma State Park system. The golf course and park area still are. But the resort, including the Lodge and cottages are owned and managed by the Choctaw Indian nation. The Lodge with its 96 guest rooms and 40 cottages is well set up to handle meeting groups of up to 200 people. They also have a restaurant and lounge.

This lovely location on the shores of Lake Eufaula provides many activities: tennis on two courts, horseback riding, an outdoor swimming pool, ping pong, baseball, hiking, their own marina and, of course, fishing.

Golf is played on the 18-hole park course. Reaching out 6,741/ 6,325/5,342 yards, it pars at 72/75.

RATES (EP) Lodge rooms: $50/$55. Parlor suites: 1-bedroom $100. Treehouse 2 bedrooms, kitchen: $90. Green fees: $12, carts $14.

ARRIVAL Air: Tulsa (75 miles). Private Aircraft: paved landing strip on property. Car: 18 miles south of I-40 on U.S. 69.

FALCONHEAD RESORT & COUNTRY CLUB
P.O. Box 206
Burneyville, OK 73430 (405) 276–9411

Falconhead, located in Red River Valley, is an incomparable blend of modern comfort and of timeless beauty. This is a large residential resort/community covering some 3,800 acres. While lodgings are available in the Falcon Inn, the focal point of the resort is the plush Country Club. The Pool and Racquet Club provides excellent dining facilities, an intimate fireside lounge, dancing and entertainment.

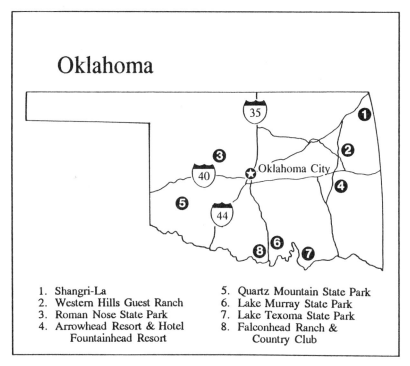

Oklahoma

1. Shangri-La
2. Western Hills Guest Ranch
3. Roman Nose State Park
4. Arrowhead Resort & Hotel
   Fountainhead Resort
5. Quartz Mountain State Park
6. Lake Murray State Park
7. Lake Texoma State Park
8. Falconhead Ranch &
   Country Club

Tennis on four lighted courts, five swimming pools and golf are a few of the amenities available. Beautiful Lake Falcon adds another dimension to the ranch, providing all manner of water activity. Falconhead has its own stable and tack room as well as facilities for boarding horses. Escorted rides are available for beginners.

Golf is played on the Falconhead Country Club's Course. Parring at 72/71 it measures 6,448/5,992/5,350 yards. While the front nine is flat, the back side brings trees, as well as some rolling terrain into play. Falcon Lake also gets into the act on four holes. There is a resident professional available to assist and a full service and well stocked pro shop, driving range and locker rooms.

RATES (EP) Falcon Inn: $48. Condominiums: 1-bedroom, full kitchen $80/$125. Green fees: $14/$17, carts $16. Golf package: 2 nights/3 days (includes 3 days golf with cart, breakfast and lunches), $239 per couple.

ARRIVAL Air: Dallas (100 miles). Oklahoma City (125 miles). Private aircraft: Falconhead Airport (4,200 feet, surfaced and lighted). Car: I-35, 18 miles south of Ardmore exit to Route 32 at Marrietta, then 14 miles west.

FOUNTAINHEAD RESORT
HC 70 Box 453
Checotah, OK 74426
(918) 689–9173
(800) 345–6343

Although the general area, including the golf course and the park, is still operated by the State Parks system the resort hotel is now privately owned. A five-story structure it offers accommodations in 202 rooms and suites, plus 22 cottages. The Terrace Room has dining and dancing with entertainment available in the lounge. Fountainhead can accommodate meeting groups of up to 600 and has many break-out rooms capable of handling groups of from 20 to 270 classroom-style.

The resort's location on the shores of Lake Eufaula, with over 600 miles of shore line, presents the opportunity for a variety of water activity: boating, fishing, water skiing and, of course, swimming. Other activities include: a swimming pool, tennis, horseback riding, archery, and, of course, golf.

Golf is played on the Fountainhead State Park golf course. With a par of 72/74, it reaches out 6,887/6,489/6,102 yards. That yardage of 6,102 is more than a fair reach for the ladies.

RATES (EP) Parkside rooms $72. Lake/Poolside: $82. Cottages: $85. Treehouses: $100/$120. Green fees: $14, carts $14.

ARRIVAL Air: Tulsa (80 miles). Private aircraft: adjacent to the property (a 3,000-foot paved runway). Car: 7 miles south of I-40 on Highway 150 and on Lake Eufaula.

SHANGRI-LA RESORT
Route 3
Afton, OK 74331
(918) 257–4204
OK (800) 722–4903
NAT (800) 331–4060

Shangri-La Resort has recently undergone a much-needed complete overhaul and renovation. Accommodations consist of the Main Lodge (126 rooms), the Golden Oaks (144 rooms) the Country Estates (32 rooms), and the Vista Towers, with 84 two-bedroom suites. They also have 48,000 square feet of convention and meeting space with a capacity to serve up to 2,000 for dinner. There are, as a matter of fact, five dining rooms, several snack and lunch bars, entertainment and dancing nightly.

Activities available include: indoor and outdoor swimming pools, the sandy beach, four indoor and four outdoor tennis courts with a professional staff to assist, four bowling lanes, a full health spa, racquetball courts, water skiing and fishing. The Grand Lake o' the Cherokees, with its 1,300 miles of shoreline, provides an unlimited variety of water activities. As a matter of fact, the river boat *Cherokee Queen* makes a stop here. You can arrange for a two-hour lake tour. The resort also provides supervised activities for the younger set.

Golf can be played on the Blue (east course) stretching out 6,972/ 6,435/5,975 and parring at 72/73. This layout shows you rolling terrain and trees with each green well trapped. The Gold (west course) is a bit more modest, playing 5,932/5,431/5,109/4,517 yards and parring at 70/71. While fairly open, with few trees, it does present its share of water and is very well bunkered. The golf shop, under the direction of Head Professional Rick Reed, is one of the better ones to be found.

RATES (EP) Main Lodge: $105. Golden Oaks: $110/$228. Country Estates: $110/$148. Vista Towers: $110/$278. Shangri-La Estates 1-bedroom condo: $190. Green fees: $25/$45 including cart. Golf package: 2 nights/3 days (includes lodging in main lodge, 3 days green fees, cart, club storage), $298 per couple. Rates quoted are for April-October.

ARRIVAL Air: Tulsa (65 miles). Private aircraft: Shangri-la (4,000-foot, paved, lighted runway). Car: I-44, take Afton exit to U.S. 59, southeast to Highway 125, then south 11 miles.

OKLAHOMA'S SCENIC FIVE STATE PARKS
500 Will Rogers Building
Oklahoma City, OK 73105
(405) 521–2464;
OK (800) 522–8565;
Limited area (800) 654–8240
NAT (800) 652–6552.

Oklahoma has five resort parks in various locations throughout the state. They all provide about the same amenities: outstanding accommodations, archery, bicycling, boating, a golf course, horse-back riding, kiddie playground, swimming pool, tennis, water skiing* and a private airstrip.**

Each resort has dining facilities and offers a golf package. These state-operated resorts are not only delightful, but represent one of the best values for a vacation buck we have seen anywhere in the country.

* Water skiing: Not available at Roman Nose.

** Airstrip: Not available at Roman Nose or Quartz Mountain.

LAKE MURRAY STATE PARK RESORT
The Lodge
Ardmore, OK 73402
(405) 521-2464

Two miles east of I-35 and seven miles south of Ardmore on Lake Murray, the Lodge has 54 guest rooms and 86 cottages.

RATES (EP) Parkside: $49. Lake/Poolside: $54. Cottages: $45/$75. Suites $100/$150. Green fees: $8, carts $14.

LAKE TEXOMA STATE PARK RESORT
The Lodge
Durant, OK 74701
(405) 521-2464

On U.S. 70, 13 miles west of Durant and adjacent to Lake Texoma, the Lodge has 97 guest rooms and 69 cottages.

RATES (EP) Parkside: $49. Lake/Poolside: $54. Cabana Suites: $85. Cottages: $55. Green fees: $8, carts $14.

QUARTZ MOUNTAIN STATE PARK RESORT
The Lodge
Lake Altus-Lugert, OK 73522
(405) 521-2464

Quartz Mountain is on Lake Altus-Lugert, 20 miles north of Altus on Highway 44 and 44A. The Lodge has 44 guest rooms, plus 69 cottages.

RATES Parkside: $44. Lake/Poolside: $49. Cottages: $60. Suites $100. Green fees $8, carts $14.

ROMAN NOSE STATE PARK RESORT
The Lodge
Watonga, OK 73772
(405) 521–2464

Roman Nose is seven miles north of Watonga on Highway 8 and 8A overlooking two small lakes. The Lodge has 20 guest rooms and 10 cottages.

RATES (EP) Parkside: $44/$54. Cottages: $55. Suites $100/$150. Green fees: $8, carts $14.

WESTERN HILLS GUEST RANCH RESORT
Box 509
Wagoner, OK 74467
(918) 772–2545

In eastern Oklahoma, Western Hills is known as "The Gettysburg of the West." A battle waged here long ago ended the Confederate influence in the Indian territory. Southwest, in Muskogee, is the Five Civilized Tribes Museum, housing historical exhibits and artifacts of the Cherokee, Chickasaw, Choctaw, Creek and Seminole Indians.

The resort has 101 rooms, 12 cabanas, 54 cottages, deluxe suites and a Western Style dining room. All rooms are air-conditioned and have color TV.

There is a trained director for the planned children's programs, offering various crafts, puppet shows and water games.

Two lighted tennis courts are available along with sailboats, power boats and paddle boats. Although there is a rental fee for boats, they provide free ramp and docking facilities for private craft.

Golf can be played on an 18-hole, par-72 course complete with pro shop and clubhouse.

RATES (EP) Rooms: $54/$59. Cottages: $45/$85. Suites: $95/$175. Green fees: $8. Carts: $14.

ARRIVAL Private aircraft: in the park is a 3,400-foot paved, lighted runway. Car: on Fort Gibson Reservoir, 8 miles east of Wagoner on Highway 51.

OREGON

BLACK BUTTE RANCH
PO Box 8000
Black Butte Ranch, OR 97759
(503) 595–6211
(800) 452–7455

Over the years, Black Butte has become one of our favorite retreats. It is, in every sense, a "family" resort. On 1,800 acres of wooded, slightly undulating terrain and surrounded by the Deschutes National Forest, it is superb. From the meadow areas the view of the many mountain peaks surrounding Black Butte is breathtaking.

Accommodations are provided in condominiums as well as many private homes. They are all extremely well equipped for housekeeping. However should you elect to "pass" on the housekeeping bit, the dining room at the lodge offers some of the finest food and service we have ever enjoyed.

The Ranch offers four swimming pools, 16 miles of bicycling paths, horseback riding (Black Butte is a working ranch), tennis on 23 courts (there is no charge for tennis), fishing, canoeing, whitewater raft trips and top movies. The fishing, by the way, is barbless fly fishing, hook and release. The kids love it and so do the fish.

Golf is offered on two of the most picturesque golf layouts anywhere. Big Meadow, stretching out a substantial 6,870/6,456/5,716 yards, pars at 72. The newer of the two, Glaze Meadows, measures 6,560/6,266/5,616 yards and also pars at 72. As an added distraction it seems that on almost every hole you are looking at one of the many mountain peaks surrounding Black Butte Ranch. These two courses have as magnificent a setting as any we have seen in this country. Each course has its own driving range, putting area and a well stocked pro shop. Both are operated under the supervision of the Director of Golf, Bunny Mason, and a very friendly staff.

RATES (EP) Rooms: $55. With fireplace: $65. 1-bedroom condo (kitchen/fireplace): $100. 2-bedroom condo: $125. 3 bedrooms:

Oregon

Astoria

❶

Portland

❷ **❹**

❸ ✪ Salem 26 84

❺ **❻**

5 **❼**

20

97

1. Gearhart-by-the-Sea
2. Rippling River
3. Salishan Lodge
4. Kah-Nee-Ta

5. Black Butte Ranch
6. Eagle Crest Resort
7. Sun River

$150. There are also private homes with capacity of 6 people: $90/$155. Green fees: $35, carts $22.

ARRIVAL Air: Redmond Airport (30 miles). Car: (135 miles from Portland). South on I-5 to Highway 20, then east on 20 (Santiam Pass) approximately 98 miles.

EAGLE CREST RESORT
Cline Falls Road
Redmond, OR 97756
(503) 923–2453
(800) 682–4786

The general setting of this property is something else. It overlooks 1½ miles of the Deschutes River, offering fishing and canoeing. Although Eagle Crest has been in operation for several years, it was primarily a resort community. As such it had no accommodations for outside guests. The completion of the hotel in late 1989 has opened up a new dimension. In addition to the 76-room Inn, there are also some townhouses available for rent. Along with the existing restaurant in the main clubhouse, the future plan is to have one in the Inn as well. The resort is capable of handling modest-size meeting groups of up to 75 theater-style.

A sample of the various activities available include: tennis (private and group lessons), racquetball, a game room, a swimming pool, use of the Equestrian Center and miles of hiking and jogging trails. The 30,000-square-foot Sports Center features, among other things, two indoor tennis courts, along with a spa and locker rooms.

During the winter months this place really comes alive as it sits near some of the finest skiing facilities to be found in Oregon. They offer ski packages including, lift tickets and transportation to and from Mt. Bachelor.

The Eagle Crest Golf Club plays a very respectable 6,673/6,292/5,395 yards and pars at 72. While fairly open it presents slight undulations and brings water into play on only four holes.

RATES Inn Rooms: $60/$75. 1-bedroom suite: $95/$105. 2-bedroom suite: up to 6 people, $155/$175. Green fees: $25, carts $20.

ARRIVAL Air: Redmond Airport (6 miles). Car: take Highway 126 west from Redmond, 4 miles, then left on Cline Falls Road.

GEARHART BY-THE-SEA
PO Box C
Gearhart, OR 97138
(503) 738–8331
OR (800) 452–9800
(800) 547–0115

Situated on the northern Oregon coast only 15 miles south of the mouth of the Columbia River, this is a "change of pace place."

The condominium apartments vary in size and floor plan, each having a spacious living room, fireplace, dining area and fully equipped kitchen.

There are two indoor swimming pools plus a therapy pool. Right in front of the resort is what may be the best razor-clamming beach in all of Oregon, with charter boat fishing available only nine miles north.

The Gearhart Golf Links is directly across the road. An 18-hole layout, it plays 6,089/5,882 yards with a par of 72/74.

RATES (EP) Suites: 1 bedroom $82/$106; 2 bedrooms $97/$139. Green fees: $18, carts $20.

ARRIVAL Air: Astoria. Car: from Portland, west on Highway 26 (80 miles) to Highway 101. North 7 miles to Seaside, then 3 miles further.

KAH-NEE-TA
Warm Springs, OR 97761
(503) 553–1112
(800) 831–0100

The lodge, owned and operated by the Confederation of Indian Tribes, rises unexpectedly from the side of a bluff. It has a sweeping contemporary design which blends well with the rugged central Oregon landscape. A visit to this facility is more of a visit to another culture rather than to a resort. And a delightful experience it is.

There are 140 rooms and suites, each with its own private balcony and spectacular view. Meeting space is also available. The village offers some unique accommodations, namely tee pees! (The children will never stop talking about the night they spent in an Indian tee pee). Neither will you if you don't bring sleeping bags or cots. The floor is concrete, *without beds.*

The dining here is outstanding. You may dine on lobster tail, rainbow trout, salmon, or get carried away with game hen, buffalo or venison.

Kah-Nee-Ta has much to offer for those who enjoy horseback riding. There are also two tennis courts and a huge swimming pool.

The golf course plays 6,288/5,418 and pars at 72/73. The resort provides a small pro shop. There is also a professional on hand to sort things out.

RATES (EP) Rooms: $80. Suites: $80/$150. Chief suites: $149/$195. Cottage: 1-bedroom $75; 2-bedroom $100. Tee Pee: $45 for up to four persons. Green fees: $25, carts $22. Rates are for May-September.

ARRIVAL Air: Redmond (60 miles); Portland (115 miles). Private aircraft: Madras. Car: 11 miles north of Warm Springs, turn-off signs are clearly marked.

RIPPLING RIVER
68010 Fairway Welches, OR 97067
(503) 622–3101
(800) 669–7666

Accommodations consist of 202 guest rooms as well as several two-
to three-bedroom condominiums. There is an excellent restaurant
(Forest Hills Dining Room) as well as a lounge. The resort has
meeting facilities with a capacity of 200 classroom- or 500
banquet-style.

If your thing is golf, tennis, hiking, swimming, fishing, or white
water rafting you are at the right place. Complimentary tennis
may be played on six courts. They also offer a staff-supervised KID
HAVEN, with many electronic games. During the winter there is
transportation provided to superb ski facilities nearby.

There are 27 holes of golf to enjoy on these gently rolling alpine
meadows. Lakes, streams and a few towering fir trees spice up the
action. Using a crossover system there is the Red/Green Course
combination reaching out 6,394/5,687 yards parring at 72/74;
the Red/Yellow nines play 5,718/5,077 yards with a par of 70/ 71.
With a par of 70/71, the Green/Yellow layouts play 6,006/ 5,246
yards.

RATES (EP) Rooms: $85/$155. Condominiums: (kitchen, living
room, fireplace), $185/$195. Green fees: $25/$30, cart $22. Golf
packages are available.

ARRIVAL Air: Portland. Car: east on I-84 to Wood Village/Gre-
sham exit. 3 miles to Burnside, turn left. Burnside will become
Highway 26. Travel 25 miles.

SALISHAN LODGE
Highway 101
Glendon Beach, OR 97388
(503) 764–2371
(800) 452–2300

Combine the majestic Pacific Ocean and its ever changing moods
on one side, a beautiful golf course on the other, along with the
outstanding architectural skill used in building the entire complex, and you wind up with a lovely resort like Salishan. Accommodations consist of 201 guest rooms and suites, some with golf

course views, others with a view of the bay. Each is well-appointed and all are within easy walking distance of the main lodge. Salishan's conference facilities can accommodate groups of up to 500 and can make meetings a fun affair.

If you have ever been fortunate enough to have dined at Salishan, you will understand why they have received the Mobil Travel Guide Five Star and the AAA Five Diamond Awards year after year. In fact, the Mobil Five Star was recently awarded for the 21st consecutive year.

Their wine cellar has become a tour attraction. Recently completed, the new wine cellar offers over 35,000 bottles and 1,100 different labels. The wine list looks a bit like a metropolitan area phone book.

As fine as the food is at Salishan, no one really enjoys eating at the same place each evening. For a change of pace and a delightful experience you might consider the Bay House. It is a couple of miles north of Salishan. Take my word for it—you will find this an eating experience long cherished and remembered.

There are three indoor lighted tennis courts, an indoor pool, hydrotherapy pool and men's and women's exercise rooms.

The golf course plays 6,439/6,246/5,693 yards with a par of 72 for men and 73 from the ladies' tees. The first nine is tree-lined and a very tight layout, while the back side is a links type and more open. Never an easy layout, it can be very difficult if the wind kicks up. They have added some potential excitement to the back nine with the planting of pampas-grass near some of the greens. Don't snicker. If you have not had the pleasure of hitting out of this stuff you have a big surprise coming!

The golf course and pro shop are under the direction of professional Grant Rogers.

RATES (EP) Rooms: $126. Deluxe South-Golf or North-Bay view: $167. Green fees: $32, cart $25. Golf package: 2 nights/3 days (includes lodging, unlimited green fees and room tax), $355/ $435 / $456 per couple. Rates are for June-October.

ARRIVAL Air: Portland. Private aircraft: Siltzer Bay Airport, 3000, foot paved runway (½ mile away). Car: south on I-5 to "Newberg and Ocean Beach" exit. Highway 18 to 3 miles south of Lincoln City limits.

SUNRIVER RESORT
P.O. Box 3609
Sunriver, OR 97707
(503) 593–1221
OR (800) 452–6874
NAT (800) 547–3922

Sunriver is a very large complex on 3,300 acres.

Accommodations range from bedrooms and suites in the Lodge Village to private homes and condominiums. Of course the suites, condominiums and homes feature a fully equipped kitchen. Daily maid service is not included in the rates for homes & condos but can be arranged. The resort can handle meeting groups of up to 400 people. The dining facilities are outstanding and include The Provision Co. with a "family" atmosphere and, The Meadows, a more formal facility.

This resort is not only large but also an extremely busy place, with a great many people and children throughout the village and shopping areas. Oh yes, baby-sitting can also be arranged.

There are many activities to enjoy: a canoe trip on the Deschutes River, fishing, a playground area for the small fry, a 28-court tennis complex, 26 miles of paved bike paths, a racquetball club and riding stables. White water rafting trips can also be arranged.

There are two 18-hole golf courses to be navigated. The older South Course measures 6,940/6,502/6,366/5,827 yards and pars at 72. We found it flat, open and not very interesting. However the North Course, a Robert Trent Jones design, is an excellent layout. Reaching out 6,823/6,208/5,912/5,446 yards, it also pars at 72. Each course, operating under the supervision of the Director of Golf, Tim Berg, has its own golf shop with professionals available to assist. For advance tee times call (800) 962–1769.

RATES (EP) Lodge: $96. Suites: $150. Homes or condominiums: $160/$205. Green fees: North Course $45, carts $25; South Course $35, carts $25. Rates are for June-September.

ARRIVAL Air: Portland (175 miles); Redmond (33 miles). Private aircraft: Sunriver 4,500 feet, paved/lighted. Car: Highway 97 (15 miles south of Bend).

TEXAS

APRIL SOUND
Highway 105 West
P.O. Box 253
Conroe, TX 77301
(409) 588–1101

April Sound is just 50 miles northwest of Houston. On the shores of 21,000-acre Lake Conroe, it offers an almost endless variety of water activities.

Accommodations consist of villas (hotel type) with verandas or balconies and one- to three-bedroom townhouses, complete with living room and kitchen. The resort is well equipped to handle meeting and conference groups with a banquet-style capacity of 225. The main dining room, the Fernery, overlooks the cove and part of the golf course.

Tennis is served up on 17 courts (four covered and nine lighted). It has its own tennis center complete with a mini-restaurant and fully equipped tennis shop.

The Lakeview Golf Course, parring at 71, reaches out 6,189/5,807/5,3233 yards. Although the course borders on April Sound, water only becomes a factor on seven holes. There is also a nine-hole par-32 executive layout.

RATES (EP) Villa 1-bedroom: $79/$139. Rates February 15-November 15. Green fees: $25/$30, carts $20.

ARRIVAL Air: Houston. Car: from Houston (50 miles) I-45 north, then west on Highway 105 (8 miles).

COLUMBIA LAKES
188 Freeman Boulevard
West Columbia, TX 77486
(409) 345–5151

While Columbia Lakes has outstanding meeting and conference facilities (15,000 square feet of meeting space and 38 breakout rooms), it also offers accommodations and the amenities of a luxury resort. Lodgings consist of cottages, many along the golf course, providing anything from a bedroom to an eight-plex with

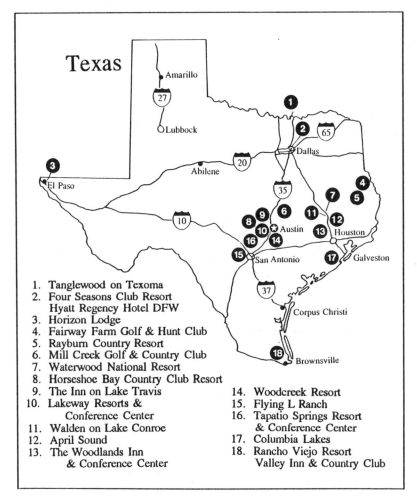

Texas

Amarillo

27

Lubbock

Abilene

El Paso

20

35

10

1. Tanglewood on Texoma
2. Four Seasons Club Resort
   Hyatt Regency Hotel DFW
3. Horizon Lodge
4. Fairway Farm Golf & Hunt Club
5. Rayburn Country Resort
6. Mill Creek Golf & Country Club
7. Waterwood National Resort
8. Horseshoe Bay Country Club Resort
9. The Inn on Lake Travis
10. Lakeway Resorts &
    Conference Center
11. Walden on Lake Conroe
12. April Sound
13. The Woodlands Inn
    & Conference Center

Dallas

65

Austin

San Antonio

Houston

Galveston

Corpus Christi

Brownsville

37

14. Woodcreek Resort
15. Flying L Ranch
16. Tapatio Springs Resort
    & Conference Center
17. Columbia Lakes
18. Rancho Viejo Resort
    Valley Inn & Country Club

living room. The restaurant and lounge are in the clubhouse. The food selection, by the way, is outstanding.

The activities available include: tennis on four lighted courts, a swimming pool, bicycles and boat rentals, a marina and some excellent fishing.

Golf can be enjoyed on the Columbia Lakes Country Club course. Measuring a substantial 6,967/6,300/5,280 yards, it pars at 72. This layout can test you. It is well trapped with many trees and a generous amount of water coming into play.

RATES (EP) Rooms: $90. Green fees: $22/$30, carts $20. Golf package: 2 nights/3 days (includes lodging, green fees and cart), weekdays $269 per couple, weekends $299 per couple. Rates are for September-November and March-May.

ARRIVAL Air: Houston (60 minutes). Car: Highway 288 south to Highway 35, then west to Country Road 25. North to Columbia Lakes.

FAIRWAY FARM GOLF & HUNT CLUB
P.O. Drawer T
San Augustine, TX 75972
(409) 275-2334

Fairway Farm, deep in east Texas, is a special type of resort. It provides many different types of recreation: golf, tennis, swimming, hunting and skeet shooting. Their location, just minutes from Lake Sam Rayburn, makes possible all manner of water activity including outstanding fishing. With guides and well-trained dogs available, the October-through-March period is a prime time for plump quail, pheasant and chukar. (No bag limit). Advanced reservations must be specifically made for this type of hunting.

All meals are served "American" style and are long remembered by those fortunate enough to have been guests. This beautifully wooded 1,400-acre retreat offers an ideal location for modest-size meetings groups and can handle from 10 to 50.

Golf is available on their own 18-hole course. Parring at only 71, it reaches out a monstrous 7,573/6,740/6,290 yards. With two lakes and Tiger Creek becoming a problem (or should I say challenge) on eight or nine holes, this one will test you.

RATES Room: $125 per couple (includes breakfast, lunch—NOT DINNER—and green fees). Cart fees: $16.

ARRIVAL Air: Beaumont (130 miles). Private aircraft: on site. Car: Highway 96 to San Augustine, then east on Highway 21.

FLYING L RANCH
HCR 1 Box 32
Bandera, TX 78003
(512) 796-3001
(800) 292-5134

The hospitality and accommodations at the resort represent a delightful blending of the old and new west. The villas, designed by

Frank Lloyd Wright Associates, consist of one- to three-bedroom suites. Some feature fireplaces, some with two double beds, others with king-size beds. The golf-view units are two-room suites. The resort, of course, has a dining room and lounge.

They offer tennis, swimming, horseback riding and hay rides along with fishing and canoeing. They also can provide a few hours entertainment for the small fry while you navigate a round of golf or whatever.

Golf, under the direction of professional Bob Looney, is played on the Flying "L" Country Club course. Parring at 72, it plays a hefty 6,787/6,320/5,813 yards.

RATES (MAP) Rooms: $160 per couple. Green fees: $11/$14, carts $14. Golf package: 2 nights/2 days (includes lodging, MAP, unlimited green fees), $220 per couple.

ARRIVAL Air: San Antonio. Private aircraft: Flying L Resort. Car: from San Antonio west on Highway 16 (45 minutes).

FOUR SEASONS CLUB RESORT
4150 North MacArthur Blvd.
Irving, TX 75038
(214) 717–0700
(800) 332–3442

The Four Seasons Inn consists of 315 guest rooms, including 13 suites. It also provides one of the most advanced meeting and conference facilities to be found anywhere. The 52 deluxe rooms set aside for meeting groups are unique in that each features a work area with a desk, special computer links and a television offering closed-circuit capabilities.

A sample of activities include: dry and wet saunas, whirlpools, herbal wraps, massages, indoor and outdoor tennis courts, swimming pools, two squash courts, as well as racquetball.

The Cottonwood Golf Club, home of the Byron Nelson Golf Classic, was designed by Robert Trent Jones, Jr. With four sets of tees, it stretches 7,002/6,532/6,096/5,707 yards with a par of 71. The first green is in the shape of the state of Texas, while the bunker immediately behind forms the state of Oklahoma. I am not sure how Oklahomans should react to that but then the water hazard off the first tee is in the shape of the Gulf of Mexico. With water plus

74 sand bunkers throughout the course, it can become an interesting layout to tour. At certain times the Cottonwood course is not available due to tournament play.

A second 18, the TPC (Texas version), is also available for guest play. Parring at 70, it reaches out 6,767/6,397/5,380 yards.

RATES (EP) $140/$190. Suites: $300 and up. Green fees: $70, carts $25.

ARRIVAL Air: Dallas/Ft. Worth.

HORIZON LODGE
13781 Horizon Boulevard
El Paso, TX 79927
(915) 852–9141

As a guest of the Horizon Lodge, bordering the Horizon Country Club, you enjoy full, temporary club membership. Accommodations consist of rooms in the lodge with some private homes available as well. The clubhouse has complete dining and bar facilities. It is also the center for various social events.

Activities include the use of four lighted tennis courts and a junior Olympic swimming pool.

The Country Club course reaches out a healthy 6,955 / 6,514/5,581 yards with a par of 71/73. There is a golf shop and a professional staff available to assist.

RATES (EP) Room: $40/$50; (with kitchenette) $55. Green fees: $13/$15, carts $16. Golf packages are available.

ARRIVAL Air: El Paso Airport. Car: 3 miles north of I-10 on Horizon Boulevard.

HORSESHOE BAY COUNTRY CLUB RESORT
Box 7766
Horseshoe Bay, TX 78654
(512) 598–2511
TX (800) 252–9363
NAT (800) 531–5105

This deluxe resort is on Lake LBJ, one of the most beautiful lakes in the state of Texas. Accommodations consist of rooms at the Inn along with some 200 condominiums. The condos, from one to three bedrooms, feature fully equipped kitchens. There are also a few private, three-bedroom homes available. Horseshoe Bay provides outstanding meeting facilities and can handle up to 200 classroom- and 250 banquet-style.

There is a full service marina and with more than 22 miles of lake you can sail, water ski or fish. The Yacht Club Restaurant offers excellent cuisine and a spectacular view of the bay.

Meanwhile, back at the Inn, they have one of the most unusual pools we have seen: an enormous black marble basin. At first glance it looks as if it had been constructed by the Romans.

If you ever considered riding, this is the place. The trails wind through hills and valleys, past spring-fed brooks with quail and deer in abundance.

Tennis can be played on 14 lighted courts (four covered) with their own tennis shop and professionals available to assist.

There are now three 18-hole courses, all Robert Trent Jones designs. The Slick Rock course, parring at 72, is 6,839/6,358/5,858 yards. The front nine is heavily wooded, while the back side is a little more open. You may rest assured the 72 traps as well as water coming into contention on 10 holes will keep you occupied. They have a super pro shop, complete with snack bar and locker rooms.

The Ram Rock course is one of the tougher layouts in Texas. Parring at 71, it plays 6,946/6,408/5,954/5,305 yards. With its 68 traps, heavily wooded fairways, and water hazards on eight holes this gem is a stem-winder.

Apple Rock golf course, the newest addition, weighs in at 6,999 / 6,536/6,038/5,480 yards, also with a par of 72. There are two first-class pro shops serving all three courses. Each has a grill, a lounge and locker rooms.

RATES (EP) Inn: (minimum 2 nights) $110. Beach House: $110/ 175. Green fees: $50/$60, cart $22. Golf package: 2 nights/3 days available weekdays only (includes lodging, 3 rounds of golf with cart, 2 dinners, all taxes and gratuities), $528 per couple. Rates mid-March to mid-November

ARRIVAL Air: Austin. Private aircraft: Horseshoe Bay Airport. Car: from Austin take Route 71 northwest 55 miles.

THE HYATT REGENCY DFW
Dallas/Ft. Worth Airport, TX 75621
(214) 453–1234
(800) 233–1234

The location of this resort, about ten minutes from this huge airport, makes it rather unusual. It is a lovely hotel with liberal use of rosewood and Italian marble throughout. While it offers many facilities, including 1,450 guest rooms, it is particularly well equipped to handle meetings with 32 corporate meeting rooms and all the amenities needed for groups large and small. They have a maximum capacity of 3,000. There are eight restaurants offering a wide variety of cuisine and four bars.

Additional activities include an extremely large health spa, a swimming pool, four lighted indoor and four outdoor tennis courts, 10 racquetball courts and golf.

The two golf courses, under the direction of a PGA professional, are five minutes from the hotel. The Bear Creek Golf Club West reaches out 6,677/6,261/5,597 yards; the East Course measures 6,670/6,265/5,620 yards. Both par at 72. Undulating terrain, many traps and water combine to produce two fine layouts.

RATES (EP) Rooms: $145. Suites: 1 bedroom $275 and up. Green fees: $30/$45, carts $22. Golf package: 1 night/1 day (includes lodging, green fees, cart and taxes), $150 per couple.

ARRIVAL The Dallas/Ft. Worth Airport.

THE INN ON LAKE TRAVIS
1900 American Drive
Lago Vista, TX 78645
(512) 267–1102

The Inn overlooks Lake Travis, which is some 65 miles long and has over 300 miles of shoreline. Lodgings consist of 54 rooms including suites. You can dine in the Captain's Table Restaurant with dancing nightly in the Windjammer Lounge. The Highland Lakes Country Club's dining facilities are open to guests as well. In addition, the resort does have excellent meeting and conference facilities and can handle groups of up to 300 theater-style.

With a swimming and wading pool, tennis on four lighted courts, basketball, volleyball, shuffleboard, boating (boat rentals), along with excellent fishing, there is more than enough to keep you busy.

Golf can be played on the Highland Lakes Country Club course. Parring at 72/71, it is a sturdy 6,599/6,331/6,003/5,488 yards. This is one of the better layouts around. The hills, traps, trees and water will keep your interest as well as your full attention. Guests also have playing privileges at Lago Vista Country Club. Measuring 6,579/6,193/5,851/5,290 yards, it pars at 72.

In addition to the two regulation courses there is the Bar-K nine-hole, par-three, layout.

RATES (EP) Room: $75. 1-bedroom condo: $125/$145. Golf packages are available. Green fees: $28, cart $22.

ARRIVAL Air: Austin (40 miles west). Car: take I-35 then I-183 north. 14 miles north of Austin turn off on FM # 1431. Travel 12 miles to Lohman's Crossing Road, turn left. Drive less than 3 miles to Boogy Ford. Turn right onto Boogy Ford, go 3 miles, then turn left on American Drive.

LAKEWAY RESORTS & CONFERENCE CENTER
101 Lakeway Drive
Austin, TX 78734
(512) 261–6600
(800) 525–3929

As the name indicates there is more than one resort: the Inn and The World of Tennis Club, located at The Hills of Lakeway. They are about two miles apart. Accommodations consist of motel-type rooms as well as hotel suites at the Inn. There are, in addition "Hillcourt Villas" (condominiums) at the World of Tennis, as well as homes and condominiums at The Racquet Club. Both the Inn and The Hills of Lakeway have meeting facilities with all the needed amenities.

A word of warning. If you are driving, do not plan to arrive at night. This is a very large complex and it is extremely difficult to find your way around.

Dining is a relaxing affair, with gracious service and fine cuisine in the Inn's Travis Room. We had the pleasure of dining in the Travis restaurant and seldom have we enjoyed more impeccable service. Dining is also provided in the Trophy Room and at the Yacht Club.

Tennis can be played on 32 lighted courts (two indoor). This is a first-class tennis complex, with pro shop, locker room, saunas, steam and whirlpool baths and a magnificent clubhouse, under the direction of a professional staff. There is an equestrian center providing instruction and trail rides. As the resort is located on the shores of Lake Travis, there are also a wide variety of water sports possible.

Golf is available to guests on two layouts: the Live Oaks with a yardage of 6,643/6,228/5,472, parring at 72/73; and the Yaupon 18, playing 6,595/5,988/5,032 yards, also parring at 72. A third course, The Hills of Lakeway, is reserved for member play only. Each course has its own fully equipped pro shop and snack bar.

RATES (EP) Inn: $160. Suites: $240. The Hills of Lakeway Racquet Club Villas: 2 bedrooms $240. Green fees: $35/$45 carts $22. Golf Packages are available. Rates are for peak golf season April to October.

ARRIVAL Air: Austin. Private aircraft: Lakeway's own airport. Car: (20 miles northwest of Austin). I-35 exit on Highway 620, continue on 5 miles after you cross the Mansfield Dam.

MILL CREEK GOLF & COUNTRY CLUB
P.O. Box 67
Salado, TX 76571
(817) 947–5141
(800) 736–3441

Mill Creek Golf & Country Club, while a private affair, allows guests to use all of its facilities including: swimming, tennis, golf and attendant social activities.

Accommodations are available in the Mill Creek Guest Homes or the Mill Creek Inn. These tastefully furnished units are on a bluff overlooking Mill Creek and are completely equipped for housekeeping. There are also a number of one-, two- and three-bedroom private homes available.

The Mill Creek Restaurant offers a relaxed and casual atmosphere. A must is a visit to the village of Salado with several good restaurants and its historical points of interest.

Golf is available on the beautifully maintained Robert Trent Jones Jr. designed course. Playing at 6,486/6,052/5,250 yards, it pars at 71/73. Salado Creek, which wanders throughout the entire layout, not only adds to the beauty but also the challenge.

RATES (EP) Guest House: weekdays $70, weekends $85. Green fees: $30/$40, carts $22. Golf package: 1 night/1 day (includes lodging, green fees and cart), weekdays $110; weekends $150 per couple.

ARRIVAL Air: Austin. Car: I-35 exit on 285, travel ½ mile.

RANCHO VIEJO RESORT
Box 3918
Brownsville, TX 78520
(512) 350–4000
TX (800) 292–7263
NAT (800) 531–7400

Flowering hibiscus, oleanders and bougainvillea welcome you to Rancho Viejo. Accommodations range from luxurious poolside suites to one-, two- or three-bedroom fairway villas. The villas all feature electric kitchen and washer/dryer. The Rancho is an ideal location for business groups, with private meeting and banquet rooms.

Dining is offered in the Casa Grande Supper Club, a gourmet experience. For less formal dining, there is the Ranchero Room at the main clubhouse. Getting there is half the fun aboard the *Delta Dawn* riverboat. Relax and sip a margarita as you wind down the three-mile Resaca to the clubhouse.

The swimming pool is unique in that it is extremely large, with a cascading waterfall and a swim up bar. Tennis is offered on two lighted courts across from the registration center. A resident professional is available to assist.

Golf is played on two championship courses: the El Diablo, a substantial 6,899/6,213/5,575 yards, parring at 70/72; and the El Angel it is, however, no Angel, measuring 6,647/6,003/5,387 yards again with a par of 70/72. Each of them will challenge you in its own way, with fairways that wind through citrus orchards and pines.

A nice touch: there is a half-way house (libation stop) on each course, to hold you together for the back nine.

RATES (EP) Rooms: $103. Suites: $113. 2-bedroom villa: $206. Green fees: $30, carts $22. Golf package: 2 nights/3 days (includes lodging, breakfast, green fees, cart, club storage, transportation to and from airport), $460/$503 per couple. Rates are for January-March.

ARRIVAL Air: Brownsville (15 minutes). Car: 3 miles off Highway 100 and less than 1 mile off Highway 511.

RAYBURN COUNTRY RESORT
Sam Rayburn, TX 75951
(409) 698–2444
(800) 882–1442

Accommodations comprise 50 hotel rooms and 54 villa rooms either near the Country Club or along the lush golf course.

In the evening you can dine at the Rayburn Country Club and afterwards dance to the music of the area's finest entertainers. The lodge has excellent meeting facilities and is supported by a full range of audio/visual equipment. They can accommodate groups of from 10 to 200.

Tennis is served up on four lighted courts adjacent to the 25-meter pool. Additional amenities consist of locker rooms, showers and a snack bar. There are a great many other activities available here: skeet shooting, fishing and sailing on Lake Sam Rayburn, to name just a few. They also offer fishing trip packages, including a professional fishing guide service.

There are now 27 holes of golf to take on. Using a crossover system you wind up with: the Green/Blue combination of nines measuring 6,775/6,210/5,274 yards; the Green/Gold playing 6,787/6,246/5,338 yards; and the Blue/Gold Course weighing in at 6,754/6,266/5,514 yards. All three par at 72. There are more than enough water hazards, traps, dogleg holes, and trees to hold your undivided attention. They had better, as these are not easy courses.

RATES (EP) Hotel: $40. Villas (1-bedroom) $55/$75. Green fees: $22, carts $18. Golf package: 2 nights/3 days (includes lodging, 2 dinners, green fees and cart), in hotel $250, weekends $290 per couple; in condo $326, weekends $350 per couple.

ARRIVAL Air: Beaumont (88 miles). Private aircraft: Pineland/Jasper Airport. Car: from Beaumont north on U.S. 96, left on Highway 255.

TANGLEWOOD ON TEXOMA
P.O. Box 265
Pottsboro, TX 75076
(214) 786–2968
(800) 833–6569

Tanglewood, 80 miles north of Dallas, is a resort community nestled among wooded hills on the shoreline of Lake Texoma. There are 65 rooms, including five master suites in the unique nine-story

"Lighthouse." There are also approximately 120 fully-equipped condominiums available. The resort is prepared to handle meeting groups of from 15 to 150 people with 13 separate meeting rooms and a full range of audio/visual equipment.

Guests can dine in the elegant Captain's Table Restaurant or in The Seachest Room. The casual Yacht Club and Moonraker lounges, atop the Lighthouse, have become the focal points of most of the social activity.

Sporting action includes: a three-tiered swimming pool, two lighted tennis courts, an equestrian center, a 21-foot ski boat and an 18-hole golf course.

Golf is played on a Ralph Plummer designed course. With three tee settings it covers a significant 6,997/6,354/5,572 yards and pars at 72/73. In addition to the yardage, some of the challenge is provided by the trees outlining almost every fairway and water in play on six holes.

RATES (EP) Rooms: $70/$85. Suites: $95. Lighthouse Tower: $145. Condominiums: $85/$155. Green fees: $20/$23, carts $20. Golf package: 2 nights (includes lodging, green fees, cart, taxes), $276 per couple. Rates are for April–October.

ARRIVAL Air: Dallas/Ft. Worth. Private aircraft: Grayson County Airport. Car: 80 miles north of Dallas on Highway 75.

TAPATIO SPRINGS RESORT & COUNTRY CLUB
P.O. Box 550
Boerne, TX 78006
(512) 537–4611

The Tapatio Springs Hotel is in one of the prettier parts of Texas.

There are 96 rooms in the hotel. There is also a full-service bar, and the clubhouse restaurant for dining. The view of the golf course from the dining area is quite spectacular. The resort is well set up to handle meeting and conference groups and can accommodate up to 350 people.

In addition to golf, there is swimming, tennis, a sauna, Jacuzzi and exercise rooms.

Surrounded by stately hills and several spring-fed lakes along Frederick Creek, the 18-hole championship course is both fun and beautiful. With a par of 72, it plays 6,543/6,233/5,849/5,277 yards. A full-line golf shop and a professional staff are available to assist.

RATES (EP) Rooms $85/$95. Suites: $125. Condominiums: 2 bedrooms $285. Weekly rates available. Green fees: $36,including cart. Golf package: 2 nights/2 days (includes lodging, green fees, cart, club storage), $256 per couple.

ARRIVAL Air: San Antonio (25 minutes). Car: I-10 north to Boerne, turn left (west) on John's Road to Tapatio Springs.

VALLEY INN & COUNTRY CLUB
Brownsville, TX 78521
(512) 546–5331

The Valley Inn & Country Club is in the heart of the Rio Grand Valley. It is only a 30-minute drive from the sandy beaches of South Padre Island on the Gulf of Mexico.

There are fairway villas (two- and three-bedroom homes), fully equipped for housekeeping, including washer and dryer. Should you experience trouble renting one of the privately owned villas we would suggest you contact one of the local real-estate brokers.

There are a great many activities available: tennis on eight lighted courts, an Olympic-size pool (a total of 15 pools throughout the complex) and, of course, golf. Matamoros, Mexico, only 10 minutes away, offers the opportunity for sightseeing and endless shopping.

The Valley Country Club course with a par of 70/71, plays 6,857/6,355/5,182 yards. This layout brings lots of water into play to keep your attention. There is also an executive nine-hole affair to sharpen up your iron play.

RATES (EP) Fairway villas: $225/$350 per week (minimum one week stay). Green fees: $18, carts $18. Rates are for January-April.

ARRIVAL Air: Brownsville. Car: Highway 77/83 and FM 802.

WALDEN ON LAKE CONROE
14001 Walden Road
Montgomery, TX 77356
(409) 582–6441

Walden's, situated on a 1,200-acre peninsula jutting into Lake Conroe, is just an hour's drive from Houston. Accommodations comprise well furnished townhouses and condominiums. There are several dining facilities: two fine restaurants, the Walden Country Club, the Commodore Room at the Yacht Club, along with the 19th Hole Grill for breakfast or lunch.

This is one of the largest yacht clubs of its type, with slips for 520 boats. There are also rental boats ranging from canoes and ski-boats to a 55-foot party cruiser. Additional activities include an outstanding tennis complex with 16 Laykold courts (10 lighted, four covered) and a professional staff.

The golf course was designed and engineered by the architectural firm of Van Hagge & Devlin. Playing 6,798/6,261/5,122 yards, it pars at 72. It is an unusual layout in that there is no duplication of holes. Each has its own character and each seems to have water problems. Water is actually in play on at least 11 holes. It is one of the more interesting courses to navigate. And I think the word navigate is appropriate.

RATES For condominium rentals call (409) 582–6995. They will quote rates for various units.

ARRIVAL Air: Houston (44 miles). Car: from Houston take Highway 45 north, off at FM 105, 12 miles west.

WATERWOOD NATIONAL RESORT
Waterwood Box One
Huntsville, TX 77340
(409) 891–5211
(800) 441–5211

Waterwood, with miles of contiguous shoreline, is on one of the most picturesque areas of Lake Livingston. Created just a few years ago, this reservoir lake serves up some of the finest bass fishing to be found anywhere.

Rooms are available in the lodge area as are lodge cabanas, each of which is equipped with refrigerator and wet bar. The clubhouse is the location of the four lighted tennis courts, the Olympic-sized pool and the dining facilities. There are also excellent meeting facilities capable of handling groups of from 12 to 200.

The Marina makes available a variety of water activities: boat rentals, including paddleboats and canoes, water-skiing and fishing.

Waterwood National, a Pete Dye designed golf course, originally opened for play in October of 1975. Carved from the east Texas pine woods, its long vistas of rolling tree-lined fairways and typical Pete Dye greens will present all the challenge you can handle. Stretching across half of Texas, this layout plays 6,872/6,258/5,480/5,029 yards, parring at 71/73.

RATES (EP) Lodge rooms: $75. Cabana: $100. Suites: $125/$150. Green fees: $25/$35, carts $20. Golf package: 2 nights/3 days (includes green fees, cart, club storage), lodge $347; cabana $404 per couple. Rates are for March-October.

ARRIVAL Air: Houston (98 miles). Car: I-45 from Houston north to exit 190. East at Huntsville. Continue east until you see signs.

WOODCREEK RESORT
One Woodcreek Drive
Wimberley, TX 78676 (512) 847–3126

Accommodations are lodge rooms, cabins or townhouses. The latter feature a living room and fully equipped kitchens. The resort also has meeting facilities and can handle groups of from 10 to 150. Although there is more than one place to eat, the Sam Houston Dining Room serves as good a meal as you will find anywhere in this area. There is also the Austin room. Recently the resort was able to obtain a liquor license. Now they have added a lounge.

There are a great many activities to enjoy—canoeing, paddle boating, fishing, tennis (10 courts), racquetball, handball, hot tubs, and a swimming pool.

The Woodcreek Resort course, measuring a modest 6,470/5,973/5,287 yards, pars at 72. There is a pesky little creek (Cypress Creek) which runs throughout the entire 18. It creates some rather interesting golf shots. There is a particularly well set up golf shop featuring an outstanding grill.

RATES (EP) Cottages: $50/$60. Townhouse suites: $75. Townhouse, 2 bedrooms: $120. Green fees: $16/$20, cart $18. Golf package: 1 night/1 day (includes 1-bedroom townhouse, green fees and cart), weekdays $80 per couple; weekends $96 per couple.

ARRIVAL Air: Austin (43 miles) or San Antonio (63 miles). Car: from either I-10 or I-35 turn northwest at San Marcus to Wimberley.

THE WOODLANDS INN & CONFERENCE CENTER
2301 N. Millbend Drive
The Woodlands, TX 77380
(713) 367–1100
TX (800) 533–3052
NAT (800) 433–2624

This is a highly fashionable resort complex, with 268 rooms and suites, many with kitchenettes. The kitchenettes, unfortunately, are not equipped for housekeeping. Woodlands is well set up to handle meeting and convention groups. Having allocated 54,000 square feet of space to group affairs, they obviously can handle a large number of people.

While there are several restaurants on the resort grounds the Glass Menagerie, with its view of the lake is one of the finest we have visited. There is, in addition, an excellent dining room at the Country Club.

There are a great many activities at your disposal: a health club, saunas, a steam room, herbal baths, whirlpools, Swedish massage, as well as golf and tennis. Tennis is served up on 17 outdoor and three indoor courts (12 lighted) and is supported by a separate and well stocked tennis shop. There is a resident tennis professional and staff available.

If you get bored here you have a problem. In addition to the foregoing there is swimming (indoor and outdoor pools), basketball and a massage.

The touring professional associated with the Country Club is John Mahaffey. Woodlands now offers play on 54 holes. Opened in late 1982, the North Course reaches out 6,881/6,339/5,765 yards with a par of 72. The West 18, parring at 72/73, plays 6,969 / 6,389/5,520 yards. The TPC layout (formerly the East Course) jumps out a substantial 7,045/6,367/5,302 yards with the par set at 72.

We were only able to play two of the courses: the West Course (home of the Houston Open) and the TPC. The introduction of water along with the tree-lined fairways makes these interesting to play.

RATES (EP) Room: $99/$136. Suites: $129/$205. Green fees: $30/$39, cart $20; TPC course $60/$75 including cart. Golf package: 2 nights/3 days (includes lodging, green fees, cart, range balls, golf clinic), $378 per couple. Play on the TPC course is not included in the golf package. Rates are for mid-March through May and for October.

ARRIVAL Air: Houston (25 miles). Car: I-45 north to Woodlands/Robinson Road exit. Turn west back over I-45 to Grogan's Mill Road. Take left, then go to second stoplight and turn right on N. Millbend Road.

UTAH

PROSPECTOR SQUARE HOTEL
P.O. Box 1698
Park City, Utah 84060
(801) 649–7100
Salt Lake (801) 322–3123
NAT (800) 453–3812

Located deep in the heart of Utah's ski country, the Prospector is only an hour's drive from Deer Valley, Alta and Snowbird. Park City, a booming silver mining center in the 1860's, later becoming a ghost town, is now a rapidly growing resort community wise enough to keep its heritage alive. The movers and shakers of this city have spent much time and money preserving the area and its old structures. While you may be in an 1860's atmosphere, the resort is definitely in the 20th century.

There is a wide selection of accommodations: 100 hotel rooms, 180 kitchenette studios, plus many one- to three-bedroom condominiums. The condos feature fully-equipped kitchen, dining room, fireplace, and washer/dryer. There are also a few private homes available. The resort has meeting and conference facilities, with a capacity of from 12 to 330 people.

While the Grub Steak Restaurant is excellent there are several others, including cafes and delis along "Main Street." Despite what you may have heard about Utah, there are state liquor stores and you may purchase mini-bottles within most restaurants for consumption on premises. Kind of "mix it yourself" action.

The hotel offers a health and athletic club. Recently refurbished to the tune of over a half million dollars, it now offers weight and aerobic rooms, an indoor pool, steamrooms, four tennis and four indoor racquetball courts, along with a resident professional.

Although our primary concern is with golf, we would be remiss in not referring to their super winter facilities. This is, by the way, the official home of the United States Ski Team. And little wonder, with 35 miles of groomed slopes, a lift capacity of 5,800 skiers per hour and much more.

While there is no golf course contiguous to the hotel, there is the Park Meadows Country Club, a Jack Nicklaus designed layout and

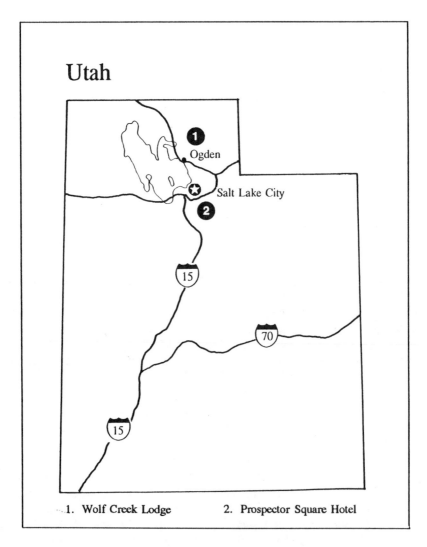

Utah

1. Wolf Creek Lodge   2. Prospector Square Hotel

the Park City Golf Course. Both are approximately one and a half miles away. In addition there is the Wasatch Mt. Golf Club 17 miles away offering 27 holes, and the Mountain Dell, also a regulation course, 12 miles from the hotel.

RATES (EP) Rooms: $55. Studio: $62. Condos $75/$125. Green fees: $34 including cart. Golf package: 1 night/1 day (includes studio room, green fees, cart), $110 per couple. Rates are May-September and include Athletic Club privileges.

ARRIVAL Air: Salt Lake City (40 minutes). Car: I-80, east-southeast of Salt Lake City.

WOLF LODGE
3615 North Wolf Creek Drive
Eden, UT 84310
(801) 745-2621

Accommodations consist of condominiums. All feature fully-equipped kitchens and wood burning fireplaces. Most border on the golf course. Dining facilities are provided in Wolf Creek Timberwolf Restaurant, offering a wide range of cuisine. There are several other restaurants in the area.

The Ogden Valley, due to its climate, is a natural setting for a four-season resort. In the winter, you are on top of some of the finest skiing available in the country—in the summer, change over to swimming in two pools, sailing and boating in Pine View Lake, the use of tennis courts, a racquetball center, horseback riding, weight rooms and a sauna.

The Country Club Resort course reaches out a healthy 6,825/6,459/5,816 yards and pars at 72/74. Whoever designed this layout obviously liked water, as it comes into play on 13 holes.

RATES (EP) Condo: 1 bedroom (sleeps up to four) $85; 2 bedrooms (sleeps up to 6) $105. Green fees: $20/$25, carts $18.

ARRIVAL Air: Salt Lake City. Car: from Ogden, take Highway 39 east to 166, north to Highway 162. Follow 162 to resort. A total of 12 miles.

WASHINGTON

ALDERBROOK INN RESORT
E 7101 Highway 106
Union, WA 98592
(206) 898-2200
(800) 622-9370

Alderbrook Inn is on the shores of Hood Canal, a fjord-like inlet of Puget Sound. The Inn has a total of 103 guest accommodations, 21 of which are cottages, each with two bedrooms, living room, fully-equipped kitchen and fireplace. The Inn can handle meeting groups of up to 150 people.

The dining room offers the standard fare, but does a special job with seafood, oysters, clams, scallops, mahi mahi, and halibut.

Activities available include: tennis on four courts, a sauna, and therapy pool. There is also a swimming pool enclosed in a year-round greenhouse.

Golf on this course is an experience you will long remember. Par-ring at 72/73, this little gem covers 6,312/6,133/5,506 yards. The professional smiles quietly *(or maybe it's a snicker)* when he hears someone threaten to "tear" up this course. While the second nine is very easy the front nine is another kettle of fish. The tight fair-ways, towering trees and sharp doglegs will test your nerves. I have seen a few golfers pray for a triple bogie on at least two holes.

RATES (EP) Rooms: $72/$85. Cottages: $110. Green fees: $20, carts $18.

ARRIVAL From Seattle: the Bremerton Ferry, then Highway 101 to Highway 106, turn right on 106 and drive 15 miles.

THE RESORT AT PORT LUDLOW
9483 Oak Bay Road
Port Ludlow, WA 98365
(206) 437-2222
WA (800) 732-1239

The Resort at Port Ludlow enjoys one of the most picturesque set-tings in the northwest. On a hill dense with towering trees, over-

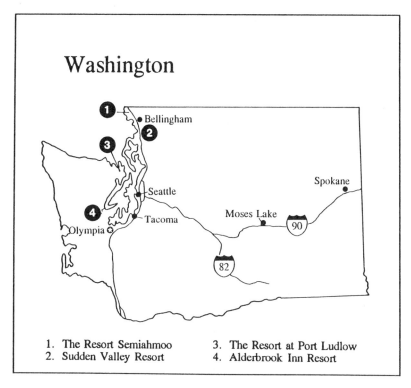

Washington

● Bellingham

Spokane

Seattle

Moses Lake

Tacoma

Olympia

90

82

1. The Resort Semiahmoo
2. Sudden Valley Resort
3. The Resort at Port Ludlow
4. Alderbrook Inn Resort

looking Ludlow Bay and the boat moorage, it is a magnificent picture. Accommodations range from one room to suites with living room, kitchen, fireplace, private decks and up to four bedrooms. Meeting facilities are available for groups of from 10 to 157.

The Harbormaster restaurant and lounge, with stunning architecture and food to match, offers nightly entertainment in the summer and on weekends during the winter.

A sample of the activities available include: tennis on seven courts, a very large heated pool, clam digging, fishing, boating, hiking, beachcombing or maybe just a relaxing posture on the beach. A new addition is an indoor swimming pool and whirlpool.

I suggest you use a cart on this course as it is extremely hilly. Reaching a significant 6,787/6,262/5,598 yards, parring at 72, it is, without doubt, one of the most beautiful golf courses we have played. Watching the deer feed on the edge of the fairway and, in some cases, crossing in front of you, can make it difficult to remember why you are out here. Should you entirely lose track of what you are doing, PGA professional Lyndon Blackwell and staff will be happy to help you get your game together.

RATES (EP) Bedroom: $90/$99. Suite loft: $130 and up. Green fees: $35/$45, carts $25. Golf package: 2 nights/2 days (includes lodging, green fees, cart), $348 per couple. Rates are for May-September.

ARRIVAL From Seattle, take the Seattle-Winslow or Edmonds-Kingston ferry, cross the Hood Canal bridge; 300 yards past the bridge turn right and follow the signs for about 8 miles.

THE RESORT SEMIAHMOO
9665 Semiahmoo Parkway
Blaine, WA 98230
(206) 371–2000
CA (800) 542–6082
CANADA (800) 854–6742
NAT (800) 854–2608

The Resort Semiahmoo, located in the northwest corner of the state, came into operation in mid-1987. The developers were very careful to blend their structures with the historic past of this area. The resort is on the tip of a sandspit, a turn-of-the-century center of the salmon canning industry, with many of these distinctive and colorful landmarks being woven into the fabric of the resort itself.

Lighthouse square was planned as a historic waterfront shopping village with festive outdoor eating spots, entertainment and local seafood markets. These activities are intermingled with those of the Inn-Athletic Club complex and the marina. As a matter of interest, of the 800 planned boat slips, over 300 are now available and in use.

The Semiahmoo Inn is a 200-room resort hotel providing 15,000 square feet of meeting and conference facilities, along with restaurants, lounges, and a complete health club. The Stars, a fine restaurant, is open for all three meals, while the Packers, the Oyster Bar & Lounge feature local seafood.

Accommodations are also available in townhouse condominiums. Clusters of townhouse groupings are built along the spit. The latter offer spectacular views of Drayton Harbor and the village complex, the San Juan Islands and the night lights of Whiterock,

Canada. Single-family homes and villas are also underway and there are lots available adjacent to the golf course.

Along with two tennis courts, located at the spa, there are two indoor racquetball courts, squash courts, an exercise room, and the most unusual indoor-outdoor swimming pool we have seen. It features pull-down garage-like doors to convert it into a warm inside entrance or an outdoor affair.

Adjacent to the Inn is a dock area offering San Jaun Island Cruises (Grayline water sightseeing tour). You can also arrange deep-sea fishing trips, departing from the resort on a regularly scheduled basis.

Now we come to the 18-hole championship golf course. Designed by Arnold Palmer/Ed Seay, and built on fully wooded and rolling terrain, it is approximately a mile from the resort. Reaching a very respectable 7,005/6,435/6,003/5,288 yards, it pars at 72.

As if the contoured hillsides and the problems introduced by densely wooded fir, hemlock, madrona and alder trees were not enough, there are four lakes which come into play on six different holes. Even though my game was a bit shaky, I found it to be one of the better and more relaxing rounds of golf I have enjoyed in some time.

RATES (EP) Rooms: $135/$185. Suites: $220. Green fees: $55, carts $22. Golf packages are available. Rates indicated are for the peak golf season mid-June to September 15.

ARRIVAL From Seattle, north on I-5 take exit 274 at Blaine. Turn left onto Bell Road which becomes Blaine Road and continue for 1 mile. Turn right onto Drayton Road and continue for about 4 miles. Follow signs.

SUDDEN VALLEY RESORT
2145 Lake Whatcom Blvd.
Bellingham, WA 98226
(206) 734–6430

Sudden Valley is on 1,500 acres, tucked away in the Chuckanut Mountains, the foothills of the magnificent Cascade range. There are 50 condominium units, each with living room, complete kitchen, cable TV, and superb views. Their meeting facilities can handle up to 150 along with suites for groups as small as 10. The dining room and cocktail lounge, housed in the main building, are excellent.

With its two miles of lakeshore the resort can provide many possibilities: a boat launch onto Lake Whatcom, fishing and canoeing, seven tennis courts, two swimming pools and hiking. There are also two recreation barns set up for children's activities.

The Sudden Valley Country Club Course is a Ted Robinson design. Weighing in at 6,553/6,143/5,627 yards, it pars at 72 and ranks among the more difficult layouts in the state. While fun, *easy, it is not!*

RATES (EP) Studio: $80/$95. Loft: $95/$110. 2-bedroom: $125 / $150. Green fees: $25/$35, cart $22. Golf package: 1 night/1 day (includes lodging, green fees),$115/$205 per couple.

ARRIVAL North on I-5, exit #240 (north of Everett). Turn right, continue through flashing light, left at stop sign (Lake Whatcom Boulevard) continue 5 miles. Traveling south take exit # 253, then left on Lakeway Drive (turns into Cable Street). At bottom of hill, the road swings sharply right and you are on Lake Whatcom Boulevard. Continue 5 miles.

WISCONSIN

THE ABBEY ON LAKE GENEVA

Fontana, WI 53125
(414) 275–6811
(800) 558–2405

The Abbey, situated in southern Wisconsin, is on the shores of Lake Geneva. Accommodations range from 340 guest rooms to approximately 32 condominium. The condo/villas feature fully-equipped kitchens and fireplaces. The resort can also accommodate meeting groups of up to 1,000.

The La Tour DeBois Restaurant presents French cuisine, while the Monaco offers less formal family dining. There is also the Waterfront Cafe. The Marina, with its 400 slips, provides boats for fishing, water skiing or just cruising this beautiful lake.

Tennis is available on six lighted courts. There are also one indoor and four outdoor swimming pools along with an indoor recreation and amusement arcade. Something new has been added—The Fontana Spa. I will not go into detail other than to say there are a thousand different ways to pamper your body—loofa scrubs, Swiss showers, Scotch hose, massage and on and on. I was afraid to ask what a Scotch hose is.

The Abbey, while having no golf course of its own, can arrange play for guests at the Lake Lawn Lodge course a few miles away. For details on this course refer to Lake Lawn Lodge. In fact there are four additional courses, including the Abbey Springs Country Club less than two miles away.

RATES (EP) Rooms: $120/$175 per couple. Suites: $250/$475. Green fees: $28, carts $25. Rates are for June-September.

ARRIVAL Air: Chicago (90 minutes). Airport limousine service is available. Private aircraft: paved runway capable of taking Lear jet, adjacent to the Lake Lawn Lodge (7 miles). Car: from Milwaukee, Highway 15 west to 67, south on 67 to Fontana.

THE ALPINE RESORT
P.O. Box 200
Egg Harbor, WI 45209
(414) 868–3000

The Bertschingers, operators of Alpine since its founding, have created a delightful resort. The main lodge has two large screened verandas overlooking Green Bay, appropriate for watching the pageant of colorful boats, fishermen and water skiers. Accommodations consist of 60 rooms in the Lodge and 40 cottages scattered throughout the grounds.

There is much to do here: tennis, riding, boating, just plain loafing, or swimming. The gently sloping beach, is safe for children. The resort recently added an outdoor heated pool. Social activities are informal and varied, with such things as an evening marshmallow roast, hayrides, lounge games or movies. It really is a family-oriented resort. The Alpine dining room prepares home cooked meals and fresh pastry from their own ovens.

The challenge on the resort's 27-hole golf course is found primarily in the rolling fairways and many trees. Using a crossover system, you have: the Red/White combination measuring 6,047/5,879 yards, parring 70/73; the Red/Blue 18 playing 5,858/5,440 yards with a par of 71/70; and the Blue/White course parring at 71/73, with a yardage of 6,207/5,837.

RATES (MAP) Room with bath: $90/$110 per couple. Duplex cottage: (living room, 1-bedroom and porch), $710 per couple per week. Green fees: $12, carts $15. Rates are for June 22-September 3.

ARRIVAL Air: Milwaukee. Car: from Milwaukee on I-43 to Manitowoc, then Highway 42 through Sturgeon Bay to Egg Harbor.

AMERICANA LAKE GENEVA RESORT
Highway 50
Lake Geneva, WI 53147
(414) 248–8811
Limited area (800) 558–3417

The Americana Lake Geneva Resort is an hour and a half from Chicago. The hotel is a complex of eight low-rise cedar, textured concrete and glass buildings. There are 340 well appointed rooms, featuring balconies or patio, each with a view of the lush Wisconsin countryside. The resort is equipped to handle group meetings of up to 1,250 banquet-style.

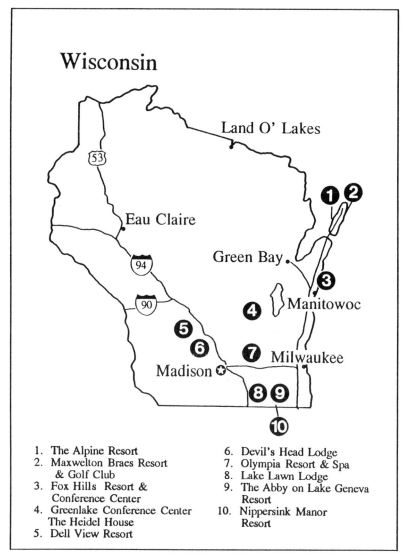

Wisconsin

Land O' Lakes

(53)

Eau Claire

(94)

Green Bay

(90)

1
2
3
Manitowoc
4
5
6
7 Milwaukee
Madison
8 9
10

1. The Alpine Resort
2. Maxwelton Braes Resort
   & Golf Club
3. Fox Hills Resort &
   Conference Center
4. Greenlake Conference Center
   The Heidel House
5. Dell View Resort

6. Devil's Head Lodge
7. Olympia Resort & Spa
8. Lake Lawn Lodge
9. The Abby on Lake Geneva
   Resort
10. Nippersink Manor
    Resort

Activities include: two swimming pools, four indoor and eight outdoor tennis courts, six racquetball courts, horseback riding, skeet
and trap shooting, boating on their 25-acre private lake, a
Nautilus-equipped health and fitness center, saunas, miniature
golf and an electronic game room. During winter you can add ice
skating and skiing.

There are a number of dining areas: Annie's Country Kitchen serving breakfast and lunch, The Americana Steak House, the Sidewalk Cafe, specializing in sandwiches and ice cream and the Cabaret Showroom featuring shows and entertainment on Friday and Saturday evenings. There is also a disco.

Golf is served up on two championship 18-hole courses. The Brute, a par-72 playing 7,258 yards was designed by Robert Bruce Harris. This aptly named course presents some 70 bunkers, many water hazards, rolling terrain and an abundance of trees. An added attraction are the greens, reputed to be the largest in the world at an average of 10,000 square feet. The Briar Patch, a Dye/Nicklaus design is a 6,900-yard par 71. Unlike The Brute it has very little water, few trees and small greens. There is a professional staff on deck to assist.

RATES (EP) Rooms: $79/$99. Suites: $199. Green fees: $50 including cart. Golf package: 2 nights/3 days (includes lodging, 2-rounds of golf, cart), $350/$398 per couple. Rates are for April-October.

ARRIVAL Air: Chicago. Private aircraft: Lake Geneva 4,100 foot. Car: from Chicago take I-90 west. Exit onto highway 12 north. Continue on to resort.

DELL VIEW RESORT MOTEL
P.O. Box 339
Lake Delton, WI 53940
(608) 253–1261

Dell View is in Wisconsin's well known Dells Lake/Delton area. Accommodations consist of rooms in the motel.

They offer indoor and outdoor pools, tennis, riding, fishing, boating, golf, miniature golf, steam rooms and a whirlpool. During the winter there is cross country skiing, snowmobiling, and ice skating.

The Gryphon Room has good food showcased in a relaxed atmosphere. The lounge offers nightly entertainment. They welcome, and are prepared to handle, modest-size meeting groups.

The course, supervised by a PGA professional, is short but can be tricky. It plays 5,750/5,497/5,363 yards with a par of 70/74. With water hazards on three holes and lateral water coming into play on another four, you need to keep alert to stay out of trouble.

RATES (EP) Rooms: $79/$98. Green fees: $22/$28, carts $22. Golf package: 2 nights/2 days (includes lodging, MAP, green fees, 25% off on cart), weekdays $198, weekends $236 per couple. Rates are for May through Labor Day.

ARRIVAL Air: Madison (45 miles). Car: from I-90/94 exit 92, onto U.S. 12, then approximately 1 mile.

DEVIL'S HEAD LODGE
Box 38
Merrimac, WI 53561
(608) 493–2251
WI (800) 472–6670

The lodge is just beneath the crest of Baraboo Bluff Range overlooking Lake Wisconsin. Accommodations are provided in the adjacent 238-room motel, with dining in the unique In-The-Round Chalet. There are meeting facilities for up to 300 people.

Tennis, swimming (indoor and outdoor pools), a fitness room, sauna, whirlpool, biking, sailing and golf are available.

Golf can be played on the Devil's Head course, measuring 6,725/6,336/5,141 yards and parring at 73. Not too much water, but dogleg holes and trees add to the tension (or fun).

RATES (EP) Rooms: weekdays $55; weekends: $70. Condominiums: $250/$350 for 2 nights. Green fees: $24, carts $22. Golf packages are available. Rates are for June-September.

ARRIVAL Air: Madison (40 miles). Car: I-90/94, then southwest on 78.

FOX HILLS RESORT & CONFERENCE CENTER
P.O. Box 129
Mishicot, WI 54228
(414) 755–2376
WI (800) 242–7615
Limited area (800) 558–7730

There are 160 rooms, including executive suites, at Fox Hills. Accommodations feature Jacuzzis and wood burning fireplaces. The resort is exceptionally well equipped to handle meeting groups. For details ask for their Meeting Planner's Kit. Special touches are the imported crystal chandeliers in the dining room and the spacious lounge featuring dancing and entertainment nightly.

There are a variety of things to keep you occupied: tennis, a game room, charter fishing on Lake Michigan, an indoor swimming pool, golf and, in the winter, skiing.

Golf can now be played on 45 holes. Parring at 72, the Fox Hills National Golf Club course is a very substantial 7,017/ 6,574/6,267/ 5,366 yards. The National is definitely a Scottish links layout. With undulating mounded terrain and water on 10 holes, it is an exceptionally well trapped golf course. This has been recognized as one of the best layouts in the area.

The Fox Hills Resort course (27 holes) plays the Front/Back nine at 6,374/6,107/5,688 yards with a par of 72/73. The combination of the Back/Blue nines measures 6,410/6,081/5,721 yards, parring at 71/73. The Front/Blue courses reach out a more modest 6,224/ 5,597/5,597 yards, with a par of 71/72. The resort provides a full time resident professional as well as a newly remodeled golf shop.

RATES (EP) Rooms: $85/$105. Suites: $140/$200. Green fees: $20/ $22, carts $20. There are several different golf packages available. Rates are for May 15-October 15.

ARRIVAL Air: Milwaukee or Green Bay. Car: from Milwaukee, I-43 exit onto highway 82 and travel east.

GREENLAKE CONFERENCE CENTER
State Route 23
Green Lake WI 54941
(414) 294–3323
(800) 558–8898

Greenlake is an American Baptist Assembly conference center. It occupies 1,000 acres on the shores of Green Lake. While this resort is ideal for meeting groups, with a capacity of up to 1200 people, it also caters to those seeking excellent golf and a relaxed vacation. The food here is not only exceptionally good, but is also modestly priced. A nice surprise indeed.

There are accommodations in the main lodge as well as various cottages and homes. The latter feature fully equipped kitchens, most with fireplaces. There are also camping sites.

A word of warning; due to the resort's church affiliation, no alcoholic beverage may be consumed on the grounds. That means no drinks are allowed, even in your own room.

Some of the activities available include: fishing, water skiing, bicycling, boating (paddleboats, rowboats, canoes, sailboards, sailboats and pontoon boats), an indoor swimming pool, tennis and golf. Hayrides can also be arranged.

Eighteen holes of the Lawsonia Links have been designed in the style of the famous Scottish links and have been rated by *Golf Digest* as one of the top 25 public courses in the United States.

The 27 holes of golf combine to play as follows. The South/West is 6,640/6,335/5,209 yards with a par of 72. The West/East combination is 6,754/6,469/5,077 yards, parring at 72/71. The East/South nines, 6,604/6,296/4,918 yards, also pars at 72/71. With several of the holes on the South Course adjacent to the lake, and noted for its deep-faced bunkers and elevated greens, you will find it a fun tour.

RATES (EP) Lodge rooms: $58. Cottages: $70/$86. Cabins: $70/$86. Green fees: $25/35, carts $22. Weekly rates as well as golf package are available. The above rates include 3 meals a day per couple.

ARRIVAL Air: Oshkosh, WI (30 miles from airport). Private aircraft: Fond du Lac (8 miles), small sod landing strip. Car: from Oshkosh travel State Highway 44 to intersection with Interstate 23. Go west on 23 to the resort entrance—2 miles west of Green Lake.

THE HEIDEL HOUSE
P.O. Box 9
Green Lake, WI 54941
(414) 294–3344
(800) 444–2812

Plan to be pampered when you visit The Heidel House. It is really something special. Accommodations are varied, to say the least, ranging from rooms, semi-suites, and suites, to the Stable House (four bedrooms) and the Grey Rock Mansion (10,000 square feet, accommodating 14 people). Small groups of up to 100 find the Mansion delightful for meetings.

You have a choice of three dining areas: the main dining room, featuring gourmet entrees, the Rathskeller and the Fondue Chalet.

Green Lake, the deepest in Wisconsin, provides not only a beautiful setting but makes available all kinds of water activities. From spring through fall they offer excursions and charter parties on the Heidel House yacht. They refer to this as "yachts of fun." *That statement I will not touch.*

There is an indoor pool, saunas and a full time professional in charge of their tennis program.

The Tuscumbia Golf & Country Club's course, in operation since 1896, weighs in at 6,301/5,833 yards, and pars at 71/72. There is a resident professional as well a delightful golf shop. There are, in addition, two other courses where play can be arranged, the Mascoutin Golf Club and the 27-hole layout at Lawsonia.

RATES (EP) Rooms: $99/$115. Lower Bungalow: $140/$160. Upper Bungalow: $155/$175. Pump House: $140/$160. Green fees: $35 including cart. Golf package: 2 nights/3 days (includes lodging, 3 days green fees covering choice of 63 holes of golf and cart, plus $40 per person of Fun Money which can be applied to meals), weekdays $450, weekends $498 per couple. Rates are for June 16-September 5.

ARRIVAL Air: Milwaukee or Madison. Car: from Milwaukee take 41, left on 23 to Green Lake.

LAKE LAWN LODGE
Box 527
Delavan, WI 53115
WI (800) 338–5296
NAT (800) 338–5253

The lodge is nestled on 275 prime wooded acres fronting on Lake Delavan. There are 284 guest rooms including suites and loft rooms. Each unit features wood paneling, vaulted ceilings and natural stone. With 28 meeting rooms they are equipped to handle groups or banquets of up to 500 people.

Dining is available in the Frontier Room and the coffee shop, with the unique Lookout Bar for an evening libation. Nightly entertainment is offered in the Frontier Cocktail Lounge.

Lake Delavan provides boating, water skiing, fishing and swimming. In addition to the lake activity, there are two indoor swimming pools, seven indoor tennis courts, horseback riding, and a health spa complete with a steam room, sauna and hydrotherapy pools.

Golf can be played from May through October. A lovely layout, the Lake Lawn Golf Course is a modest 6,418/6,173/5,215 yards and pars at 70. You will find it a challenge, with traps and trees in great abundance. There is an excellent clubhouse and a first rate teaching professional on deck.

RATES (EP) Lodges: $109/$125. Loft rooms: $129/$145. Suites, 1-bedroom: $225/$275. Green fees: $28, carts $25. Golf package: 2 night/3 day (includes lodging, MAP, green fees, club storage, and gratuities on food), $430/$470 per couple. Rates are for July-September.

ARRIVAL Air: Chicago (75 miles). Milwaukee (50 miles). Private aircraft: The Lodge, 4,400-foot, lighted runway. Car: from Chicago, I-94 north to Highway 50, then west to Delavan.

MAXWELTON BRAES RESORT & GOLF CLUB
Bonnie Brae Road
Baileys Harbor, WI 54202
(414) 839–2321

The name Maxwelton Braes comes from the song "Annie Laurie" whose home, located near St. Andrew's Golf Course, was called Maxwelton House. Due to the similarity in setting, the resort was given the same name.

You can stay in lodge rooms or cottages, with living room, two bedrooms, and either one or two baths. They have the facilities to handle modest-size groups on a seasonal basis. Dining is provided in the new Scottish Grill & Lounge. There is also dancing each evening. Less formal dining is available at the Wee Inn Coffee Shop.

In addition to two lighted tennis courts, they now have a large swimming pool. There is also boating, horseback riding, bicycling and excellent fishing.

Golf is played on the Maxwelton Braes Country Club course. This links layout with rolling fairways, unusually large bent grass greens and dotted with bunkers, plays a modest 6,019/5,867 yards. It pars at 70/74.

RATES (MAP) Lodge: $98/$102 per couple. Cottages: $100/$110 per couple. Green fees: $20 carts $18 Golf packages are available. Rates are for June-September.

ARRIVAL Air: Green Bay. Car: from Green Bay, north on Highway 57.

NIPPERSINK MANOR RESORT
P.O. Box 130
Genoa City, WI 53128
(414) 279–5281
WI (800) 541–5442
Limited area (800) 647–7465

When you start with outstanding accommodations, add fine dining and excellent service, you produce a superior resort such as Nippersink Manor. Lodgings consist of hotel rooms, new suites and recently renovated cottages. The Manor has convention facilities for groups of 10 to 500. There is also a baby sitting service available.

The resort serves food that is not only of excellent quality but is also varied. For example, one of the appetizers on the menu was *"sweetwater gefilte fish."* I was not up to this one, but I did my part on a filet mignon, and destroyed a homemade banana cream pie. Cocktail patio dancing and nightly entertainment are also provided.

Even if golf is not your thing, there is much to do here. Possibilities include an outdoor swimming pool, boating on adjacent Lake Tombeau (including water skiing), tennis on six courts, along with horseback riding nearby. The golf course with its two tee settings weighs in at 6,289/5,905 yards with a par of 71/76. Although there is little water on this layout it features very small greens, many traps and rolling hilly terrain.

RATES (FAP) Cottage: (private bath) $175 per couple. Hotel deluxe room: $192 per couple. Green fees: $18/$20, carts $22. Rates are for the July-August period.

ARRIVAL Air: Chicago (60 miles). Car: north on U.S. 41 or I-94 to Illinois 173, west to U.S. 12, right for ¼ mile, right on Burlington Road (Highway "P"). Follow signs for 3 miles.

OLYMPIA RESORT & SPA
1350 Royale Mile Road
Oconomowoc, WI 53006
(414) 567–0311
(800) 558–9573

The Olympia is one of the more "posh" resorts. The evidence can be seen in the beautiful lobby with its fireplace wall that seems to reach the sky, as well as the beamed ceilings and massive skylights. The general setting of the resort further enhances this evaluation with its beautiful forested hills, rivers, lakes and meadows.

The 400 rooms have a view of either the course or the lake and are nicely furnished, with the suites featuring open fireplaces and wet bars. The meeting facilities are equally impressive, with a capacity of up to 1,500 banquet- and 2,000 theater-style.

For dining there is a choice of four restaurants. The Royal Cellar is a gourmet dining room supported by an outstanding wine cellar. There is also the Garden Room Coffee Shop, the Terrace Room, and the Beach House located on Silver Lake.

A tennis program is offered on four indoor and seven outdoor courts (four lighted). In addition to tennis and golf there are many activities to keep you busy, four new racquetball courts, indoor and outdoor swimming pools and spa facilities which are among the best in the country. The Spa, under the supervision of a professional staff, offers men's and women's gyms, whirlpool baths, steam rooms, saunas, Grecian showers, and massage. Should you care to venture out on Silver Lake you can add, sailing and water skiing to the mix.

If you are having "control" problems with your golf game you might consider taking up sailing. There is enough water to accommodate you right on the course. Playing at 6,567/6,364/6,056 yards, it pars at 71/75. With water a factor on 10 holes, lots of trees and traps, you will find this a most interesting and challenging layout. If things get too tough, professionals are on deck to help with lessons and a well stocked golf shop.

Recently added are two polo fields adjacent to the golf course. If your game gets out of hand you may elect to watch the polo games instead. Just don't hit the wrong ball as it won't fit in the cup.

The Olympic, open year-round, has an excellent winter sports package, including downhill as well as cross country skiing. They also have time-share condominiums.

RATES (EP) Hotel: $105. Suites: $190. Villas: 1-bedroom, $95 / $125; 2-bedroom, $175. Green fees: $20, carts $22. Golf package: 2

nights/2 days (includes lodging, 1-dinner, 1-lunch, 1-breakfast, 36 holes of golf with cart), $366 per couple. Rates are for late June to mid-September.

ARRIVAL Air: Milwaukee (30 minutes). Chicago (2 hours). Car: from Milwaukee, I-94 to exit 282, continue on Route 67 1½ miles to resort.

WYOMING

GRAND TETON-JACKSON HOLE AREA

The sheer, stark, beauty of this country is difficult to describe. It is truly "High Country". As a point of interest the highest point in Wyoming is 13,804 feet (Gannett Peak), but what is not generally realized is that *the lowest point of elevation in the entire state* is still a very substantial 3,100 feet above sea level (Belle Fourche River).

Seven miles west of Jackson, in Teton Country, is a 40-mile-long, 8-mile-wide valley. Set within this valley is Teton Pines Golf Course. There are two resorts—the new Teton Pines, which came into operation in late 1989, and the Jackson Hole Racquet Club Resort, which has been established for several years.

On the floor of the valley, surrounded by mountains on all sides, this Arnold Palmer designed golf course will give you all you can handle. A few of its more challenging features include: the distraction created by the magnificent Teton Mountain views, 40 acres of water either threatening or coming into play on 11 holes, and three acres of sand spread over 50 bunkers. There is more than enough water coming into play to make you feel you are in Florida. With its undulating fairways the course plays, 7,401/6,888/6,333/5,486 yards, parring at 72. It is without doubt one of the most beautiful layouts we have seen.

Due to the outstanding scenery you may spend more time "looking up" than usual, in which case Director of Golf, Bob Marshall, or teaching professional, John Godwin, are available to assist you in breaking this foolish and, most often, very costly habit. A second golf course, The Jackson Hole Country Club is also available for play. Near the airport this course measures a sizable 7,168/6,783/6,036 yards.

The Teton Pines clubhouse (finished in late 1988) is 23,000 square feet and has a formal as well as an informal dining room. Other amenities include a bar and lounge. On the lower level may be found the men's and women's locker rooms, the men's card room and the rod and gun club. On the upper level, in addition to the main lobby, there is a ladies' card room, the aforementioned dining areas, conference facilities and the pro shop.

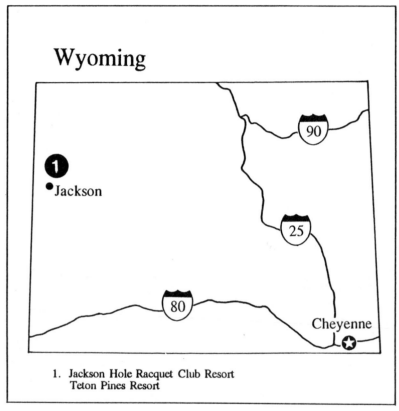

Wyoming

1 ●Jackson

90

25

80

Cheyenne

1. Jackson Hole Racquet Club Resort
   Teton Pines Resort

The tennis pavilion, a separate structure, supports the seven-court complex (three indoor with a center stadium court). There is a tennis shop, a video instruction room, juice bar, shower rooms and Jacuzzi. The resident professional conducting the "John Gardiner Tennis Center" is Dave Luebbe. Their outstanding tennis school uses all the latest state-of-the-art equipment (video replay and ball machines) to make the game more enjoyable.

There is an unusual attraction available—a fly fishing school. Headed up by nationally recognized fly fishing expert Jack Dennis, the instructions cover how to tie a fly, read a stream, casting for trout, and all the other fine points. They really get into it in a most sophisticated manner, using videotape replay to critique and analyze your casting technique.

It is almost redundant to cover the winter sports activities at your disposal. On the property is a 10-kilometer cross country ski course, within four miles is the Teton Village, with downhill facilities. This area represents the greatest vertical drop (4,139 feet) and is one of the largest ski areas in the United States. With 22 miles of groomed trails and spanning two mountains, its slopes are also equipped for night skiing.

While the ski areas are outstanding for the accomplished and expert ski nut, a great percentage of the slopes, and attendant facilities, are designed to accommodate the beginner and/or the intermediate ski enthusiast. Both resorts provide (during the winter) shuttle service.

A few additional activities within the immediate area include river rafting, horseback riding and polo.

A WORD OF WARNING: while it can get pretty warm during the lazy summer days, warm clothing is recommended for evening as it can turn equally cool.

In addition to the Country Club restaurants there are two "eating experiences" awaiting you. Located in Jackson and open for lunch as well as dinner is The Blue Lion. I will not go into detail, but one menu selection was "Jalapeno Garlic Shrimp". It was as good as it sounds. Another excellent restaurant, found at the Racquet Club Resort, is Stieglers, featuring Austrian/continental cuisine.

JACKSON HOLE RACQUET CLUB RESORT
Star Route Box 3647
Jackson, WY 83001
(307) 733–3990
(800) 443–8616

The Jackson Hole Racquet Resort is nestled at the base of the Teton Mountain Range. There are 120 well appointed condominiums ranging in size from studio and one-bedroom units to luxurious three-bedroom/loft townhouses. Each condo (including studios) features a fully-equipped kitchen, cable TV, washer/dryer along with a wood burning fireplace. A nice touch—firewood is provided at no additional charge.

Guests of the Racquet Resort have complimentary use of the private athletic club including: saunas, whirlpools, steam rooms, a Nautilus-equipped workout room, as well as the outdoor heated swimming pool. Although requiring court fees, racquetball and tennis are also available.

A few additional amenities, located on premises, include Stiegler's Restaurant & Bar a full service grocery store and a liquor store. Something new has been added in the form of meeting facilities. The resort is now capable of handling meeting or conference groups up to 100.

RATES (EP) Studio: $120. 1-bedroom unit: $145. 3 bedrooms plus loft with 2½ baths: (up to 6 people) $274. Rates are for the summer of July and August.

ARRIVAL Air: Jackson Hole Airport (8 miles). Car: 7 miles from Jackson on Highway 390 (also known as the Teton Village Highway), 13 miles to Grand Teton National Park and 63 miles to the south entrance of Yellowstone National Park.

TETON PINES RESORT
Star Route Box 3669
Jackson, WY 83001
(307) 733–1005
(800) 238–2223

While Teton Pines Resort is basically a residential resort community they have recently completed accommodations for overnight or weekly guests. Consisting of "Country Club Suites," these very posh units are rented as bedrooms or as full suites. None of the units are equipped with kitchens.

In addition to the facilities of the clubhouse which, by the way, is located on premises, the Teton Village (four miles away) has a selection of restaurants, shops, art galleries, and live stage shows. The town of Jackson (seven miles away) offers some distinctive restaurants and shops along with the Grand Teton Music Festival, art exhibits and so forth.

A heated swimming pool, adjacent to the clubhouse, is now in place. All of the amenities described under the "Grand Teton-Jackson Hole Area" on the proceeding pages are available to guests of the Pines Resort.

RATES (EP) 1-bedroom (with deck): $265. 1-bedroom (fireplace, deck and living room): $370. Green fees: $48, carts $24.

ARRIVAL Air: Jackson Hole Airport (8 miles). Car: 7 miles west of Jackson (on Highway 390, also referred to as the Teton Village Highway); 13 miles from Grand Teton National Park; 63 miles to Yellowstone National Park; 82 miles to Idaho Falls; 280 miles to Salt Lake City.

CANADA

ALBERTA

BANFF SPRINGS HOTEL
P.O. Box 960
Banff, Alberta
T0L 0C0 Canada
(403) 762–2211
Canada (800) 268–9411
Ont & Que (800) 268–9420
U.S. (800) 828–7447

The architect of the Banff Springs Hotel, confronted with the same breathtaking, awesome scenery as that dealt with by the architect of Jasper Lodge, chose the opposite solution. He did not attempt to blend in or hide the buildings. Rather he took these massive mountains head on. The result was this magnificent fortress-like structure. Although the resort's original facilities date back to the late 1800s, the current buildings originally opened in 1928, becoming a year round operation in 1969. During that period a major restoration was started and is, as a matter of fact, still underway. The hotel now offers accommodations in 829 rooms and suites, including a total of 245 rooms added in 1987. With The Ballroom and 15 break-out rooms, Banff can accommodate (classroom-style) 350 and banquet-style from 25 to 800.

You can enjoy a wide selection of dining areas: The Alberta Dining Room (breakfast, luncheon, dinner), The Alhambra Room for breakfast and dinner, The Rob Roy Room for intimate dining and the Samurai Japanese Restaurant for a taste of the Orient. Located at the Banff Manor is the new 250-seat Coffee Shop, as well as the outdoor Terrace Restaurant. Should you still be hungry there is the Pot Pourri Deli for selections of pastries and sandwiches, the Espresso Cafe, open 24 hours, and (weather permitting) the Red Terrace for outdoor barbecues and cocktails. I am really not trying to make you ill, but there is also 17-hour room service in case you need something to tide you over.

There are as many bars as there are restaurants: the Rundle Lounge, the Grapeswine Bar, the Golf Clubhouse serving light snacks and with a full-service bar, the Cafe and, something new added in 1985, "The Works", a night club open until 2:00 AM.

The Hotel is, in reality, a city, operating within the walls of a huge castle. In addition to the facilities indicated above there are the following activities available: an indoor Olympic-size swimming pool as well as a smaller outdoor pool, Jacuzzis, a sauna, an exercise area and five tennis courts (with professional Al Robinson on deck to assist).

If water activity is your thing you may want to try your hand at fishing or sightseeing aboard, *The Great Escape*. If you can yank yourself back on dry land, a few more avenues of activity await you: horseback riding (including overnight pack trips and a morning breakfast ride), bicycling and, of course, hiking and mountain climbing. For the more adventurous, rafting tours including a two-day trip can be arranged. These tour groups supply everything— guides, rafts, tents, sleeping bags, waterproof storage for your clothing, and food. There are a variety of sightseeing tours leaving throughout the day which will allow you to see as much of this truly spectacular scenery as you wish.

Should you opt to just relax around the hotel, you will find that between the lobby, the arcade and the lower arcade, there must be a total of 40 different shops or services available. There is a tanning salon and masseuse, a post office, a money exchange "bank", and a beauty and barber shop. This is one very busy place. I recommend that you spend the time to really explore its many delightful shops, alcoves and various levels.

One thing I did not mention: the entire area is surrounded by mile upon rolling mile of beautiful dense forests. Beautiful that is until a few trees get in front of you on the golf course. At that time they seem to lose some of their appeal. It is not at all unusual to see elk on this course, particularly in the morning.

The Banff Golf Course now consists of three nines. Using a crossover pattern, you may play the Rundle/Sulphur combination, stretching 6,626/6,391/6,282/5,964 yards with a par of 71. The Sulphur/Tunnel nines weigh in at 6,721/6,420/6,014 yards, also parring at 71. They must grow their ladies big and strong as that yardage (6,014) is a bit much. The final combination is the Rundle/Tunnel course which reaches out 6,443/6,117/5,652 yards and pars at 72.

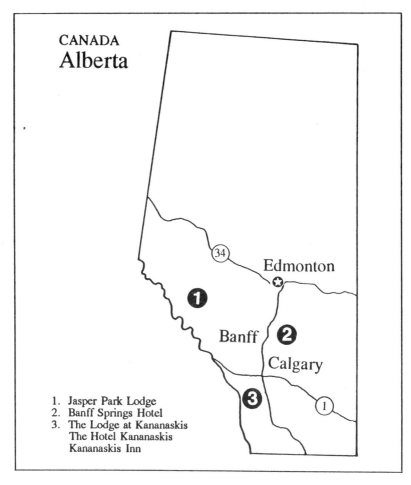

CANADA
Alberta

(34)

Edmonton

Banff   ❷
Calgary

❶

❸

(1)

1. Jasper Park Lodge
2. Banff Springs Hotel
3. The Lodge at Kananaskis
   The Hotel Kananaskis
   Kananaskis Inn

The Rundle and the Tunnel nines each bring water into play on only three holes. The Sulphur layout is, however, a different kettle of fish as the Bow and the Spray Rivers present an interesting challenge on at least six holes.

The architects, Cornish/Robinson, went to great lengths to blend the new creation with the original Stanley Thompson design. It is said the new nine has views even more spectacular than those provided on the original layout. I am not sure that is at all possible—but I certainly, want to see it. There is also a new clubhouse. Put into operation in the fall of 1988, it features a circular design and provides an outdoor patio, a lounge and dining room, coffee shop, locker rooms and a well stocked golf shop. It also offers a spectacular view of the entire area. Head professional Doug Wood, and staff, are on deck to assist.

RATES (EP) Twin room: $165/$270. 1-bedroom suites: $390 / $470. Green fees: $39, carts $26. Rates are for peak season May 15-October 11th.

ARRIVAL Air: Calgary (about 85 miles). Car: from the south take Highway 2 to Calgary. From Calgary go west on the four-lane Trans-Canada Highway 1.

JASPER PARK LODGE
P.O. Box 40
Jasper, Alberta
T0E 1E0 Canada
(403) 852–3301
Alberta (800) 642–3817
U.S. (800) 828–7447

We were pleasantly surprised by our first view of the Jasper Park Lodge. I think we expected something more massive and imposing. Located within the heart of the Jasper National Park, this famous resort complements and blends beautifully with the surrounding countryside. The architect was indeed a wise man, recognizing the fact that there was little built by man that could compete with the spectacular backdrop formed by the Canadian Rocky Mountains. These magnificent mountains dominate every aspect of the area.

Do not be misled by the above comments, for this is not a small operation. On the contrary, there are 400 rooms and suites including the deluxe Beauvert Suites. Some of the features include sitting rooms, living and dining rooms, patios and log burning fireplaces. The Lodge, including the adjacent chalets, can accommodate up to 800 guests.

Should you still have a doubt as to the scope of this resort, their 10 fully equipped conference rooms can accommodate up to 1,000 people. They also provide the following amenities: a full money exchange bank, a gift shop, fur, jewelry, clothing and sportswear shops, and a hairdresser.

There are three dining rooms to choose from—The Beauvert, Moose's Nook and The Henry House, each featuring a different selection. With a relaxing lounge, live entertainment and dancing nightly, you may never see the inside of your room.

The recreational facilities are almost endless: tennis on four hard-surfaced courts (with a professional staff), a heated outdoor swimming pool, exercise rooms, and a whirlpool. There are men's and women's locker areas (with saunas and steamrooms), a game room featuring table tennis, shuffleboard, pool and various video games.

A sample of the other activities include: facilities for croquet, a fully-equipped equestrian center offering trail and overnight rides, bicycling, as well as jogging and hiking on the 3.8-kilometer trail surrounding Lac Beauvert. Speaking of the lake, they also offer fishing, rowboats, canoes, sailboats, windsurfing and pedal boats. If you really want to get serious, white water paddle rafting can be arranged on the mighty Athabasca River. There are a number of different sightseeing excursions scheduled each day enabling you to explore as much of this magnificent area as you wish.

If you can bring yourself to withdraw from the lodge and its various activities you might consider a round of golf. The Jasper Golf Course originally came into being in 1925. It was virtually plowed under at the end of World War II, then completely rebuilt, with the present clubhouse opening in May of 1968. Parring at 71/75 it measures 6,598/6,323/6,037 yards. With gently rolling terrain, each fairway lined by trees, more than a fair number of sand bunkers coming into play, and with water becoming a nuisance on four holes—this layout will keep your undivided attention.

I hate to keep harping on a point, but the view of the surrounding mountains does, in fact, become a definite factor. Should you keep gawking, instead of paying attention to business, you may well find yourself unable to pay your hotel bill.

The operation of the course, as well as the outstanding pro shop, is under the direction of head professional, Ron MacLeod.

RATES (MAP) Regular room: $294/$326 per couple. Beauvert Suites: $439 per couple. Green fees: $44, carts $28.

ARRIVAL Air: Jasper Hinton Airport (30 minutes). Car: from Calgary take Highway 1 west to the junction of Highway 93. Take Highway 93 (Banff/Jasper Road) north to Jasper. A total of 260 miles.

KANANASKIS VILLAGE

This beautiful 4,000-square-kilometer wildlife sanctuary, with its hundreds of picnic areas, has three provincial parks within its boundaries—Kananaskis, Bow Valley and Bragg Creek.

Approximately 55 miles west of Calgary, the Kananaskis Village was put together for the prime purpose of supporting the 1988 Winter Olympics. Of course, each of the facilities operates year-round.

Adjacent to Nakiska at Mount Allan (location of the 1988 Winter Olympics), the area includes: a ski run with a vertical drop of 2,493 feet, one fixed-grip double chair, one fixed-grip triple chair and a detachable quad chairlift. The total lift capacity is 8,600 people per hour.

It is aptly named a village, as it provides lodgings in the Hotel Kananaskis, the Lodge at Kananaskis and the Kananaskis Inn. There is also a Village Center Building, a facility to provide visitors as well as overnight hotel guests some of the essential services--a post office, an information center, sports equipment rentals, showers, lockers, saunas, a lounge, two meeting rooms, and so forth. There are also various shops housed within each of the hotel properties. The centerpiece of the village, fronting each hotel, is a most delightful outdoor ice skating rink (during the summer a pond). The hotels surrounding the skating rink are within 100 yards of each other, allowing guests to walk with ease from one to the other.

While writing the above I have been avoiding a description of the surrounding area. It is not easy to do justice to this scenery. I have seen the rugged mountains in Alaska, China, Japan and the magnificent mountains of western Colorado. While all of them are, most certainly, breathtakingly beautiful none come close to these mountains. While the Canadian Rocky Mountain range is most spectacular as it stretches out from Jasper Park in the northwest, it becomes even more awesome as you travel southeast and reaches a visual crescendo in the Kananaskis area. These mountains are a great deal more than just beautiful or awesome—they are, in fact, intimidating. While Alaska's mountain ranges are startling, I think the difference is the fact few of us can really get close to them. These mountains, on the other hand, are right on top of you. As you approach Kananaskis from the northeast along Highway 40, the emotional impact is unsurpassed.

Within five minutes of the village, and within this magnificent area, are two of the most interesting golf courses you will find anywhere. The Kananaskis Country Club course is, in reality, two superb 18-hole layouts. Specifically the Mt. Lorette course weighs in at a more than substantial 7,102/6,643/6,155/5,429 yards and pars at 72. While designed by Robert Trent Jones,Sr., it must have been during a period in which he discovered that water can become a definite irritant to golfers. On the front nine, eight holes bring water into play. On the back side the Kananaskis River decides to get into the act and five holes become involved. Then to add to the excitement which nature had provided in the form of trees, Mr. Jones tried to outdo by adding sand bunkers. They are scattered around both courses like snowflakes. As I recall there are some 136 in total.

Now we come to the Mt. Kidd layout, which operates out of the same clubhouse. It measures a masochistic 7,049/6,604/6,068/5,539 yards. Like the Mt. Lorette course, it pars at 72. On the front nine, you may think you are playing in Florida as eight of the first nine holes introduce water into play. Our old neighbor, the Kananaskis River, is back and brought a friend along by the name of Evan Thomas Creek. I assume they tire of being a nuisance because on the back nine water only becomes a factor on two holes. While the Mt. Lorette course presents large, undulating and irregularly shaped greens, Mt. Kidd has somewhat smaller ones. One thing you must keep in mind—you have not gotten stronger, you are not ready for the tour, but you are a bit over 4,800 feet above sea level. That is why you are driving so far—so tuck your ego back in and carry on.

After a round you can relax in an exceptionally fine clubhouse— offering a lounge, excellent dining facilities, in the form of a dining room, as well as two outdoor terraces, plus two snack bars. There are also men's and women's locker rooms. The well stocked pro shop, the hub of action, operates under the guidance of the Director of Golf, Brian Bygrave, and Head Professional, Wayne Bygrave.

For tee times call within Alberta (800) 372–9215 or outside Alberta call (800) 661–1581 or (403) 261–4653. The courses are public and are open to guests of all of the hotels. Green fees: $30, carts $25.

During the summer months you can add to the mix: fishing (21 stocked lakes), camping, hiking, bicycling and horseback riding (there are four guest ranches in the area), as well as use of the tennis complex (six courts).

ARRIVAL Air: Calgary (1 hour, 55 miles). Car: from Calgary travel Highway 1 west to Highway 40. Turn south to Kananaskis. The resort is 49 miles from Banff via Highway 1 and 40.

THE HOTEL KANANASKIS
Kananaskis Village Resort
Kananaskis Country, Alberta
T0L 0C0 Canada
Canada (800) 268–9411
Ont & Que (800) 268–9420
U.S. (800) 828–7447

In early 1988 the Hotel Kananaskis, a 70-suite VIP affair adjacent to the lodge, came into being. It was designed as a luxurious manor-style hotel, featuring a lobby lounge along with a dining room specializing in French cuisine. Additional amenities include a sauna, a steam room and Jacuzzi, an exercise room and, of course, access to all of the services provided by the village.

For details on the golf courses refer to "Kananaskis Village".

RATES (EP) Rooms: $160. Executive suites: $210/$220. 1-bedroom suites: $300/$370. Green fees: $30, carts $25.

KANANASKIS INN
Kananaskis Village, Alberta
T0L 2H0 Canada
(403) 591–7500
Alberta (800) 332–1013
Canada (800) 661–1064

The Inn, also in the village, has 96 rooms and suites. Many of the suites feature fireplaces, private whirlpool baths and balconies. Thirty-two of the suites are equipped with kitchenettes.

The dining room is adjacent to the lobby and is a sunroom type with large windows giving a stunning view of the surrounding area. Woody's Pub on the ground floor offers an opportunity to meet friends and enjoy a cool one.

Amenities include an indoor swimming pool, hot tubs, a steam room and Jacuzzi, a patio deck for sunning, a gift shop and access to the shopping plaza of the village. There is also an underground parking garage. The Inn also is capable of hosting meeting or conference groups of up to 250.

For details on the golf courses refer to "Kananaskis Village".

RATES Standard: $105. Executive: $115. Loft: $135. Suites: $250/$295. Rates are for the period of June through September. Green fees: $30, carts $25.

THE LODGE AT KANANASKIS
Kananaskis Village Resort
Kananaskis Country, Alberta
T0L 0C0 Canada
(403) 591–7711
Canada (800) 268–9411
Ont & Que (800) 268–9420
U.S. (800) 828–7447

The Lodge at Kananaskis came into being in mid-1987 and was designed as a year-round operation. There are 255 rooms, including 64 suites with fireplaces. There is a 190-car underground heated garage beneath this three-story structure. The meeting and convention facilities are outstanding. The main ballroom can be divided into three reception or meeting rooms. Kananaskis also has a banquet capacity of 800 as well as two private dining rooms for intimate groups.

The main guest dining room can handle 300 people. There is also a Japanese restaurant, the Sushi & Shabu Shabu bar. In fact the dining facilities range from casual to gourmet.

Available activities include a fully equipped health club, steam rooms, a tanning salon, an exercise room, an indoor swimming pool, whirlpools and a sauna.

For details on the golf courses refer to "Kananaskis Village."

RATES (EP) Rooms: $150. Executive suite: $180/$210. 1-bedroom suite: $300/$370. Rates quoted are for the peak golf season—late June through early October. Green fees: $30, cart $25.

BRITISH COLUMBIA

CHATEAU WHISTLER RESORT
4599 Chateau Blvd., Box 100
Whistler, BC V0N 1B0
(604) 938–8000
Canada (800) 268–9411
Ont & Que (800) 268–9420
U.S. (800) 828–7447

It is more than 100 years since a grand chateau hotel has been built in Canada. One need only look at the enormous cost involved to understand why it has been so long. A bit over $50 million. In late November of 1989 the massive 12-story Chateau Whistler Resort greeted its first quests. It reflects a strange mixture—the motif is of the 1800's but it is a new structure with all of the modern amenities available to us in this century. The setting does little to dispel the grandeur, with beautiful Blackcomb Mountain forming the backdrop.

To say that it is elaborate may be one of the great understatements. There are 343 guest rooms including 36 suites as well as 14,000 square feet of space set aside for convention/meeting groups. The resort can handle groups of up to 750 theater- or 400 classroom-style.

The dining and entertainment facilities are also in the grand style. The Wildflower Cafe is an informal setting during the day and switches to a more intimate dining atmosphere in the evening. La Fiesta presents an international menu and features live entertainment, music and dancing. The Mallard Bar offers a light luncheon or supper menu.

A few of the activities include: a health club featuring an indoor-outdoor swimming pool, whirlpools, an exercise room, massage, saunas, steam rooms and, of course, locker rooms. Other activities are tennis, hiking, fishing, biking, canoeing, rafting and horseback riding. During the winter months the Chateau really comes into its own. The resort sits on top of some of the finest skiing facilities on the North American continent. For details refer to the "Whistler Resort Association" section below.

While Chateau Whistler has started construction on its Robert Trent Jones II golf facilities, it will be a few years (1992) before it comes into play. In the interim the Arnold Palmer designed course, located close by, is available to guests. For more detail on the golf facilities as well as the tremendous number of things to do and places to eat, refer to the "Whistler Resort Association."

RATES (EP) Rooms: $140. Suites: $260/$550.

ARRIVAL Air: Vancouver (airport is 100 miles away). Private aircraft: charter flights can be arranged into Pemberton Airport (30 minutes).

FAIRMONT HOT SPRINGS RESORT
P.O. Box 10
Fairmont Hot Springs,
British Columbia, Canada VOB 1LO
(604) 345–6311
(800) 663–4979

We were pleasantly surprised by the excellent condition of the Canadian road system. We entered Canada from northern Idaho and were not at all impressed with the U.S. highways leading to the border.

Fairmont Hot Springs is nestled within the magnificent British Columbia Rocky Mountains. Our prime thrust is golf and associated summer activities. Not to apprise you, however, of the outstanding winter action available would be a gross disservice. This family ski area has a triple chair (4,000 feet long). There is a 1,000-foot vertical beginner's ski area, with a platter lift, a free pony tow for the younger set, night as well as cross country and Alpine skiing (nearby 3,100 vertical feet).

Accommodations include a 140-room lodge complete with a restaurant and lounge, a coffee shop, two saunas, indoor hot and cold plunge pools and a view of the mountains which has to be seen to be believed. There is also a 265-unit trailer park (135 with full service) and about 116 time-share one- and two-bedroom villas, the latter fully equipped for housekeeping. These are on the golf course. They are some of nicest condos we have seen at any resort. Fairmont is also capable of handling meeting groups of up to 350.

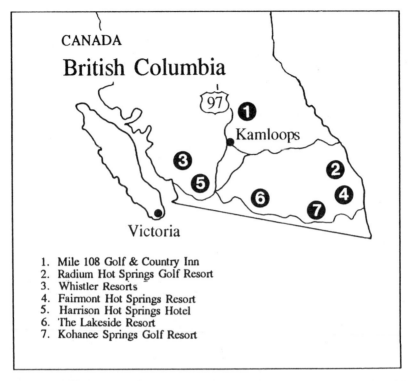

CANADA

British Columbia

Kamloops

Victoria

1. Mile 108 Golf & Country Inn
2. Radium Hot Springs Golf Resort
3. Whistler Resorts
4. Fairmont Hot Springs Resort
5. Harrison Hot Springs Hotel
6. The Lakeside Resort
7. Kohanee Springs Golf Resort

Various activities include: swimming in four natural hot mineral outdoor pools (with temperatures ranging from 96 to 108 degrees), tennis, horseback riding and hiking. Recently the resort has added a new "Sportsplex", offering squash, racquetball, weight rooms, an indoor swimming pool, three Jacuzzi pools and a sauna. Two tennis courts are also at your disposal.

Nearby Windermere and Columbia Lakes provide swimming, windsurfing, sailing and water skiing. The various streams make available white water kayaking, river raft tours and excellent trout fishing.

A few other things you may be pleased to find available include: a coin-operated laundry, two gift shops, a general convenience store, a grocery and liquor store, a gas station and a barber and beauty salon.

Golf can be played on the resort's two championship layouts. Playing from its two tee settings, the Fairmont Mountain Course measures 6,510/5,938 yards, parring at 72. It is in an area directly below the lodge, adjacent to the villas. The view and scenery, as viewed from the fairways, are magnificent. In fact it can be a distraction, most detrimental to your game. Should you allow your attention to wander, make sure you are not playing for the family homestead.

The new 18-hole Riverside Course came into play in early 1989. It boasts a par-three which must carry across the mighty Columbia River. However, to be honest, it is near the headwaters and not really the "mighty" Columbia at this point. As a matter of fact, the Columbia River does a number throughout the course, coming into play on at least 15 holes. Parring at 71, the Riverside layout plays 6,507/6,102/5,349 yards.

The clubhouse, contains the golf shop, restaurant and lounge. There is also a beautiful clubhouse at the new course, complete with restaurant and locker rooms.

RATES (EP) Lodge: $105. Suites: $135. Villas: 1-bedroom $155, weekly $1085. Green fees: $35, carts $22. There are a variety of golf package plans offered. Rates shown are for late March-September.

ARRIVAL Air: Calgary (190 miles). Private aircraft: a new 6000-foot paved runway within half a mile of the resort (equipped for commercial flights). Car: from Calgary—west on Canada 1 to Highway 93. Turn south, continue to Radium Junction. Intersect Highway 95 south to Fairmont Hot Springs (190 miles). From Spokane east on I-90 to Coeur d' Alene. North on Highway 95 to the resort (260 miles).

HARRISON HOT SPRINGS HOTEL
Harrison Hot Springs,
B.C. VOM 1K0, Canada
(604) 796-2244
Limited Area (800) 663-2266

The Harrison is a mixture of evergreens and formal lawns blended with stately old trees and lovely flower beds. It is bordered by 46-mile-long Lake Harrison on one side and the meandering Miami River on the other, with mountains surrounding the entire area.

Originally put together in 1926 on 700 acres, it has undergone repeated and continuing expansion. It was recently purchased by a

Japanese investment group and anticipation is high that many needed improvements will take place—a full 18-hole golf course will be built and interior refurbishing will be done.

There are 81 rooms in the main hotel, 80 in the Tower, 40 in the West Wing, 14 rooms in the Lodge, as well as 15 suites and Executive Bungalows. The resort is well qualified to handle meeting groups of from 15 to 600. They are also able to supply needed audio/video equipment.

The Copper Room, offering excellent dining, also has nightly dancing (with an orchestra) and live entertainment. The Terrace Dining Room is open for breakfast and lunch, while the Terrace Lounge is available for cocktails and also has live entertainment. If you want a little more activity you may well wish to make it an evening at The Good Queen Bess Pub—an English Tudor neighborhood-style pub with dancing.

The garden area at the back of the hotel is well worth a visit. If you enjoy a spectacular showcase of color, then a visit to the 27-acre Minter Gardens is a must. Located 10 miles away, this theme garden will charm you. April and May are the time to be dazzled by magnolias, dogwood and azaleas and overwhelmed with 100,000 tulips, massive rhododendrons and daffodils. In the summer the rose gardens, enchanting ferns and the annuals are in their glory. In the fall add the magnificent backdrop of autumn golds and greens on 7,000-foot Mt. Cheam. Whatever else you do—bring your camera.

There are an endless number of activities to enjoy: walking or hiking trails, horseback riding, tennis, sauna and whirlpools, their famous natural hot springs, massages, croquet, the health pavilion (exercise equipment), jogging trails, bicycle riding, shuffle board, pickle ball, ping pong and swimming in the outdoor heated pool (equipped with an adjacent outdoor bar). The lake offers an additional range of activity: power boating, sailing, water skiing, fishing and two miles of sand beaches for sunbathing and swimming.

The Harrison has a children's playground and an organized children's program with the director involving the youngsters in various games, taking them for hikes, and introducing them to creative crafts.

The Harrison golf course, while only nine holes, is a very interesting layout. With more than an ample number of trees, underbrush,

OB stakes and lateral water hazards, this par-36 course will keep your attention. It plays 3,420/3,241/2,930 yards.

RATES (EP) Main hotel: $85. Tower-West Wing: $115. East Tower: $160. Suites: $185/$385. Bungalows: $95. Green fees: (18 holes) $20, carts $20. Golf packages are available. Rates are for May-September.

ARRIVAL Air: Vancouver (80 miles). Private aircraft: seaplane landing facilities in front of the hotel. Car: take Highway 1 (Trans Canada) east. Watch for Agassiz-Harrison turn-off signs beyond Chilliwack. From Vancouver, 129 kilometers (80 miles).

KOKANEE SPRINGS GOLF RESORT
P.O. Box 49
Crawford Bay, BC V0B 1E0
Reservations (604) 227–9292
Golf Tee Times (604) 227–9362

Kokanee Springs Resort is in a beautiful cedar forest setting of Crawford Bay. Situated along the shores of Kootenay Lake, it provides a magnificent vista of the Kokanee Glacier as well as of the lake. The original 10 cedar A-frame chalets installed in 1967 have now been increased to 18. They feature private bedrooms, bathroom, living room, a fully equipped kitchen and color TV. Ranging from one to three bedrooms, each chalet can accommodate from two to eight people. The tent and trailer park facilities feature: water and electricity, fire-pits, children's playground, washrooms with showers, a coin operated laundry and a sani-sump.

The clubhouse is the location of the dining room and licensed lounge as well as the well stocked golf shop.

Swimming and picnicking can be enjoyed on the sandy beach of Crawford's Bay (a five-minute walk). Fishing and a public boat launch ramp are at nearby Fishhawk Bay Marina. Fishing is, by the way, outstanding for dolly varden, kokanee salmon and rainbow trout.

While accommodations may be on the modest side, the golf course is not. Designed by Norman R. Woods in 1967, it plays 6,755/6,320/5,870 yards with a men's par of 71, ladies' at 76. The yardage is only a sample of the challenge awaiting you. The immense rolling greens (some of the largest in Canada), coupled with 66 sand traps and 12 water hazards backed up by mountain ash, chestnut, oak and beech trees sprinkled throughout the course, combine to make any golfer a bit more cautious and alert than normal. At the very least, I suggest you approach this layout with due respect.

To illustrate the care with which the golf course was put together, Mr. Woods was in residence during the complete construction period and had the entire course hand-raked to ensure that no rocks were on the surface.

RATES (EP) Chalet rooms: $45. Tent and trailer park: $13. Green fees: $35 (all day), carts $18. Golf package: 3 nights/3 days, weekdays (includes lodging, green fees, cart), $380 per couple. Rates quoted are for late May to early September. This resort is open 6 months of the year—from mid-April until mid-October.

ARRIVAL Air: a 2700-foot grass airstrip, maintained in the spring, summer and fall. Car: 45 miles north of Creston, BC on Highway 3A. Located about 177 miles from Spokane, WA.

THE LAKESIDE RESORT
21 Lakeshore Drive
Penticton, BC
V2A 7M5 Canada
(604) 493–8221
(800) 663–9400

The resort is just where it says it is—lakeside. Built along the shores of the southern tip of Okanagan Lake, this six-story hotel can offer its guests a great variety of activities. There are 204 rooms and suites—each with a balcony. A few of the amenities include: laundry and valet service, room service, color TV and in-room movies. The Lakeside is also well set up to handle meeting groups with a ballroom capacity of 600. There are also five fully equipped break-out rooms.

The restaurant, Peaches and Cream, is open from early morning until late evening and offers a menu ranging from full meal service to lighter fare. For more formal dining, Ripples, an elegant dining room, has not only fine cuisine but a breathtaking view as well. Then there is the "patio" where the aroma of barbecued food may very well snare you. For a libation, the hotel offers the relaxation of the Leading Edge Lounge. With its warm, glowing fireplace this becomes a nice way to wind up the day.

An indoor heated swimming pool, whirlpool, two outdoor tennis courts, a Health Center complete with saunas and games room, a lakeshore jogging track, canoes, paddleboats and a sandy beach are but a sample of the activities available. About a block away is a marina where you can arrange boat rentals, fishing or a stern wheeler tour of Okanogan Lake.

Golf may be played on the Penticton Golf Club layout. Located in town, it measures 6,365/6,120/5,952/5,459 yards parring at 70 / 72. There is a full-line golf shop, a clubhouse and restaurant.

There are several other courses you can make arrangements to play. The Summerland Golf & Country Club is a few miles away. It has an 18-hole, par-72 course sporting a full pro shop, lounge and dining facilities. About 40 minutes south is the Osoyoos Golf & Country Club, again a par-72, 18-hole layout. There are, in addition, several nine-hole courses in the area.

RATES (EP) Room: $125/$140. Rates are for July-August. Green fees: $22, carts $20.

ARRIVAL Air: Penticton. Car: from the Okanogan Valley in Washington take Highway 97 north.

MILE 108 GOLF & COUNTRY INN
R.R. #1 100 Mile House
British Columbia, Canada V0K 2E0
(604) 791–5211
From Vancouver 687–2334

This resort surprised us a bit. It had a great deal more to offer than we had expected. Each room is fully carpeted, has its own private balcony and is equipped with color television. Each has a view of the pool area, practice putting green and the golf course. There is also a very nice extra we wish all resorts offered—a coin operated laundromat

Within the lodge complex itself there are: saunas, whirlpools, an outdoor heated pool, barbecue pits, volleyball, horseshoes, a large playground for the younger set and much more.

The 108 Restaurant, with its beautiful view, offers a very diverse menu. There is also cocktail service. The resort is well set up to handle meeting groups and can provide all of the audio/visual aids required.

Activities available include: five plexipave tennis courts (with a professional available to assist), bicycle rentals, horseback riding (a large stable of horses with one to match every level of expertise or lack thereof), open country riding and barbecues or bonfire sing-a-long rides.

The beach is on a 360-acre lake just 500 yards from the resort and boat rentals are available. It is also heavily stocked, providing outstanding trout fishing.

Lake Watson, a bit further away, has 13 float planes as well as some conventional land aircraft which are used for fishing or wilderness trips. There is also a one-mile-long, lighted, fully paved, landing strip.

The resort's wildlife preserve area includes hundreds of acres of open wilderness trails stretched along some of the most incredible marsh breeding grounds found within Canada.

The golf course, which virtually surrounds the resort, plays 6,669/6,401/6,246 yards with a par of 72/75. At first glance the Ranch Course looks easy. Do not be misled. Winding its way over slightly undulating terrain, bordered by pine and maple trees, it is no "push-over." The rough is deep and you can be punished even more by straying into marsh-like areas adjacent to some of the fairways. There is not much water on the front side (just two holes as I recall), but the back side has water in the form of a lateral ditch as well as a stream, providing a challenge on six holes. There is a large and well stocked golf shop and a resident professional to assist.

RATES (EP) Room: $95. Kitchenettes: $82/$92. Housekeeping: $105. Executive suite: $110. Green fees: $25, carts $20. Golf packages are available. Rates are for June-September.

ARRIVAL Air: Vancouver or Williams Lake. Private aircraft: 1-mile long-paved runway at the resort. Car: take Highway 97 north to Mile 108 BC.

RADIUM HOT SPRINGS GOLF RESORT
Box 310
Radium Hot Springs, BC
V0A 1M0 Canada
(604) 347–9311
(800) 528–1234

Radium Hot Springs, on the western slopes of the Rocky Mountains, has a natural beauty which is difficult to describe. In the winter it is a virtual wonderland and in the summer the mountains seem to reach out forever—the tops powdered with snow, the trees stretching out like an endless carpet. Their brochure describes the atmosphere: "We wanted a place where our guests would be removed from everyday pressures, casual, comfortable, lots to do, NO PRESSURE TO DO ANYTHING".

Accommodations at the Inn consist of studio or one- to two-bedroom suites with mini-bars. The Radium Condominiums/Villas are either one- or two-bedroom accommodations with separate living and dining rooms, fully equipped kitchens with dishwashers, two baths and complete laundry facilities.

If you don't think this resort is golf oriented, here are the names of a few of the various wings of the resort: St. Andrews, Gleneagles and Carnoustie. To carry it even further, the menu reads like a golf course map. Salads are under the heading of *"Picked from the Rough"*, the seafood selection is named *"Fished from the Water Hazard and Sand Traps"*, and the meat entrees are under the heading of *"Found Grazing on the Fairway"*. The children's menu is called the *"Pitch & Putt."*

A sample of the activities available include: an indoor swimming pool, hot tub, whirlpool and sauna, an exercise gymnasium, massage facilities, tennis, racquetball and squash courts.

The dining room and pro shop overlook the 9th and 18th holes. The patio deck is available for lighter meals and, most certainly, for a slight libation. There is also the Piper Cocktail Lounge.

Operating first as a nine-hole layout, the Radium Hot Springs Course was enlarged to 18-holes in September of 1979. While not long, it is demanding. At 5,271/5,068 yards, it pars at 69/68. Although lightly trapped, there is water coming into play on five holes. With the fir trees which line the fairways, this course will demand your full concentration.

RATES (EP) Inn studio suite: $80/$98. Condo/Villas: 1-bedroom $90. Green fees: $26, carts $22. Golf package: 1 night/1 day [includes lodging, green fees), weekdays $110, weekends $135 per couple.

ARRIVAL Air: Calgary (156 miles). Car: from Spokane—north on Highway 95 (278 miles).

WHISTLER RESORT ASSOCIATION

P.O. Box 1400, Whistler,
British Columbia, Canada V0N 1B0
(604) 932–4222
Vancouver Toll Free 685–3650
Limited (800) 663–8668
From Seattle 628–0982

Whistler Village, originally put together for ski buffs, is today considered one of the finest ski facilities in Canada, or for that matter, in North America. One of Whistler's many attributes, the spectacular scenery and setting, also contributes to it becoming an outstanding summer and golfing destination.

The drive from Vancouver (75 miles), is quite picturesque. There is also train service from North Vancouver (for information call B. C. Railway 604–984–5246). Once you have arrived at the village an automobile is no longer needed.

Whistler is, in reality, an alpine-style village, consisting of many different types of accommodations ranging from hotels to condominiums to chalets. In fact, within the village itself there are 18 different types of lodgings, while outside the village proper (the so-called Valley Accommodations), there are another 16 locations.

Some of the lodgings provide amenities such as: swimming pools, saunas, Jacuzzis, fireplaces, fully equipped kitchens, on-premises restaurant, lounge and tennis courts. When making reservations make clear your requirements. While a few of the inns within the village provide their own restaurants, they are all grouped near a number of places to eat. The food selection is almost limitless, ranging from the most sophisticated European cuisine to fast food. Oh yes, they have not neglected the night life. There are 18 nightspots ranging from neighborly pubs and rock clubs with live entertainment to romantic lounges.

Also within the village are a number of service and/or retail establishments: delis, bakeries, a post office and bank, a grocery, drug and liquor store, candy and ice cream shops along with high quality stores offering brand names in knitwear, miscellaneous sport and ski wear. In addition to a visiting dentist, there are two doctors on call.

A nice feature—cars are banished to convenient underground parking. The village thus becomes a "people place" with no motor vehicles to get in the way. The village is, in fact, the focal point for almost all activities, providing more than ample seating for just plain people watching on a lazy summer afternoon.

Their Conference Center building boasts over 100,000 square feet of space. The center can accommodate 2,000 people. There are also eight break-out rooms which can handle from 15 to 230.

The activities provided by this resort are almost as limitless and varied as the accommodations. Whistler's five lakes and nearby rivers offer white-water canoeing, kayaking, river rafting, sailing, windsurfing and, of course, swimming and fishing.

Should you tire of water action, you can wade ashore and try tennis, racquetball, squash, horseback riding, hiking, walking trails, guided mountain tours, chair lift rides, helicopter glacier skiing (that's right—glacier skiing in the summer), jogging and cycling paths. In addition arrangements can be made to pan for gold, tour a mine, climb a giant monolith, watch logging championships, visit hot springs, take a train ride to the desert-like Southern Cariboo or explore the interior of British Columbia by car. Of course, you may just elect to relax and take it easy in this fabulous area.

Finally, we get to the main focus of interest (as far as we are concerned)—golf. Opened in 1983, the Whistler Golf Course, designed by Arnold Palmer, is both beautiful and a real tester. It measures 6,502/6,074/5,381 yards and pars at 72. While this layout is fun, the second nine can give you problems. At one time this was a swamp area and a great deal of water was redirected to form hazards. There is one creek which really becomes a nuisance, paralleling and then crossing one fairway no less than three times. As I recall, it was the par-five, 11th hole.

The first two holes are very gentle and may lead you to believe it will all be smooth sailing. Not so. On the third, you will get acquainted with your first bit of water, in the form of a pond and a stream. At this point, you may begin to get the idea that you had better pay attention. If you do not, prepare yourself for a bad afternoon.

Should you plan to stay overnight, tee times can be reserved at the same time you make your reservations. If your visit is for golf only, you should call—no less that five days in advance—(604) 932–4544.

Reservations Can Be Made At The Following Locations Using The Whistler Resort Association Telephone Numbers

BLACKCOMB LODGE

72 rooms, indoor swimming pool, common use sauna and jacuzzi. Fireplaces in some units, kitchens in most.

CARLETON LODGE

16 rooms, a Jacuzzi, fireplace and kitchen in most units. Satellite TV, restaurant and lounge.

CLOCKTOWER HOTEL

15 rooms, common-use sauna, kitchen in most units, cable TV, restaurant and lounge.

DELTA MOUNTAIN INN

290 rooms, outdoor pool, sauna, Jacuzzi, fireplace and kitchen in some units. Satellite TV, restaurant, lounge.

FAIRWAYS HOTEL

194 rooms, an outdoor pool, sauna and Jacuzzi, restaurant and lounge. Cable TV.

FIREPLACE INN

37 rooms, Jacuzzi, fireplace and kitchen in most units. Restaurant and lounge, cable TV.

FITZSIMMONS CONDOS

10 units, sauna, Jacuzzi, fireplace, kitchen in most units. Cable TV. Restaurant and lounge.

HEARTHSTONE LODGE

10 units, sauna, fireplace, kitchen in most units. Satellite TV.

LISTEL WHISTLER HOTEL

97 rooms, a sauna and Jacuzzi. Restaurant, lounge and satellite TV.

MOUNTAINSIDE LODGE

90 units, an outdoor swimming pool. A sauna, Jacuzzi, fireplace, kitchen in most units. Restaurant, lounge and satellite TV.

NANCY GREEN LODGE

137 units, an outdoor swimming pool, sauna and Jacuzzi. Fireplace and kitchen available in some units. Restaurant, lounge and satellite TV.

TANTALUS LODGE

76 units, an outdoor swimming pool, a sauna and Jacuzzi. Fireplace and kitchen in most units. Cable TV.

TIMBERLINE LODGE

42 units, an outdoor swimming pool, a sauna and Jacuzzi. Fireplace in some units. Restaurant, lounge and cable TV.

VILLAGE GATE HOUSE

20 units, Jacuzzi in some units. Fireplace, kitchen in most units. Cable TV.

WESTBROOK WHISTLER

49 units, Jacuzzis in some units. Fireplace, kitchen in most units. Cable TV.

WHISTLERVIEW

9 units, sauna, fireplace, kitchen in most units. Jacuzzi in some units. Restaurant, lounge, cable TV.

WHISTLER VILLAGE INN

88 units, outdoor swimming pool, a sauna and Jacuzzi. Fireplace and kitchen in most units. Restaurant, lounge and cable TV.

WINDWHISTLE CONDOS

4 units, Jacuzzi, fireplace, kitchen, satellite TV. Restaurant and lounge.

RESORTS ON BLACKCOMB MOUNTAIN

FOXGLOVE

36 units, fireplace, kitchen and cable TV.

GABLES

9 units, jacuzzi, fireplace, kitchen available in most units. NO TV.

GLACIER LODGE

112 units, outdoor swimming pool. Fireplace, kitchen in all units. Cable TV.

STONERIDGE

9 units, fireplace, kitchen in all units. NO TV.

WILDWOOD LODGE

33 units, outdoor swimming pool. Fireplace and kitchen in all units. Cable TV.

LODGINGS OUTSIDE THE VILLAGE

FITZSIMMONS CREEK LODGE

45 units, kitchen in some units. Restaurant, lounge and cable TV.

GONDOLA VILLAGE

45 units. Fireplace and kitchen in most units. Cable TV.

HIGHLAND VALE

55 units, a sauna and Jacuzzi. Fireplace and kitchen in some units. Restaurant, lounge and satellite TV.

LAKE PLACID LODGE

104 units, outdoor swimming pool, a Jacuzzi. Kitchen in most units. Cable TV.

THE SEASONS

13 units. Fireplace and kitchen in most units. Cable TV.

WHISTLER CREEK LODGE

43 units, outdoor swimming pool, a sauna, Jacuzzi, tennis courts. Fireplace, kitchen in most units. Restaurant, lounge, cable TV.

WHISTLER ON THE LAKE

24 units. Fireplace and kitchen in most units. Cable TV.

WHISTLER RESORT & CLUB

42 units, outdoor swimming pool, a sauna, Jacuzzi and tennis courts. Fireplace and kitchen in most units. Restaurant, lounge and cable TV.

WISKI JACK RESORT

15 units, a sauna. Jacuzzi in some units. Fireplace, kitchens in most units. Cable TV.

BED & BREAKFAST INNS

ALTA VISTA CHALET

6 units, sauna, Jacuzzi and fireplaces. Cable TV.

CHALET LUISE

6 units, sauna, Jacuzzi. Fireplace in most units. No TV.

DURLACHER HDF

7 units, sauna. Fireplaces in most units. No TV.

EDELWEISS

6 units, sauna, fireplaces, No TV.

HAUS HEIDI

6 units, sauna, Jacuzzi. Fireplace in most units. NO TV. In addition to the above lodgings there is an alternative. Should you wish to stay in some of the private homes in the area call WHISTLER CHALETS—from Vancouver (604) 683–7799 or toll free (800) 663–7711.

ARRIVAL Air: Vancouver, BC (75 miles, from airport 100 miles). Car: from Vancouver take Highway 99 northbound along Howe Sound (allow about 2 hours). Avis has a car rental office at Whistler. There is also taxi service operating year-round from Whistler Village to Vancouver International Airport (call 932–5455).

MANITOBA

FALCON LAKE RESORT & CLUB
Falcon Boulevard
Falcon Lake, Manitoba
R0E 0N0 Canada
(204) 349-8400
Winnipeg 943-3400

The Falcon Lake Resort, a little less than two hours driving time east of Winnipeg, is at the southern end of Whiteshell Provincial Park. Accommodations vary from motel rooms to executive apartments, with kitchenette, patio, air-conditioning, color TV, VCR, and barbecue grill. Some of the aforementioned equipment must be specifically requested and at an additional charge.

The resort is well set up to handle conference, banquets or meetings/seminars and can work with groups of from 10 to 250. There is a dining room and lounge available, as well as a games room and a children's arcade.

Situated as it is on the shores of magnificent Falcon Lake, all kinds of water activities are possible. Within this 1,000-square-mile park setting you will find everything from wilderness to a small shopping mall. In the town (a short walk from the hotel) is a professionally maintained sports complex offering tennis, horseback riding, lawn bowling and miniature golf. Activities located on premises include: an indoor heated swimming pool, a spa and sauna, boating, lake swimming and, of course, fishing. During the winter months you can add downhill and cross country skiing, snowmobiling, ice fishing and indoor curling.

The par-72 golf course is operated by the Provincial Parks Department.

RATES (EP) Motel rooms: $57/$69. Executive apartments: $85/$95. Weekly $530. Green fees: $17, carts $17. Rates quoted are for the peak summer season of late June through early September.

ARRIVAL Air: Winnipeg (90 miles). Car: take Trans Canada Highway 1 due east to Falcon Lake.

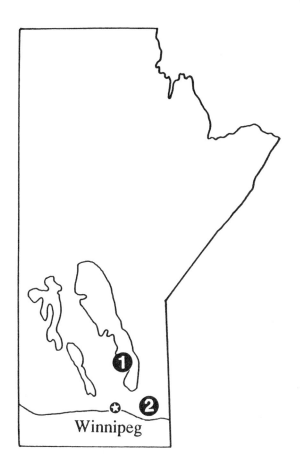

CANADA
Manitoba

Winnipeg

1. Gull Harbour Resort
2. Falcon Lake Resort & Club

GULL HARBOUR RESORT
General Delivery
Riverton, Manitoba
R0C 2R0 Canada
(204) 475–2354

This area has a most interesting history. In 1876 volcanic erup-
tions on Mount Hekla sent thousands of Icelanders fleeing to Manitoba. A few of these hardy souls, in quest of prime fishing grounds,
came to Lake Winnipeg where they discovered and settled on what
is now called Hecla Island.

Gull Harbour Resort, some 110 miles north of Winnipeg, is on the
northeastern tip of Hecla Island. Remains of the original fishing
village may still be found and restoration work has been done.

There are 91 guest rooms plus two suites. Most ground floor rooms
provide a patio area, while the suites feature spacious living areas
and a fireplace. All rooms are equipped with satellite TV.

The resort can handle meeting and conference groups with a capacity of from 5 to 125 people. The audio/visual aids are state-of-
the-art, including TV camera, monitors and VCR equipment for
taping practice sessions.

The dining room has a wide choice of cuisine, ranging from country fare and seafood, to Icelandic baking and elegant dining. With
the dining and banquet rooms the resort has the capacity to host
groups of 260 people banquet-style. In addition to the lounge there
also is a coffee shop. During the summer months, the resort operates an outside bar and grill for quick lunches or even an evening
barbecue.

A few of the indoor activities include: swimming pool, sauna,
whirlpool, and (in the gym) basketball, volleyball or badminton.
For the children they provide a wading pool, an arts and crafts
program and scavenger hunts. Step outside and you can enjoy tennis, baseball shuffleboard, windsurfing and even horseshoes.
There is, of course, always the added adventure of exploring this
historic island.

Since the resort is open year-round, during winter you can add:
cross country skiing, ice fishing, tobogganing, ice skating and,
should you really want to wreck yourself, try snow shoeing.

The Hecla golf course is adjacent to the parking lot of the lodge
and runs along the lake itself. Parring at 72, it measures 6,022/

5,735/5,060 yards. There is a fair amount of water on this layout with ponds in play on #15, #16 and #17. There is also an inlet from Lake Winnipeg becoming a nuisance on numbers #10, #11 and #12.

The course, owned and operated by the Manitoba Parks System, is under the supervision of golf professional Jim Mayer.

RATES (EP) Standard Rooms: $75. Deluxe $85. The resort also offers golf packages. Green fees: $15/$18, carts $20.

ARRIVAL Air: Winnipeg (110 miles). Private aircraft: Riverton (limited airstrip). Car: from Winnipeg take Highway 8 north.

MEXICO

The physical aspect of Mexico is relatively easy to describe: it is a country of some 760,000 square miles, bordered on the north by the United States, on the south by Guatemala and Belize, on the east by the Gulf of Mexico as well as the Caribbean Sea and on the west by the majestic Pacific Ocean. But the land, the rich history and the people are not so simple to write about.

They are a people with a heritage rich in historical background, who are reaching for a more modern society. Exceptional art forms have been produced since the eighth century BC. Pyramids and temples in the mountains, jungles and valleys along with old churches and colonial palaces hidden away in many small villages can provide a history buff with a lifetime of exploration.

Situated between the two Sierra Madre mountain ranges lie the flatlands of Mexico. At an elevation of 2,500 to 10,000 feet this area enjoys a moderate climate. It also is where most of the larger cities and the bulk of Mexico's almost 68 million people can be found.

Along the coastal lowland areas, where most of the major resorts are sited, the general climate is definitely tropical. While extremely warm during the summer months, the temperature is pleasant during the winter.

Don't be reluctant to shop—Mexico is a bargainer's paradise. Don't be reluctant to take tours. You will see a better selection of things and places at a lower cost that way. And when the sun goes down Mexico comes alive. Take part, as there is much to see and to do.

When all is said and done the best part of Mexico is the people. They are still warm and friendly. And, amazingly, they are graciously tolerant of our mutilation of their beautiful language.

THINGS YOU NEED TO KNOW

For international flights you need to arrive at the airport an hour and half prior to departure. For flights within Mexico one hour is fine. Baggage limit: two checked pieces and one carry-on.

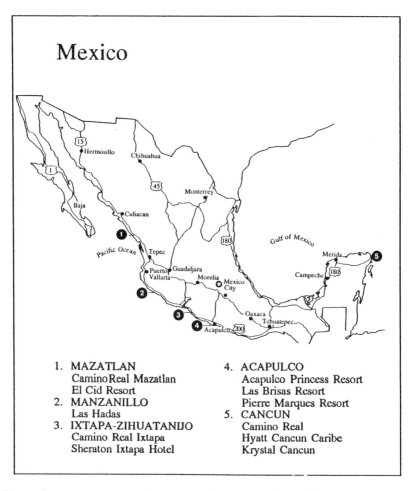

Mexico

1. MAZATLAN
   Camino Real Mazatlan
   El Cid Resort
2. MANZANILLO
   Las Hadas
3. IXTAPA-ZIHUATANIJO
   Camino Real Ixtapa
   Sheraton Ixtapa Hotel
4. ACAPULCO
   Acapulco Princess Resort
   Las Brisas Resort
   Pierre Marques Resort
5. CANCUN
   Camino Real
   Hyatt Cancun Caribe
   Krystal Cancun

If you have a passport be sure to bring it. If you do not, then you must have a certified birth certificate and a voter's registration card. You must have a "tourist card" to enter Mexico. DO NOT MISPLACE IT. IT IS MANDATORY THAT YOU HAVE IT UPON DEPARTURE.

The electricity is 120 volt/60 cycle (same as U.S.). Thus there is no need to bring converters.

While most resorts will accept major credit cards, we found that none would take personal checks.

The climate is mild, in fact warm, but the nights can get cool. It is wise to have a jacket or sweater for the evening hours.

There are certain remote areas where travel by private vehicle is not recommended and, in fact, can be dangerous. Check with your resort management.

THE ACAPULCO-GUERRERO AREA

Acapulco, 150 miles south of Zihuatanejo/Ixtapa, has been referred to as one of the world's greatest playgrounds. With its magnificent bay, miles of beaches, shops galore and many beautiful resorts, that may well be an apt description. It has become very crowded so careful advance planning is necessary to assure yourself of reservations which fit your style and pocket book.

ACAPULCO PRINCESS RESORT
P.O. Box 1351
Acapulco, Guerrero
Mexico 39868
011–52–748–4 –31–00
(800) 223–1818

Set on 480 acres along Revolcadero Beach, the Princess is one of the largest resort facilities in Mexico. The main building is formed in the shape of an Aztec Pyramid with an atrium soaring some 16 stories. Within this structure are 423 rooms plus junior suites and six penthouses. A short distance away, connected by a covered walkway, is the 10-story Princess Tower with additional rooms and suites. Alongside the shopping arcade is the 10-story Marquesa Tower. In total there are 1020 rooms.

All rooms have a private terrace, a bathroom with tub and shower, separate dressing area with a walk-in closet and air-conditioning. The Princess has been awarded the AAA Five Diamond Award for 12 years in a row.

The eight restaurants (not including those at the golf courses) offer a wide variety of cuisine. The Veranda features authentic Chinese food. La Posadita, an open air affair overlooking the pools and the beach area, starts with an international breakfast, features a seafood menu for lunch, then switching to a BBQ Mexican buffet during the evening. The Chula Vista offers a buffet dinner and has a marimba band performing each evening. La Princesa, the main dining room, provides continental fare as does El Jardin. Should you prefer French cuisine there is La Gourmet. Then there is the wonderful Mexican food presented in La Hacienda, one of Acapulco's most popular dining spots and a Holiday Award winner. One final point—the dress code is casual at all times.

I am happy to report that this is a civilized and 20th century operation—while there are eight restaurants, they have provided NINE bars throughout the property. Included in the count are a nightclub, a dance pavilion and two-swim up bars. This resort is well equipped to handle meeting groups and/or banquets with a capacity ranging to as high as 2000 theater and- 1200 banquet-style.

The recreational facilities are almost endless. Tennis is offered on nine outdoor and two indoor courts (there is grandstand seating for 200 and all courts are lighted). Four fresh water pools plus a salt water lagoon featuring a water slide as well as a children's wading pool are available. Other activities which can be arranged by the hotel include: scuba diving, deep sea fishing, parasailing, waterskiing, sailing, catamaran cruises, a yacht cruise, even night club tours. Finally all of the facilities—restaurants, tennis courts, golf course at the nearby Pierre Marques Hotel (also a Princess Resort property) are at the disposal of guests of the Acapulco Princess.

There are two golf layouts: the Acapulco Princess course and the testier Pierre Marques course. The two, side by side, are directly across the street from their respective hotels.

The Acapulco, playing 6,355/6,085/5,400, pars at 72. A Ted Robinson design it presents its own challenge in the form of water introduced into play on 10 holes and many trees. For detailed coverage on the more difficult Pierre Marques course, refer to the text on the Pierre Marques Resort listed below. Both the Princess and the Marques courses are supported by a driving range as well as an excellent pro shop.

RATES During high season (mid-December through Easter) the resort per-day cost is based on MAP, while during the off-season (after Easter to mid-December) the resort is on an EP basis.

(MAP) Rooms: $200 per couple. Jr. suites: $290 per couple. Executive suites: $310 per couple. Golf package: 3 nights/3 days (includes MAP, lodging, all taxes, green fees on either course, golf cart and bag storage), $954/$1058/$1164 per couple.

ARRIVAL Air: Acapulco International Airport. Government-run taxi service is available from the airport to the hotel.

LAS BRISAS RESORT
P.O. Box 281
Acapulco, Guerrero
Mexico 39868
011–52–748–4–15–80
(800) 228–3000

I think our love affair with Las Brisas began upon arrival. Having flown from Mexico City and then driven to the hotel our tongues were literally hanging out. Before I could even get my room confirmation forms out some delightful person placed a tall cool tropical drink in my hand. What a great way to start a relationship. Las Brisas is more of a village than a resort/hotel. As a matter of fact it is more a fantasy land than a place. This magnificent resort is the essence of a posh, luxuriant life style.

Along the side and on top of Las Brisas hill the resort contains over 300 casitas. Each unit is sited in such a manner as to provide a maximum amount of privacy as well as views of Acapulco Bay. These views, outstanding during the daylight hours, are beyond description at night as you look down on the various ships in the harbor and across the bay to brilliantly lighted Acapulco.

A few of the thoughtful amenities include: fresh flowers flown in from Mexico City each day placed on your pillows and sprinkled in the swimming pool; a continental breakfast left in a little slide-through door of your room each morning; a complimentary bowl of fresh fruit replenished daily and a fully-stocked bar. In each casita is a louvered wall which glides back to reveal a delightful pool (either private or shared). As there are 250 pools on the property this means only 96 casitas share a pool while all others have their own.

The main dining room, "Bella Vista", is a terrace patio open on three sides. It lives up to its Spanish name—Beautiful View. When evening falls you can enjoy gourmet cuisine along with music and dancing. There is also El Mexicano, located at the top of the hill, offering charcoal broiled Mexican specialties. The dress code is casual. No ties or jackets are worn. Another nice touch, *NO TIPPING IS ALLOWED.* The very best of all, however, is having dinner served on the patio next to your private pool.

Tennis can be played on five lighted courts, or join a jeep caravan for an excursion to the bullfights (available only during the winter season). You can take a jeep safari for a visit to nearby fishing villages, plantations or tropical lagoons; or you can arrange for your own jeep to explore the area. Las Brisas has over 300 separate casitas sprinkled over 110 acres. Jeeps decorated in the same color scheme as the buildings (pink and white) get you from one place to another. There are many of them and never a delay in getting where you need to go.

Descend to the beach area and another world opens up. At the foot of the bluff is the Concha Beach Club. Available only to members and guests of the resort, there is windsurfing, parasailing, water-skiing, snorkeling, sailing and even a private scuba diving club. The world famous La Concha Restaurant is something to long remember.

Golf can be arranged for quests of Las Brisas at either of two courses: the Acapulco Princess or the Pierre Marques golf courses. For detail on either of these layouts refer to "Acapulco Princess Resort" or "Pierre Marques Resort".

RATES (EP) Casitas: (shared pool) $185/$195; with (private pool) $265/$400. 1-bedroom suites: (private pool and whirlpool) $500. All rates include continental breakfast. You are charged a fee (about $20) each day of your stay to cover ALL tipping. This includes check-in and departure.

ARRIVAL Air: Acapulco International Airport (20 minutes). Government operated taxi service is available from the airport to the resort.

PIERRE MARQUES RESORT
P.O. Box 474
Acapulco, Guerrero
Mexico 39868
011–52–748–4–20–00
(800) 223–1818

Near the Acapulco Princess, the Pierre Marques enjoys the same ideal setting. A much more intimate hotel, the Marques offers a total of 344 rooms. The main building, with its 86 rooms, 10 junior suites and five-story tower accommodations all have ocean views. There is also the villa section of the hotel with its assortment of rooms and suites offering garden views. Each room has a private bath/tub shower, radio, either a terrace or patio and is air-conditioned.

La Terraza, an informal outdoor restaurant, overlooks the pools and beach area and specializes in Mexican dishes. The Tabachin Room features continental cuisine. The newest addition is the Amigo Restaurant, serving Italian cuisine. There is also a snack / bar at the golf course, offering sandwiches as well as bar service. The Pierre Bar also provides nightly dancing during high season. The dress code is casual at all times throughout the hotel. The Pierre Marques is capable of handling meeting groups of 280 school-room to 500 in a theater-style setting. They also have four breakout rooms to accommodate smaller groups.

Tennis can be played on five lighted outdoor courts. Other amenities available include: three freshwater swimming pools plus a children's wading pool, aerobics classes, theme parties, cooking classes and Spanish orientation classes. In addition, all of the activities offered by the Acapulco Princess Hotel are available to guests of the Pierre Marques. Additional recreation activities which can be arranged through separate concessions include: scuba diving, deep sea fishing, waterskiing, parasailing, catamaran or yacht cruises and night club tours.

The Pierre Marques golf course has not only been recognized as one of the finest in Mexico but also was selected by *Golf Digest* as one of the top 100 in the world.

Originally designed by the well known Percy Clifford, it was redone by Robert Trent Jones, Jr. in time for the 1982 World Cup Tournament. Redesigning 65 bunkers and adding many mounds turned this course into a championship layout. While fun to navigate (water in play on 13 holes), it places a premium on accuracy off the tee and delivers immediate chastisement for erratic shots. The yardage alone should give you some indication as to what you may face. Measuring 6,855/6,557/6,112/5,197 yards it pars at 72/73. As a guest of the Pierre Marques Hotel, you may elect to play the Acapulco Princess layout as well. For more detailed information refer to the Acapulco Princess Resort listed above. Both courses are supported by excellent pro shops as well as their own driving range.

RATES (MAP) Rooms: $200 per couple. Jr. Suites: $280 per couple. Suites: (separate living rooms) $320 per couple. Golf package: 3 nights/3 days (includes lodging, MAP, green fees on either the Marques or Princess courses for 3 rounds, cart, club storage), $954/$1058/$1164 per couple.

ARRIVAL Air: Acapulco International Airport. Government operated taxi service is available from the airport to the hotel.

YUCATAN PENINSULA

The Yucatan Peninsula is as deeply immersed in history as any place on earth. In fact, the continuing mystery surrounding the Maya civilization is one of the greatest enigmas to face archaeologists. At a period just prior to 250 A.D. this culture began to form. From 900 to approximately 1500 it flourished and, by some estimates, reached a population of some 16 million. During this six-century period, a dynamic and sophisticated society was created with nobles, priests, artists, scribes, craftsmen, warriors, and farmers. This very structured civilization built a great many Mayan cities and temples. Their technical and architectural achievements have continued to astonish the world.

The two basic questions which linger on are: how did they accomplish what they did with the limited equipment available during that period and, of course, what happened to them? True, there are some four million descendants still speaking the Maya languages, but the once proud and magnificent cities no longer rule.

On the northeastern tip of the peninsula is an area known for its magnificent beaches and mild climate—Cancun. There is much evidence, in the form of ruins, that the Mayan people also came here to play and enjoy the sand and sea.

Golf is our main purpose but to visit this area and not explore at least some of the history all about you would indeed be a travesty.

Cancun, a Mayan word, means "Pot of Gold". With an average of 240 cloudless days a year—it is little wonder the Mayan people came here for a respite from the interior rain forest areas. Cancun is an island connected to the mainland by two bridges and is the site of several resorts as well as a golf course.

Golf can be played on the Pok-Ta-Pok Golf Club course. Just so we stay even on the name, it comes from the Mayan language and means "game played with a stick". You can't get more basic than that. The course is a Robert Trent Jones, Jr. design. Playing to a par of 73/74, it reaches a respectable 6,721/6,142/5,586 yards. The clubhouse facilities include a pro shop and a cafeteria serving breakfast and lunch.

CAMINO REAL
P.O Box 14
Cancun, Quintana Roo
Mexico, 77500
011–52–988–3–01–00
(800) 228–3000

The Camino enjoys a unique setting in that it literally projects into the ocean. In fact, from a distance, it appears to be partially in the water. The hotel is a modified pyramid-style structure with 379 rooms, including suites. A recent addition, the 18-story Royal Beach Club, houses 87 of the hotel's rooms and 18 of the deluxe suites. Some of the units sport a private whirlpool spa. All accommodations are air-conditioned and have color TV.

Restaurants include the Calypso specializing in Caribbean cuisine, Azulejos and the open-air La Brisa, featuring steak and the daily catch of seafood. There is also El Tucan, featuring regional specialties. As a matter of vital interest, the Camino has its own water purification system. The resort can handle up to 550 Banquetstyle with their excellent meeting facilities.

Along with two outstanding beaches (water on three sides), some of the activities available include tennis on four lighted courts and swimming in a heated fresh water pool. The pool features a swim-up bar. Snorkeling, waterskiing, sailing, deep-sea fishing, and excursions in glass bottom boats can also be arranged. For those wishing to venture a bit further, you may set up a trimaran trip, including a five-hour excursion to the Isla Mujeres. You can, of course, elect to spend a subdued, quiet day on the beach doing NOTHING AT ALL.

Golf can be arranged on the Pok-Ta-Pok golf course. For details refer to the "Yucatan Peninsula" above.

RATES (EP) Rooms: $185. Beach Club: $225. Suites: $500 and up. Green fees: $24, carts $18.

ARRIVAL Air: Cancun International Airport (approximately 12 miles).

HYATT CANCUN CARIBE
P.O. Box 353
Cancun, Quintana Roo
77500, Mexico
011–52–988–30044
(800) 233–1234

This deluxe Hyatt was built along one of the finest secluded white sand beaches in Cancun. There are 202 rooms, plus 21 beachfront villas. They also have meeting facilities and can handle groups of up to 150.

The restaurants are the Cocay Steak House, the Blue Bayou and La Concha, offering Mexican specialties.

A few of the available activities include a swimming pool, tennis courts and, of course, golf. For details on the golf facilities, located nearby, refer to the "Yucatan Peninsula".

RATES (EP) Rooms: $160/$215. Suites & villas: $395/$425.

ARRIVAL Air: Cancun International Airport.

KRYSTAL CANCUN
Pasea Kukulcan
Cancun, Quintana Roo
77500, Mexico
011–52–988–311–33
(800) 231–9860

The Krystal is a high-rise directly on the beach. It is also across from the 17,000-square-foot convention center. There are 330 air-conditioned rooms and suites. Some of the units feature a private swimming pool, while all are equipped with mini-bars and satellite TV.

Amenities include: Bogart's Casablanca Restaurant, an outstanding disco, "Christine", a coffee shop, two large swimming pools, lighted tennis and racquetball courts, and a health club containing all manner of exercise equipment including a gymnasium, a Jacuzzi and sauna, as well as a massage service.

They also have excellent convention and meeting facilities.

Guests may play the Pok-Ta-Pok Golf Course. For details refer to the "Yucatan Peninsula".

RATES (EP) Rooms: $160/$190. Suites: $190/$210.

ARRIVAL Air: Cancun International Airport.

THE IXTAPA-ZIHUATANEJO AREA

Located 150 miles north of Acapulco, the area is one of tropical tranquility. While the resorts described in Ixtapa are modern and sophisticated, "Old Mexico" can be found six miles south in Zihuatanejo. A quiet fishing village of 40,000 people, it is a sharp contrast to Ixtapa. An interesting bit of trivia. The most acceptable origin of the word Zihuatanejo and its literal translation is "Land of Women". It seems that this area was, in ancient times, ruled by women.

CAMINO REAL IXTAPA
Playa Vista Hermosa
Ixtapa-Zihuatanejo
Guerrero, Mexico 40880
011–52–743–4–33–00
(800) 228–3000

The Camino Ixtapa, surrounded by dense jungle growth, was built directly above the magnificent white sand beach of Vista Hermosa. The architectural motif of the hotel might be compared to that of an Aztec pyramid. It is an unusual structure and offers a delightful view of the beach and ocean. The beauty of the resort has been enriched by the liberal use of palm trees, bougainvillea, hibiscus and the dramatic organ cactus. Even though this is a modern structure a traditional feeling has been introduced by the use of elegant terracotta floors, ceiling fans and Mexican-tiled baths. The setting, the mood, the unhurried yet gentle service combine to turn this into an extraordinary experience to be savored and enjoyed.

There are 428 lanai rooms, each with an ocean view. Each room also has an intimate, partially covered terrace and is equipped with a hammock and a fully stocked bar. *WHAT MORE COULD YOU DESIRE?* Although the rooms do sport ceiling fans each is air-conditioned. In addition, there are Junior, Fiesta and Viceroy Suites. The Camino Real Suite (4,500 square feet) has three bedrooms, living and dining room, private pool and whirlpool. The Jr. Suites feature a Jacuzzi while the Viceroy Suites have a private pool.

Dining here can also be a delightful experience. You may elect to dine at El Mexicano (gourmet Mexican fare), Le Pavilion (French cuisine) or La Esfera (international menu). In addition Le Club (bar and disco) is available for your pleasure. Twenty-four-hour room service is also an option. One very important point—Camino Real Ixtapa has its own water purification system.

The hotel has excellent meeting facilities and can handle groups of from 500 banquet- to 700 theater-style. They also have a convention services department to assist as well as a complete selection of audio/visual aids.

There is a wide selection of activities including: tennis on four lighted courts with pro shop, swimming in any or all of the four pools which, by the way, are connected to one another by cascading water falls. Or you may elect to try a swim at the secluded beach. If you really want to get into it you can arrange sailing, scuba diving, snorkeling, windsurfing, parasailing and deep-sea fishing trips. A wide variety of tours may be arranged or you can rent a jeep at the hotel to explore on your own.

About half a mile away is the Palma Real Golf Club. A Robert Trent Jones, Jr. design, playing to a par of 72, it reaches 6,898/6,408/5,801 yards. Water becomes a factor on nine of the 18 holes. While it is flat there are enough trees and traps to keep you busy. A nice point—there is no charge for transportation to or from the golf facilities.

RATES (EP) Lanai/rooms: $150. Jr. Suites: $330. Fiesta Suites: $380. Viceroy Suites $500. The magnificent, 3-bedroom Camino Real Suite with all of its amenities is $900. Not too bad split three ways. Green fees: $27, carts $20. Golf packages are available.

ARRIVAL Air: Ixtapa/Zihuatanejo International Airport (30 minutes away). Taxi service is available from the airport to the hotel.

SHERATON IXTAPA HOTEL
Pasa de Ixtapa
Ixtapa, Zihuatanejo
Guerrero, Mexico 40880
011 52 (743) 318–58
(800) 325–3535

Thirty minutes from the airport, the Ixtapa Sheraton has a great many things to offer. Entering the hotel you are reminded a bit of

Hawaii in that everything opens to the outside. It is a multi-storied, atrium-style structure. The view from the various levels of the dining room and bar is outstanding.

There are 358 guest rooms (including suites). Each features individually controlled air-conditioning, an FM radio, cable TV, a mini-bar and a small balcony.

Dining is available in the Veranda Restaurant with a menu that is truly international. The Casa Real, a very special gourmet restaurant with its beautiful view of the ocean, features Mexican cuisine as well as various fish specialties. There are a number of bars, including a swim-up affair, to keep things in proper balance. The resort is also equipped with a water purification plant. A nice extra—baby sitting service can also be arranged.

The Sheraton meeting facilities can accommodate groups of 400 theater- and 250 classroom-style.

Activities include tennis on four lighted courts and pool as well as ocean swimming. Sailing, snorkeling and sport-fishing can be arranged.

Golf is available on one of the more interesting layouts. A Robert Trent Jones, Jr. design, the Palma Real Golf Club is located directly across the road. Parring at 72, it shows a yardage of 6,890/6,408/5,801. While flat, plenty of challenge is introduced by water (nine holes) and more than its share of trees and traps.

RATES (EP) Rooms: $110/$140. Suites: $205. Green fees: $27, carts $20.

ARRIVAL Air: Zihautanejo Aeropuerto. Car: from the airport take a taxi to your destination.

THE MANZANILLO AREA

We were very impressed with Manzanillo. The trip from the airport (30 miles) passes through beautiful countryside. The lovely tropical setting has not been spoiled by the roadside trash (bottles, newspapers) prevalent in some other parts of Mexico.

About 150 miles south of Puerto Vallarta, this area was pretty well cut off until about 15 years ago. At that time a highway opened, allowing traffic into Manzanillo. The wide, uncrowded and unspoiled beaches stretch for more than 10 miles. They provide an endless array of water activity ranging from snorkeling and scuba diving to sailing and charter fishing trips.

There are a number of excellent restaurants in Manzanillo along with a few stores and boutiques. Accommodations include condominiums and hotels such as Maeva, Roca del Mar or El Pueblito. The star of the show, however, is the world-class Las Hadas. A place of magic, fantasy and complete enchantment, it truly is "the ultimate resort".

LAS HADAS
P.O. Box 158
Manzanillo, Colima
Mexico 28200
011–52–333–3–00–00
(800) 228–3000

Las Hadas must be classified as a premier destination resort. In our opinion this magnificent property ranks very high in the list of the top 25 golf resorts in the U.S., Canada and Mexico.

At the tip of the Santiago Peninsula on a hill just across the bay from Manzanillo, the white Moorish spires of Las Hadas rise dramatically. As a matter of fact you almost expect to see Tyrone Power at any moment.

Compared to many of the larger 1,000-room hotels, Las Hadas is be an intimate affair with its 220 guest accommodations. The very deluxe rooms and suites (the word deluxe is an understatement) feature marble floors as well as tile-floored private verandas and are air-conditioned. They are also equipped with two channels of taped music and each has a fully stocked bar. The overall Moorish architectural motif of the resort is even carried out in the guest rooms, with their graceful arched doorways and windows. The views looking down onto the beach and Manzanillo Bay are, to put it mildly, spectacular. All in all we would rate these accommodations as the finest we have ever seen.

Las Hadas can handle meeting groups of up to 200 and has all the state-of-the-art audio/visual equipment which might be required.

There are a variety of restaurants. The Legazpi Restaurant & Lounge, overlooking the upper level swimming pool, enjoys a very elegant indoor/outdoor setting. El Terral, specializing in Mexican food, can also provide either indoor or outdoor dining from its beautiful terrace overlooking the bay. For a lighter meal El Palmer, with its view of the lagoon pool, offers a delightful and casual atmosphere for all three meals. If fresh fish intrigues you perhaps you will enjoy Los Delfines. There is 24-hour room service also available. With the beautiful setting provided from your private patio you might well consider a private dinner for two. At poolside should you twitch an eyebrow a libation is sure to appear.

When the sun goes down the action starts at the lounges and the lively disco and keeps percolating until the wee hours. After a full night at the disco, if you think you can still handle it, there is tennis on 10 courts (eight hard-surface, two clay).

Between the beach and the 70-vessel private marina there are all types of water sports at your disposal including sailfishing, scuba diving, snorkeling, water skiing, sailing and trimaran cruises. The Puerto Las Hadas Marina & Yacht Club is the largest privately built marina in Mexico.

Then there are always the swimming pools, one with a lovely swim-up bar, and another which is reserved for adults only. Or you might consider joining me on the beach doing nothing but soaking up some sun and watch those other foolish people exhaust themselves. Meanwhile the ladies may well enjoy the shopping arcade as well as the beauty shop.

Golf is played on the La Mantarraya course, just minutes away. A Roy and Pete Dye design, it has been rated among the world's top 100 by *Golf Digest*. Not only is it challenging but it is scenic as well. If you get by the first three holes without developing the shakes you have got it made. Reaching a relatively modest 6,495/ 5,994/5/531/4,691 yards it pars at 71. Don't let the yardage fool you as this course is tough.

RATES (EP) Santiago rooms: $195. Romantica rooms: $225. Royal Beach Club: $275. Fantasia suites: $300. Green fees: $20, carts $25. Caddies ($8) are also available. Rates quoted are for the peak season, mid-December to late April.

ARRIVAL Air: Playa De Oro International Airport. Mini-bus and taxi service is available to the hotel (30 miles).

MAZATLAN, SINALOA AREA

Settled by the Spanish in the early 1600's Mazatlan developed very slowly over the years. Long known by sport fishing enthusiasts this quiet fishing town was "discovered" and over the past twenty years has developed into one of the largest cities in Mexico (almost 600,000). There are many reasons for this growth. It's just two hours by jet from Los Angeles and 900 miles south of the Arizona border. The climate is fabulous (winter in the daytime 70's— summer in the high and humid 80's). While Mazatlan is modern, it has kept its traditions and is definitely "Old Mexico" in flavor.

There is much to do, with beautiful beaches, water sports, shopping in many fine boutiques, back-country tours, night life activities (your hotel can direct you) and, of course, fishing and golf.

CAMINO REAL MAZATLAN
P.O. Box 538
Mazatlan, Sinaloa
Mexico 82100
011–52–678–3–11–11
(800) 228–3000

The Camino Real Mazatlan is on a rocky promontory of the rugged Punta del Sabalo and is a short distance north of Mazatlan. There is a spectacular view of the entrance to the Sea of Cortez, the Pacific Ocean and the beautiful beach area directly below the hotel. All rooms have either a view of the ocean or of the lagoon area. Many have private balconies facing the sea and each is air-conditioned.

Dining at the Camino is a special treat. Las Terazas, available for all three meals, features Mexican cuisine but specializes in prime ribs. They were the best I have ever enjoyed. It is supported by one of the better wine cellars. Open from 10 AM until 2 AM, the Chiquita Banana Beach Club serves up tropical drinks and fresh seafood. Live music and dancing until midnight are to be found at Camino Real's very posh Lobby Bar.

A few of the guest services include: purified water and ice machines, laundry and dry cleaning service, room service from 7 AM to 11 PM and a number of interesting shops.

Mazatlan has long been recognized as one of the premier fishing areas in the world. The hotel can arrange deep sea fishing trips where record catches of black marlin or sailfish are not uncommon. For those who prefer to be in, rather than on, the water there is a freshwater swimming pool and two white sand beaches. The beaches come equipped with picturesque palapas (straw huts). Of course water skiing or snorkling and skin diving, can be arranged by the hotel. Something extra—the surf here can provide some big-wave surfboard excitement. In addition to all of the water action there are also two excellent tennis courts. Horseback riding facilities are nearby.

The outstanding hunting in the Mazatlan area is not well known. The countryside abounds in wild fowl, deer, duck, mountain lion and ocelot and provides some of the best hunting in Mexico. Should you have an interest, you should make all arrangements and obtain permits prior to your arrival.

Golf can be played on the El Cid Country Club course nearby. With a par of 72, this layout reaches 6,712/6,393/5,252 yards.

RATES (EP) Rooms: $100/$110. Jr. suites: $152. 1-bedroom suite: $2084. 2-bedroom suite: $352. Green fees: $25, carts $20. Caddies are also available.

ARRIVAL Air: Mazatlan International Airport (17 miles or 35 minutes south of the city). Car: from the airport take either a mini-bus or a taxi.

EL CID RESORT
P.O. Box 813
Mazatlan, Sinaloa,
Mexico 82110
011–52–678 3–33–33
(800) 525–1925

Perhaps the complete title of El Cid Resort—"Hotel, Country Club and Marina"—will give you some idea of its scope. It is big and it is busy.

Set on 900 acres, some of the accommodations front directly on the beach while others reach inland to the country club area. El Moro tower, a 25-story structure on the beach, has deluxe suites, most with ocean views. El Cid tower is the location of the main lobby and reception area. There are additional accommodations across the road and connected by an overhead pedestrian walkway. In total El Cid has some 1000 rooms and suites. Each room is equipped with either a king or two double beds, is air-conditioned, and has a private balcony. Some rooms contain color satellite TV. This hotel does NOT have a water purification plant. Do not drink the tap water. Each room is supplied with bottled water. BY ALL MEANS USE IT.

The Los Tapices convention center is ideally set up to handle group affairs ranging from 2000 theater- to 1000 classroom-style. There are, in addition, many break-out rooms as well as a trained staff to help you handle those last minute problems which always seem to arise.

Restaurants include: El Alcazar, featuring an international gourmet menu; The Prime Rib House; La Cava Supper Club offering Italian cuisine as well as live entertainment; El Corral (what else but Mexican fare) and steaks; La Concha with its seafood specialties; the 19th Hole with its bar and restaurant. And if that's not enough there is always room service. Finally, there is El Patio, a poolside bar and grill. For evening entertainment, and considered a Mazatlan must, visit El Caracol Tango Palace for dancing or listening.

A few of the adult activities at your disposal include: 17 lighted tennis courts, squash and racquetball courts. There are five swimming pools, two of which are enormous (one 20,000 square feet) and include waterfalls and a swim-up-bar. One of the pools, by the way, is set up with a water-slide specifically designed for children. There are also jogging trails and bicycle paths. At the Clubhouse are a few additional amenities including a hot tub, gym, and sauna. The Aqua-Sports Center, directly in front of the hotel, can serve up virtually every water-related activity you can bring to mind.

At this time El Cid is the only 18-hole golf facility in the area. There are, however, plans to add an additional 18. The course, located on the property, stretches 6,712/6,393 yards from the hombres tees. From the senoritas tees the yardage is set at 5,252. Parring at 72, this layout will give you all you want and then some.

RATES (EP) Rooms: $105/$115 per couple. Suites: $195/$700. Green fees: $25, carts $20. Golf packages are available.

ARRIVAL Air: Mazatlan International Airport (17 miles, or 35 minutes south of the city). Car: from the airport take either a taxi or mini-bus to the hotel.

INDEX

USA

Abbey, The, WI: 247
Alderbrook Inn Resort, WA: 242
Alisal, The, CA: 57
Alpine Resort, The, WI: 248
Americana Lake Geneva Resort, WI: 248
Angel Fire, NM: 205
April Sound, TX: 223
Arizona Biltmore, The, AZ: 1
Arizona Golf Resort, AZ: 2
Arlington Resort Hotel & Spa, AR: 31
Arrowhead Resort & Hotel, OK: 210
Avondale Country Club, CA: 82

Barbara Worth CC, CA: 82
Bay Valley Inn, MI: 168
Big Sky, MT: 192
Birchmont Ruttger Resort-o-Tel, MN: 182
Black Butte Ranch, OR: 216
Boulder Creek Lodge, CA: 46
Boulders, The, AZ: 2
Boyne Highlands, MI: 168
Boyne Mountain, MI: 171
Breezy Point Resort, MN: 182
Broadmoor, The, CO: 100

Carlton Oaks Lodge & CC, CA: 64
Carmel Valley Ranch Resort, CA: 40
Cathedral Canyon CC, CA: 83
Cathedral Canyon Resort Hotel, CA: 83
Cliffs, The, HI: 130
Coachella Valley Desert Area, CA: 80

Columbia Lakes, TX: 223
Copper Mountain Resorts, CO: 103
Crystal Lakes Resort, MT: 194
Crystal Mountain Lodge, MI: 171

Dawn Hill Golf & Racquet Club, AR: 32
DeGray State Park, AR: 34
Dell View Resort Motel, WI: 250
Desert Inn Hotel & Casino, NV: 198
Devil's Head Lodge, WI: 251
Dogwood Hills CC & Resort, MO: 187
Double Eagle CC Resort, NM: 206
Double Tree Resort, CA: 84
Dunes Hotel Casino & CC, NV: 200

Eagle Crest Resort, OR: 217
Eagle Ridge Inn & Resort, IL: 158
El Camino Inn & CC, CA: 66
Elkhorn Resort, ID: 152

Fairfield Bay Resort, AR: 34
Fairfield Flagstaff, AZ: 6
Fairfield Green Valley, AZ: 7
Fairfield Pagosa, CO: 103
Fairmont Hot Springs Resort, MT: 194
Fairway Farm Golf & Hunt Club, TX: 225
Falconhead Ranch & CC, OK: 210
Flying L Ranch, TX: 225
Fountainhead Resort, OK: 212

Four Seasons Club Resort,
TX: 226
Fourwinds, A Clarion Resort,
IN: 165
Fox Hills Resort, WI: 251
Francisco Grande Resort,
AZ: 7
French Lick Springs, IN: 163
Furnace Creek Inn & Ranch
Resort, CA: 47

Gearhart by-the-Sea, OR: 218
Gold Canyon Resort, AZ: 8
Grand Hotel, MI: 172
Grand Hyatt Wailea, HI: 137
Grand Teton National Park,
WY: 259
Grand Traverse Resort Village,
MI: 173
Greenlake Conference Center,
WI: 252
Grouse Mountain Lodge,
MT: 195
Gull Lake View Golf Club,
MI: 175

Half Moon Bay Lodge, CA: 48
Hanalei Bay Resort, HI: 128
Handlery Stardust Hotel &
C C, CA: 67
Hawaiian Islands Resorts Inc,
HI: 130
Heidel House, The, WI: 253
Hidden Valley Club & Resort,
MI: 175
Horizon Lodge, TX: 227
Horseshoe Bay CC Resort,
TX: 227
Hot Springs Village, AR: 35
Hyatt at Lake Tahoe, NV:
201
Hyatt Grand Champions Re-
sort, CA: 85
Hyatt Regency DFW, The,
TX: 229
Hyatt Regency Maui, HI: 142
Hyatt Regency Monterey, The,
CA: 41

Hyatt Regency Scottsdale,
AZ: 9
Hyatt Regency Waikoloa,
HI: 119

Incline Village, NV: 201
Indian Lakes Resort, IL: 160
Indian Palms CC & Inn, CA: 86
Indian Wells Racquet Club Re-
sort, CA: 87
Inn at McCormick Ranch,
AZ: 5
Inn at Spanish Bay, CA: 42
Inn at Silver Lakes, The,
CA: 58
Inn of The Mountain Gods,
NM: 206
Inn on Lake Travis, The,
TX: 229
Inn Rancho Santa Fe, The,
CA: 66
Iron Horse Resort & Retreat,
CO: 104
Ironwood CC, CA: 88
Island of Hawaii, The, HI: 116
Island of Kauai, The, HI: 127
Island of Maui, The, HI: 135
Island of Molokai, The, HI: 149
Island of Oahu, The, HI: 114

Jackson Hole Racquet Club
Resort, WY: 261

Kaanapali Alii, HI: 147
Kaanapali Beach Hotel,
HI: 142
Kaanapali Beach Resort Area,
HI: 141
Kaanapali Plantation, HI: 147
Kaanapali Royal, HI: 148
Kalua Koi Hotel & G C, HI: 149
Kah-Nee-Ta, OR: 219
Kalua Koi Hotel, HI: 149
Kapalua Bay Hotel, HI: 143
Ka'u Coast Area, The, HI: 125
Keauhou Beach Hotel, HI: 117
Keauhou-Kona Beach Area,
HI: 116

Ketchum-Sun Valley Area,
    ID: 151
Keystone Resort, CO: 105
Kiahuna Plantation, HI: 133
Kimberland Meadows, ID: 156
Kohala Coast Area, The,
    HI: 118
Kona Surf Resort, HI: 118

La Casa del Zorro, CA: 88
La Costa, CA: 68
Lahaina-Kaanapali-Kapalua
    Areas, The, HI: 141
Lake Lawn Lodge, WI: 254
Lake Murray State Park Re-
    sort, OK: 214
Lake of the Ozarks, MO: 187
Lake Shastina Golf Resort,
    CA: 49
Lake San Marcos Resort,
    CA: 69
Lakes Country Club, The,
    CA: 89
Lake Texoma State Park Re-
    sort, OK: 214
Lakeway Resorts, TX: 230
La Quinta Resort, CA: 90
Lawrence Welk Village, CA:
    70
Lodge at Pebble Beach, The,
    CA: 44
Lodge of the Four Seasons,
    The, MO: 188
Loews Ventana Canyon Resort,
    AZ: 11

Madden's on Gull Lake,
    MN: 184
Marina Cay Resort, MT: 196
Marriott's Camelback Inn,
    AZ: 12
Marriott's Desert Springs Re-
    sort & Spa, CA: 91
Marriott's Lincolnshire Resort,
    IL: 161
Marriott's Mountain Shadows,
    AZ: 13

Marriott's Rancho Las Palmas,
    CA: 92
Marriott's Tan-Tar-A Resort,
    MO: 189
Maui Eldorado, HI: 148
Maui Inter-Continental Wailea,
    The, HI: 138
Maui Marriott Resort, HI: 144
Maui Prince Hotel at Makena,
    HI: 139
Mauna Kea Beach Hotel, The,
    HI: 120
Mauna Lani Bay Hotel, HI: 122
Maxwelton Braes Resort & CC,
    WI: 255
Mill Creek Golf & CC, TX: 231
Monterey Country Club,
    CA: 93
Monterey Peninsula Area,
    CA: 38
McGuire's Motor Lodge & Re-
    sort, MI: 176

Nippersink Manor Resort,
    WI: 256
Nordic Hills Resort, IL: 160
Northstar at Tahoe, CA: 49

Ojai Valley Inn & CC, CA: 59
Oklahoma's State Parks,
    OK: 213
Olympia Resort & Spa, WI: 256
Orange Tree Golf Resort,
    AZ: 14

Pala Mesa Resort, CA: 71
Palm Desert Resort & CC,
    CA: 94
Palm Valley Country Club,
    CA: 95
Pasatiempo Inn, CA: 50
Paradise Hills CC & Lodge,
    NM:
PGA West, CA: 96
Pheasant Run Resort, IL: 161
Phoenician Resort, AZ: 16
Pima Golf Resort, AZ: 17
Princeville Mirage Resort
    Area, The, HI: 127

Princeville Travel Service,
HI: 130
Prospector Square Hotel,
UT: 239

Quadna Mountain Resort,
MN: 185
Quail Lodge, CA: 45
Quartz Mountain State Park
Resort, OK: 214

Radisson Resort Arrowwood,
MN: 186
Rams Hill, CA: 97
Rancho Bernardo Inn, CA: 72
Rancho De Los Caballeros,
AZ: 17
Rancho Murieta, CA: 51
Rancho Viejo Resort, TX: 232
Rayburn Country Resort,
TX: 233
Red Apple Inn & CC, The,
AR: 36
Registry Resort, The, AZ: 18
Resort at Port Ludlow, The,
WA: 242
Resort Semiahmoo, The,
WA: 244
Rio Rancho Inn, NM: 208
Rio Rico Resort & C C, AZ: 19
Ridgemark, CA: 52
Ridge Tahoe, The, NV: 202
Rio Verde Resort & Ranch,
AZ: 20
Rippling River Resort, OR: 220
Ritz Carlton Laguna Niguel,
The, CA: 73
Roman Nose State Park Re-
sort, OK: 215
Royal Lahaina Resort, HI: 144
Royal Waikoloan Hotel, HI: 123

Salishan Lodge, OR: 220
San Luis Bay Inn, CA: 61
San Luis Rey Downs, CA: 74
San Vicente Resort, CA: 75
Scanticon Denver Resort,
CO: 106

Schuss Mountain Resort,
MI: 177
Scottsdale Princess, AZ: 21
SeaMountain at Punalu'u,
HI: 125
Shangri-La Resort, OK: 212
Shanty Creek/Schuss Mountain
Resort, MI: 178
Sheraton At Industry Hills,
CA: 61
Sheraton Kauai, HI: 134
Sheraton Makaha Resort & CC,
HI: 114
Sheraton Maui Hotel, HI: 145
Sheraton Mirage Princeville,
HI: 129
Sheraton Round Barn Inn,
CA: 52
Sheraton San Marcus, AZ: 23
Sheraton Steamboat Resort,
CO: 108
Sheraton Tucson El Conquista-
dor, AZ: 24
Showboat Hotel & CC, NV: 203
Silverado CC Resort, CA: 54
Singing Hills CC & Lodge,
CA: 76
Skyland Resort & CC, CO: 108
Snowmass Club, The, CO: 109
Southeast "Poipu Beach" area,
The, HI: 132
Stallion Springs Lodge, CA: 62
Stouffer Esmeralda Resort,
CA: 98
Stouffer Wailea Beach Resort,
HI: 140
Stouffer Waiohai Beach Resort,
HI: 135
Sudden Valley Resort, WA:
245
Sugar Loaf Resort, MI: 179
Sunriver Resort, OR: 222
Sun Valley Lodge & Inn,
ID: 154
Sylvan Resort, MI: 180

Tahoe Donner G & CC, CA: 55
Tamarron, CO: 110

Tanglewood on Texoma,
    TX: 233
Tapatio Springs, TX: 234
Temecula Creek Inn, CA: 77
Teton Pines Resort, WY: 262
Toro Hills Resort, LA: 166
Torrey Pines Inn, CA: 78
Tropicana Resort & Casino,
    NV: 204
Tubac Valley CC & Inn, AZ: 25
Tucson National Resort & Spa,
    The, AZ: 26
Turtle Bay Hilton, HI: 116
Twin Lakes Village, ID: 157

Vail-Beaver Creek Area, The,
    CO: 111
Vail/Beaver Creek Resort Asso-
    ciation, The, CO: 113
Valley Inn & CC, TX: 235
Volcano House Inn & CC, The,
    HI: 126

Waikoloa Villas, HI: 124
Wailea Area of Maui, The,
    HI: 136
Walden on Lake Conroe,
    TX: 235
Waterwood National Resort,
    TX: 236
Western Hills Guest Ranch,
    OK: 215
Westin Kauai, The, HI: 130
Westin La Paloma, The, AZ:
    27
Westin Maui, HI: 145
Whaler at Kaanapali Beach,
    The, HI: 148
Whispering Palms Lodge & CC,
    CA: 78
Wigwam Resort & CC, AZ:
    28
Wolf Lodge, UT: 241
Woodcreek Resort, TX: 237
Woodlands Inn & Conference
    Center, TX: 237

CANADA

Alta Vista Chalet, BC: 287

Banff Springs Hotel, ALB: 263
Blackcomb Lodge, BC: 284

Carleton Lodge, BC: 284
Chalet Luise, BC: 287
Chateau Whistler Resort,
    BC: 272
Clocktower Hotel, BC: 284

Delta Mountain Inn, BC: 284
Durlacher HDF, BC: 287

Edelweiss, BC: 287

Falcon Lake Resort & Club,
    MAN: 288
Fairmont Hot Springs, BC:
    273
Fairways Hotel, BC: 284
Fireplace Inn, BC: 284
Fitzsimmons Creek Lodge,
    BC: 286
Fitzsimmons Condos, BC: 284
Foxglove, BC: 285

Gables, BC: 285
Glacier Lodge, BC: 286
Gondola Village, BC: 286
Gull Harbour Resort,
    MAN: 290

Harrison Hot Springs, BC: 275
Haus Heidi, BC: 287
Hearthstone Lodge, BC: 284
Highland Vale, BC: 286
Hotel Kananaskis, The,
    ALB: 270

Jasper Park Lodge, ALB: 266

Kananaskis Inn, ALB: 270
Kananaskis Village, ALB: 267
Kokanee Springs Golf Resort,
    BC: 277

Lake Placid Lodge, BC: 286
Lakeside Resort, The, BC: 278
Listel Whistler Hotel, BC: 284
Lodge at Kanaskis, The,
    ALB: 271

Mile 108 Golf & Country Inn,
    BC: 279
Mountainside Lodge, BC: 284

Nancy Green Lodge, BC: 285

Radium Hot Springs Resort,
    BC: 280

Seasons, The, BC: 286
Stoneridge, BC: 286

Tantalus Lodge, BC: 285
Timberline Lodge, BC: 285

Village Gate House, BC: 285

Westbrook Whistler, BC: 285
Whistler Creek Lodge, BC: 286
Whistler On The Lake, BC: 286
Whistler Resort Association,
    BC: 282
Whistler Resort & Club,
    BC: 286
Whistlerview, BC: 285
Whistler Village Inn, BC: 285
Wildwood Lodge, BC: 286

Windwhistle Condos, BC: 285
Wiski Jack Resort, BC: 287

MEXICO

Acapulco Princess Resort,
    Acapulco: 294

Camino Real, Cancun: 301
Camino Real Mazatlan,
    Mazatlan: 309
Camino Real Ixtapa,
    Ixtapa: 303

El Cid Resort, Mazatlan: 310

Hyatt Cancun Caribe,
    Cancun: 301

Krystal Cancun, Cancun: 302

Las Brisas Resort,
    Acapulco: 296
Las Hadas, Manzanillo: 306

Pierre Marques Resort,
    Acapulco: 297

Sheraton Ixtapa Hotel,
    Ixtapa: 304